Suntanning in 20th Century America

KERRY SEGRAVE

McFarland & Company, Inc., Publishers
Jefferson, North Carolina, and London

ISBN 0-7864-2394-3 (softcover : 50# alkaline paper) ∞

LIBRARY OF CONGRESS CATALOGUING DATA ARE AVAILABLE

British Library cataloguing data are available

Cover image ©2005 Stockbyte Photography

Manufactured in the United States of America

*McFarland & Company, Inc., Publishers
Box 611, Jefferson, North Carolina 28640
www.mcfarlandpub.com*

Contents

Preface

This book looks at suntanning in America in the 20th century, from beginnings fueled by medical considerations to a point, less than a century later, when different medical considerations suggested that suntanning disappear from the scene. Overwhelming praise for the sun as healer drove society to accept tanning and make it an integral part of the fashion scene. People came to believe that a tan made them look and feel better, healthier, more attractive.

Initially the tan was adopted for its supposed medical properties, but in a fairly short time those reasons receded into the background as the arbiters of fashion came to relate sunbathing to social significance. Its popularity led to the birth of the home sunlamp in the 1920s and even to the search for a window glass that admitted ultraviolet light (ordinary glass did not). Parents were urged to give their infants and children long and regular sunbaths.

A change in medical opinion after World War II led to more critical articles about the sun and to many articles on the damaging effects of the sun. Tanning behavior slowly changed as the full weight of the medical establishment came down on it. But because it was so entrenched as a fashion statement by then, it proved harder to eradicate than had been expected. In the wake of this anti-sun sentiment, an entire industry—sunscreens—came into existence and prospered. Questions about the effectiveness of sunscreens have been raised since the rate of skin cancer has continued to rise, but as the sale of sunscreens has risen in tandem over almost the same time period, those questions remain unanswered. The tanning parlor was also born and survived, at least in a small way, while the search for the no-sun suntan continued.

Research for this book was done at the University of British Columbia, Simon Fraser University, and the Vancouver Public Library, using various online and hard copy databases.

1

Coco Chanel Had Nothing to Do with It: The Years to 1920

"I like a tomato for tan [removal] ... Whenever I can I get a big ripe tomato and I rub it on my face. It takes off the tan...."

Los Angeles Times, January 27, 1907

Today it is widely publicized, and accepted, that fashion maven Coco Chanel was responsible for the suntan becoming a fad and eventually a craze among people the world over. Single-handedly, went most accounts, Chanel caused the practice of suntanning to become pervasive, all from a supposedly single personal experience. The first report that linked the pair seemed to have been an unsigned piece in *Mademoiselle* magazine in May 1971. According to that article, "Up until the '20s, tans carried about as much social cachet as calluses, then suddenly Coco Chanel dared to turn up with a deep Deauville [France] glow and voilá— the bronze age began." No source was provided for that information. Others then started to pick up and repeat the story. For example, June Weir, in a May 1982 issue of the *New York Times Magazine*, explained that in the 1900s women took every precaution to avoid the sun, for example, by using wide-brimmed hats and parasols. "Then in the 1920s Coco Chanel, the legendary Paris designer, launched sunbathing as an in — that is to say, acceptable — sport as she exposed her face and figure to the sun for hours." Weir also provided no source for the information.[1]

The story spread more rapidly in the 1990s. Writing in the *FDA Consumer* in 1991, Alexandra Greeley observed, "Ever since fashion designer

Coco Chanel sported her new tan after a yachting vacation in the 1920s, many Americans have equated tanned skin with good health, great wealth, leisure time, social status, beauty and high fashion."[2]

Later that same year *Time* magazine reported it had been 70 years "since Coco Chanel's bronzed mannequins helped make the perfect tan a symbol of leisure and affluence...." (One of the more popular versions of the pairing argued that Chanel used tanned mannequins to display her wares and thus sparked the fad. Proponents of this version of the tale were usually silent as to whether or not Chanel had personally tanned.)[3]

Emily Prager, in *Harper's Bazaar* in 1996, declared that until the 1920s, women of higher classes did not tan at all since having a tan was considered to be a mark of membership in the working class. Those upper class females stayed out of the sun whenever possible and wore hats, when avoidance was not possible. Then, wrote Prager, "In the late 1920s suntanning became an upper-class recreation — thanks in part to Coco Chanel, who came back from Deauville (where she opened her first shop) with a tan." Also in 1996, Susan Brink, in *U.S. News & World Report*, asserted that one could "Blame it on Coco Chanel, who in the 1930s returned to Paris from the south of France with her skin a shocking bronze." (Dates of the events varied from account to account.)[4]

An Internet search in the summer of 2004 (using the string "Coco Chanel" Suntan*) produced a total of 206 hits on the Google search engine and 143 on Yahoo. Those hits contained the same types of variation with respect to dates (from 1920 to the 1930s) and specifics as mentioned for the citations above. That Coco Chanel single-handedly established the act of suntanning as a fad and as something worthy of emulation was well on its way to being an established "fact," if not already done. Yet Coco Chanel had nothing whatsoever to do with it. Prior to 1971 her name had never been mentioned in connection with tanning, which was established as a fad before 1920. One of the reasons the stories about Chanel and the origins of suntanning had so many variations was likely due to the fact that Chanel had nothing to do with the fad. If Chanel got herself a tan in the 1920s and/or started to use bronzed mannequins, she was simply doing what people all over the world were doing and had been doing for some time — following an existing fad.

The groundwork for establishing the suntan as an admirable, healthy and worthy goal was laid in the 1890s as medical science refocused on the power of the sun as healer. Claims were made, exaggerated enormously, and spread among the general public by a growing number of journalists and medical personnel, the latter often feeding almost miraculous statements about the power of the sun as healer, to a credulous band of journalists only too happy to report such material uncritically. Beginning with a few reports the flow soon became a torrent as medical personnel beat the drum and sang the praises of the sun, urging people to get into it whenever and wherever possible. People did so, but not right away. First it was necessary for old attitudes about the sun to be broken down. In the period around 1900, people did avoid the sun, if possible. A tan was considered a mark of the lower classes. It was, at least partly, a racist perspective — white good, not-white bad. Beauty advice of the time told women that a tan was as sophisticated and fashionable as acne. Before suntanning could be established as a fad and a fashion statement, all those old attitudes had to be eliminated.

Some of the changing attitudes toward the sun could be seen in a *New York Times* editorial in 1905 wherein the editor attacked what he felt to be an increasing practice — the habit of men and women to go about bareheaded under the summer sun. More and more people were doing this, explained the editor, "And they do it under the queer delusion, for which there is no foundation of fact whatever, that thus are they getting back to nature and laying in a stock of health for future use. The truth is that they are taking rather desperate chances of wrecking what health they have and are storing up large quantities of future trouble." Noted was that in hot countries people such as Arabs, Turks, and Indians never went bareheaded in the sun, but he allowed that blacks could and did go bareheaded anywhere since they had "a natural thatch of extreme imperviousness to light." Hoping hatless people would reflect on that and reconsider the habit, the editor added, "And, at any rate, it is full time that the utter irrelevancy of 'tan' to health should be generally understood. It is true that in acquiring 'tan' an assortment of healthful things are usually done, and it is also true that 'tan' is in itself to some degree protective, but it is neither a proof of physical well-being nor a direct aid to it." He worried that so many beautiful complexions "should be permanently coarsened and ruined simply because of a modern superstition that sunshine is always desirable and nobody can get too much of it is much to be lamented by all in whom the aesthetic sense has even begun to develop."[5]

Two years later a long article summarized the theories of Major Charles E. Woodruff, M.D., Surgeon, U.S.A. Stopping in New York on a lecture tour, Woodruff gave an interview to an unnamed reporter. At the time of the article Woodruff was Medical Officer of the U.S. Army camp at the Jamestown Exposition. The reporter observed that it had been nearly two years since the surgeon had published his "great" work, *Effects of Tropical Light on White Men*, a book the journalist claimed to be seminal, and worthy of being classed with Charles Darwin's *Origin of Species*, although it was admitted that the book by Woodruff remained largely unknown. While the author acknowledged the fact the sun killed bacteria, he argued that people failed to see the problems it caused: "God's sunlight is producing neurasthenia and cardiac feebleness and anemia, is promoting tuberculosis, and increasing insanity and suicide every day, not only in the tropics, but here in New York." Cloudiness, shade, awnings, and so forth, were, he said, promoting health, sanity and long life. The very future of the Aryan people living in America, those of English, Irish, Dutch, and German stock, Woodruff felt, depended on their getting this "God's sunshine nonsense out of their heads."[6]

Woodruff's thesis was, in brief, that man, originally a dark-skinned and hairy animal, a forest denizen or a cave-dweller with nocturnal habits, afraid of the sun and injured by it, survived as the creature into which he had evolved only by virtue of the pigmentation of his skin in proportion to the degree of light to which he was exposed. Men had evolved to creatures suited to the zone where they lived. That is, the blacks at the tropics, brown and olive-skinned races "further into the less fiercely lighted zones" and the blonder, whiter races at the cloudy north. Any attempt by a northern race (Aryan) to establish itself in a more southerly zone had always failed, and always would, declared Woodruff, because the Aryan was unfit to survive anywhere except "in a land of Winter and of mists. He comes to the South, conquers and dies." And that was because sunlight had properties that were destructive to life, and the worst rays of the sun were "those which we cannot see at all, but know as the ultra-violet rays [UV] — the actinic rays."[7]

In his view, a black person had a natural shield against the sun's UV rays in the pigment of his skin but "The white man is out of place in the tropics and cannot live there, except by hiding away from the light, and even then he rapidly deteriorates. With the utmost carefulness he gradually goes to pieces, and if he leaves any children they are frail." Even the U.S.A., he claimed, was mostly too sun-filled for the Aryan, as nervous breakdowns in America were frequent, suicide was on the increase, and "The American girl is a bundle of nerves. She is a victim of too much light." Only in the extreme Northwest of America and in Alaska were conditions sunless enough to be an amenable home for the Aryan. Singled out by Woodruff as a city unfit for habitation by white men was Denver, because it had "too much light." He went so far as to argue that in the U.S., other things being equal, "the death rate of a place is proportional to its sunshine and inversely proportional to its latitude. The death rate decreases steadily from Florida to Vancouver, with its fogs."[8]

According to Woodruff "light is a deadly enemy of life. In small quantities it is a stimulant; in excessive amounts — and very little is excessive — it is destructive." He added "A bright day affects one like wine, but too many bright days madden as surely as too much alcohol — and with far more permanent results. Men go to the Philippines and praise the climate — and in two years come home to die." In his view "We are daft over the idea of plenty of God's sunlight in schoolrooms and factories. We forget that miners are proverbially healthy." (Both Woodruff and the editor cited before him displayed some of the changing attitudes toward sunlight then under way in society. Both accepted traditional thinking about avoiding the sun, at least for white people, but felt compelled to rail against the beginnings of the movement to worship the sun as healer and to seek it out.)[9]

A few years later, in 1911, Dr. Percy Brown of Harvard Medical School argued that the intense brilliancy of sunlight was a likely cause of nervous energy and restlessness, which he claimed, characterized the typical American's quest for success. He thought there might be a similarity in effect between long exposure to the sun's UV rays and to X-rays, declaring, "Exposure to the X-ray over a long period of time in many instances might tend to increase what has been called Americanitis, or, in other words, a condition of irritability and extreme activity."[10]

An ad in the *Los Angeles Times* (disguised as a news item), in January 1901, pitched Mme. Ribault's complexion beautifier. Women could write to a Cincinnati address for a free trial box of the preparation that was promoted as a cure for all sorts of facial afflictions. [That revealed how tan was perceived at the time.] According to the ad, "The treatment is harmless, a natural beauty maker, and will permanently remove all tan, freckles, moth patches, pimples, blackheads, flesh worms, sunburn, chaps, roughness and any and all skin imperfections, no matter what they may be."[11]

Mrs. Henry Symes penned a long article, in 1902, that was mostly about how to keep the arms and hands beautiful. Mentioned were several bleaching treatments to apply to the arms and hands to make them white; one used oatmeal as a base, another used buttermilk, while a third was based on bread dough. Summer presented special problems, warned Symes, "Upon the woman with the lily face the sun's ravages show soonest; and if she comes home at night with a coat of tan her lily skin is gone." Yet another bleaching remedy Symes mentioned contained half a pint of rose water, an ounce of lemon juice and a tablespoon of borax. When a woman came home from being out in the sun, she was advised to rub that preparation on her arms, let it stay on for five minutes, and then wash it off with soap and hot water.[12]

A year later Symes returned with another long beauty article, containing various recipes and formulas to be made up at home to remove dandruff, to make rouge, shampoo, and for "whitening the skin — a liquid powder" and "Antiphelic Lotion for Removing Tan and Freckles" and "Lime Juice Lotion for Tan" (removal of, that is). That Antiphelic Lotion contained bichloride of mercury, sulphate of zinc, acetate of lead, and distilled water. Symes said, "It is efficacious, but painful."[13]

Yet another beauty article, in 1907, advised its female readers on how to be beautiful on the cheap — pretty on $1 a week. Included in the piece were several tips on how to bleach the skin — how to make it white and how to keep it white. Favored by the author of the piece were a cucumber and "I like a tomato for tan and for taking out yellow spots and whenever I can I get a big ripe tomato and I rub it on my face. It takes off the tan, stimulates the cuticle and makes the cheeks red." She also made it a habit to keep a bit of fresh fruit on her dresser because "Nothing removes tan, sunburn, freckles and pimples like ripe fruit juice." Also of use was the potato. "Take a raw potato and rub it upon your hands and see how quickly they will begin to whiten."[14]

Class and racial interpretation of white skin go far back in time. When the original European migration to Australia took place in the 1800s, two social mores combined to promote skin protection in immigrants living in Australia, wrote researcher Simon Chapman. One was a moral code that proscribed the removal of too much clothing in public and a second code "that dictated that suntans signified lower- or working-class status." But in the early 20th century, both of these codes were reversed. Tans became a sign of upward social mobility, indicating that a person had the financial wherewithal to take holidays.[15]

Researcher Marvin Harris said that as the history of the parasol indicated, civilized people had always considered it a privilege to be able to avoid the heat and glare of the direct rays of the sun. And those parasols were adopted with as much enthusiasm by the kings of West Africa as by the Chinese emperors and the popes of Rome. Everywhere, he added, ordinary people were forbidden to protect themselves with such devices. "By staying out of the sun, royalty — from Japan to Spain — kept itself several shades lighter than the peasants who worked in the fields," explained Harris. "Where people's skin could be appreciably darkened by exposure to solar radiation — and this includes almost everyone of Asian and European descent — pallid skin became a mark of upper-class status." It meant that being noble and not being suntanned became synonymous.[16]

Harris argued that the idea "white is beautiful" became an esthetic canon among the upper classes. Beautiful women were described by European court poets as having necks as "white as alabaster" or breasts "as white as snow." White face powders were said to have been used in ancient times in both Japan and China by the upper classes to create the effect of pallor. Eventually, continued Harris, "whiteness" was internalized by the Eurasian lower classes and became their own ultimate psychological standard of beauty and excellence. It was said to be in that way that the brown, yellow, and red peoples of Europe and Asia acquired prejudice against skins darker than their own.[17]

Another factor that turned attitudes toward favoring tanning was the shifting class distinction that took place in the industrialized world in the latter part of the 19th century. There was, argued Harris, a reversal of the prevalence of sun and shade with respect to social class. With the spread of the factory system, the principal location of menial labor moved indoors. A pallid complexion ceased to be the hallmark of the parasol-wielding elites; instead it became the mark of the lower-class industrial workers— the men, women and children who were capitalism's wage slaves. The high-density urban settlements prevented sunlight from penetrating while the high level of consumption of coal created a permanent pall over working-class districts. At the same time, the upper classes were spending more time outdoors engaged in sports such as tennis and polo and in a general back-to-nature movement. The tan was losing its lower-class distinction. But more important was the effort to promote the sun as healer; an effort that managed to erase many of the negative ideas held about the sun by people in all classes.[18]

One of the earliest accounts to indicate such efforts were successful and that the suntan was in fashion, something to be sought after and attained, appeared in May 1908, in the *New York Times*. It was an article about the expected happenings in the coming summer season at Newport, Rhode Island, the "in" summer spot for America's society people. "Women of both the older and younger sets are already having some marvellous creations in bathing suits made for the season at Bailey's Beach," said the article. "They are to be more beautiful than ever in view of the newest fad of sun baths on the beach, which are to be indulged in more generally next Summer than ever before in Newport." Health benefits were also mentioned, "These beach baths in the sun are supposed to be wonderful reliefs for rheumatism and such afflictions."[19]

A 1912 article in the *Los Angeles Times* observed that "Most people feel disappointed if after their summer holiday they have not something to show for it in the shape of a healthy coating of sunburn [that is, tan. In the early years the words "tan" and "sunburn" were sometimes used interchangeably]." Also noted by this article was that in recent years more than one patent medicine preparation had appeared on the market (chemicals to be rubbed on the skin to create a tan) that guaranteed to produce a permanent tan. Undoubtedly they did not work but their existence was further evidence that the suntan had arrived as a fad.[20]

In Chicago, Health Commissioner John Dill Robertson visited the different bathing beaches in his city on a Sunday in July 1917. Worried about people getting real sunburn, he observed, "On my visit to the beaches I found hundreds and thousands of men, women and children lying about in the sun, their arms and necks and faces blistered from the sun." Robertson advised people not to lie on the beach all day, adding, "Many people think it is the proper thing to get the body tanned and burned."[21]

By this time the fad had extended to where it was felt that young children should also receive long-term sun exposure. In Los Angeles the Women's Alliance, as of 1915, had been running a nursery for low-income women for some nine years. Their main project then was to raise enough money to add a sun-parlor, for 100 babies, to their facility. Mrs. William Baurhyte, president of the Alliance, did not feel a sun-parlor was a luxury because fresh air and sunshine were looked upon as better medicine for babies than just about anything. At the facility, in warm weather, the children, none of whom were more than two years of age, spent nearly all of their waking hours in the open air and sun and were said to "thrive amazingly." To deprive them of the air and sun even for the few months of a Southern California winter, worried Baurhyte, "would seriously militate against their health."[22]

A reference to the subject turned up in *The Beautiful and Damned*, by famed American novelist F. Scott Fitzgerald. Published in 1922, the brief part concerned with tanning was set in 1913-1914. All three of the characters involved were between the ages of 22 and 27 and were wealthy members of the upper class. Anthony Patch was talking with Maury Noble about Gloria Gilbert, whom he had just met, by saying, "She talked about skin too—her own skin. Always her own. She told me the sort of tan she'd like to get in the summer and how closely she usually approximated it." After a few short exchanges with Patch, Maury reminisced, "I began thinking about tan. I began to think what color I turned when I made my last exposure about two years ago. I did use to get a pretty good tan. I used to get a sort of bronze, if I remember rightly."[23]

Thus, tanning was established as a fashion by around 1908, at the latest, and was well entrenched by the time of World War I. It would become even more of a fad and more pervasive as a fashion in America after World War I and especially through the 1920s. Partly that change was due to a shifting notion of what skin color was appropriate to the lower classes and to the upper classes and partly due to a decline in the idea that white was good and that the whiter, the better. Mostly though, it was due to the endless hype of the sun as healer, often from the medical profession. That incessant drumbeat reached its height in the 1920s, although it had begun much earlier. So, Coco Chanel had nothing to do with it. She deserved no blame, or credit, for suntan fashion. Almost all blame, or credit, lay with the medical establishment.

2

The Sun as Healer: 1890s–1945

"We almost dare say sun baths would cure every ill except erythema solare [sunburn]. We even know sunlight has cured skin cancer (epithelioma)."

Dr. William Brady, 1914

"It seems that the curative effects [of the sun's rays] do not come into play until the skin is well pigmented by exposure. No tan, no cure."

Scientific Monthly, 1923

"Sun ray baths save baby."

New York Times, 1925

Sun worship is probably as old as humankind: that homage is most likely due to the fact that the sun is responsible for all life, in a general sense. Perceiving the sun, however, as a healer of specific ailments in individuals is a somewhat different matter. Reportedly the treatment of disease by sunlight was systematically practiced by Hippocrates. Sunbaths for the cure of disease were also recommended by Galen, Celsus, and Herodotus. Almost 2,100 years ago, a great temple dedicated to Aesculapius was built on the sunny side of a mountain slope and used for sun bathing. The Romans followed the Greeks, and both Herodotus and Antyllus recommended sun bathing for disease of the skin.[1]

The Romans are said to have made great use of the sun for healing of sores and maintenance of health. Pliny, in writing about his aged friend Spurinna, noted the latter undressed and went out for a walk in the sun every day.[2]

Still, little mention was made of the sun as healer until the 1800s.

Sometime around the 1830s, Dr. George Boddington of Sutton Coldfield, near Birmingham, England, began to put his consumptive patients out-of-doors for extended periods. He claimed that this treatment of disease by light and air was successful, but so unorthodox was the treatment that it was largely ignored by the medical establishment.[3]

In 1845, Bonnet of Lyons, France, in *Treatise on Diseases of Joints*, stated that white swelling of the knee (tuberculosis) was greatly benefited by exposure to the sun. Florence Nightingale, in 1856, vigorously but unsuccessfully protested against the orientation of Netley Hospital, observing that no sunlight could ever enter its wards. In 1876, Benjamin Ward Richardson praised sunlight in his *Hygeia, The City of Health*. A year later, Downes and Blunt demonstrated that sunlight would kill anthrax bacilli. In many writings in this period, John Ruskin praised sunlight and complained about the "plague-cloud of smoke above our cities." Using the geographical method in 1890, Dr. Theobald Adrian Palm showed that lack of sunlight was the chief factor in the causation of rickets. Robert Koch and others showed that sunlight killed tubercle bacilli.[4]

A Dr. Poncet made use of heliotherapy (as sun treatment came to be called in the early years of the 20th century) for treating osteo-articular tuberculosis (TB) as early as 1892, and impressed the value of sun exposure on all his pupils. In 1899 Poncet declared he believed the beneficial effect of the exposure of tubercular manifestation to solar rays (from a prolonged sun bath) extended not only to local tuberculosis (of the bones, and so on) but even to those of internal organs.[5]

Dr. Niels R. Finsen, a young Dane, began to cure lupus, a form of cutaneous TB by the local use of sunlight, in 1893. Reportedly he obtained results superior to any other treatment method in use at the time. It was believed that the ultra-violet (UV) rays were the most useful in treating disease and steps were taken either to filter sunlight, or to use artificial light that was rich in the rays of shorter wavelength. The red rays and heat rays of the sun were hot and burning and were not thought to be therapeutic and, in any case, because they could burn severely, the patient had to be protected from them.

Finsen continued the scientific study of ultraviolet light and the skin first begun in 1859 when an aide to renowned French physician Jean Charcot accidentally got in the way of an electric arc and ended up with a tan on one side of his face. Charcot wondered how the tan got there and traced it to the short-wavelength UV rays emitted by the arc (that is, 2800 to 3200 Angstrom units — one unit equalled a hundred millionth of a centimeter). When Finsen later painted part of his arm with lampblack and exposed it to UV rays, he found the skin under the painted region was not burned but the bare skin was. Thus, Finsen felt he had proven that sunburn had little to do with heat since the temperature of the black area of his arm was higher than that in the unpainted region. In 1900, on May 1, the London Hospital began the cure of lupus by the local use of sunlight.[6]

Then, in 1903, in Leysin, Switzerland, Dr. A. Rollier opened the first clinic for the treatment of so-called surgical tuberculosis by sunlight; and in 1910 he applied his idea to prevention by the establishment of the "school in the sun" at Cergnat, just below Leysin.[7]

By the start of World War I, the promotion of the sun as healer was pervasive and incessant. Early in 1914 the popular general magazine, *Literary Digest*, argued that while the healing virtues of sunlight had been known in a general sense for centuries, it had remained "for our generation to discover that direct sunlight is not merely beneficial in stimulating the general health and raising the tone of mind and body, but possesses a therapeutic value in certain maladies which borders on the marvellous." This new method of treatment by means of prolonged exposure of the naked body to solar rays—termed heliotherapy—was particularly helpful in treating tuberculosis of the bones, joints and ganglions. "But it has met with marked success in other diseases also, including acute rheumatism and even certain affections of the eye." Dr. Armand Delille told other French physicians, in a French medical publication, "All the forms of external tuberculosis, known as surgical tuberculosis, are amenable to heliotherapeutic treatment and receive benefit thereby, with results at times so stupefying that they seem to touch on miracle."[8]

In this account Rollier was described as a man who talked the method up tirelessly before congresses and other learned societies. Of 369 "invalids" suffering from external TB and treated by heliotherapy, said Rollier in 1911, 284 cures (78 percent) were effected, 48 cases improved, 21 showed no change, and 16 (four percent) died. According to the Swiss physician, the transformation of the subject under the solar rays was characteristic: "pigmentation of the skin is very rapid; at the end of a month or two, brunettes take the color of rosewood and actually look like negroes; blondes become mahogany-colored. The general aspect is modified and becomes blooming; the muscles are regenerated; the digestive functions are regularized. This rapid amelioration of the general condition is accompanied by notable local modifications." Because heliotherapy was said to be good for other conditions, such as muscular rheumatism and trachoma, this account suggested that, in the suburbs of cities, solaria equipped to apply the sunbath to patients and convalescents not requiring the usual hospital treatment be established all over the country.[9]

Later in 1914, Dr. Guy Hinsdale of Hot Springs, Virginia, described

Rollier's method by observing that the patient was clothed in linen or white flannel, depending on the season, and wore a hat. Also, he wore smoked or yellow glasses while a screen protected his face from direct sunlight. "The whole system of heliotherapy aims at acquiring a progressive pigmentation of the skin.... Bronzing of the skin varies from a copper to a chocolate color. Without it no one could endure the sun-cure for many hours a day." According to Hinsdale, Rollier's record consisted of treating 1,200 patients with tuberculosis and achieving 1,000 cures.[10]

American physician William Brady declared, in the pages of *The Independent* in 1914, that while it was common knowledge that exposure to the sun was good for the health, "it is not sufficiently taught that sun baths should be, and in actual practice are, a curative measure for many serious diseases." Not only were modern homes being planned with a view of getting more direct sunlight in all the rooms, he added, "but special rooms or porches are being built into the houses to give the occupants the benefit of sun baths." Numerous hospitals and sanatoriums were said to be installing sunrooms for the use of patients.

Brady argued that one of the first noticeable effects of exposure to direct sunlight was an increase in hemoglobin, with an average increase of 10 percent noted in invalids in the course of the first three days of sun bathing. At Leysin, Rollier's patients were exposed to the sun on open porches by gradual degree — 10 minutes the first day, 20 minutes the second, and so on, until sun baths of two or more hours daily could be taken. Gradual exposure was used to avoid sunburn. Lavish in his praise of heliotherapy, Dr. Brady explained, "Every form of tuberculosis, both surgical and pulmonary, responds to sun baths. Some of the results attained in children with hip disease and Pott's disease of the spine are admitted by the world's best surgeons to be superior to anything surgery has offered in such cases." In the case of patients with tuberculosis, sunbath treatment could last, in the worst cases, for two to three years, or more. Brady also observed that in California "sun bathing has become almost a popular fad for all sorts of ills." Admitting he did not know what the physiological effect of sunlight on the body was—"too mysterious for understanding"— Brady went on to declare that sunlight was the greatest activator of general metabolism, having positive effects on blood pressure, sleep, digestion, respiration and circulation as great as from any agents available then to the medical profession. "We almost dare say sun baths would cure every ill except erythema solare [sunburn]," enthused Brady. "We even know sunlight has cured skin cancer (epithelioma)." Wild exaggerations with regard to the sun's powers were clearly evident, although Brady may have been alone in his claim that sun bathing cured skin cancer.[11]

Under the title "Doctor Sun," a 1918 article in *Literary Digest* explained that sunlight was then being used successfully in the treatment of wounded men in many of the military hospitals in France, according to American physician Dr. Willis C. Campbell, who had himself used sun therapy for five years with "marked success" in treating diseases of the bones and joints and who believed that treatment could be successfully extended to the treatment of other disorders, especially in military surgery. Campbell concluded, "Heliotherapy is far-reaching in its effects and undoubtedly will be found of great value, not only in the treatment of affections of bones and joints, but for the cure of various disorders elsewhere in the body."[12]

Dr. Randle C. Rosenberger argued in 1920 that people did not get enough sun and that we would all be better off if we adopted the old Roman fashion of using a solarium. He added that Dr. Kellogg, of Battle Creek, Michigan, believed that through heliotherapy "debilitated functions are exhilarated, nutrition is very markedly improved, activity of secretions is marked, and internal organs are oxygenated." According to Rosenberger, "During the late war it was discovered that the sun's rays were beneficial for compound fractures and suppurating wounds." In his view the sun "will always be our friend." And, sunbaths, "most physicians claim, give not only energy to the bather but help to cure insomnia, malnutrition, anemia, neurasthenia, chlorosis, and tubercular troubles." Declaring that sunlight was the birthright of everyone, he argued that more of the energy-giver be provided in all homes, schools, factories, workshops, churches and prisons. Concluded Rosenberger, "More, not less, sunlight is needed by all of us, and this great republic will have a healthier and happier race of citizens when laws are made to provide plenty of sunlight as a natural environment for all."[13]

A brief article in *Scientific American* in 1921 asserted, "That the rays of the sun can be used for curing many skin diseases and that the sun baths are advantageous even to those who are in perfect health has long been well known to the general public."[14]

A 1921 piece in the UK publication *New Statesman* urged, "Let us seek the sun and place therein our ill folk whom we have hitherto failed to cure with our best efforts of surgery and medicaments. In certain common and chronic diseases, notorious especially throughout the temperate zones, we achieve results unapproachable by any other means." Rollier was described as "The High Priest of Modern Sun-Worship" in this account. While the reporter noted that patients at Rollier's facilities in Switzerland also got pure air, good fresh food, were protected from the chance of further infections, and so on, he was convinced "whilst other facts aid, and none should be neglected, the sunlight is the therapeutic agent." Herein Rollier's patients, after the initial gradual exposure build-up, were given sunbaths that lasted three to six hours daily. "Properly aired and lighted, the skin becomes a velvety, supple, copper-coloured tissue, absolutely immune from anything of the nature of pimples or acne...." Even more impressive to the reporter was that in many cases those patients had, practically speaking, never moved a muscle, were not massaged, and so forth. They were bound to their beds. "But always the muscles are firm and well-developed under the warm skin." The pigmentation of the skin, or the tanning process, speculated the account, caused the more complete absorption by the body of the ultraviolet rays—thought to be a good thing. Also declaring he did not know how the sun cured diseases, he asserted, "Processes vastly more subtle than the killing of bacilli by radiation are at work, as we see by the value of the light, generally applied to the skin, upon deep-seated local infections, and by the curative results of heliotherapy in many affections which no one believes to be of microbic origin."[15]

A month later, a report in the same publication said that Rollier had assured the reporter that patients who did not pigment (tan) did not thrive under the sun, a sentiment said to be shared by "all other observers." Yet the more tanned skin got, the more it was believed to block out the UV rays—the supposed healing part of the sun's rays, which created confusion in the minds of the medical profession. No one knew how the sun performed its supposed healing functions.

However, there was a consensus that the sun healed through its light and not through its heat. Despite all the uncertainties, this piece declared, "And again, it is certain that sunlight is of value against local microbic lesions when applied to the skin elsewhere, and also when used in forms of disease where microbes are not concerned at all."[16]

Dr. C. W. Saleeby, writing in *Nature* in 1922, remarked that Rollier's methods were followed in many countries, including France, Italy, Spain, the UK and America. "We shall do well not to associate the sun cure exclusively with tuberculosis nor solely with the proved antiseptic power of sunlight," explained Saleeby, because recent American work, both at Columbia University and at Johns Hopkins Hospital, "has shown that sunlight has potent influences upon nutrition and metabolism, and is capable, for instance, of preventing and curing rickets in a fashion hitherto unsuspected."[17]

An account in *The Survey*, in October 1922, said the new sun worship began with the "great international campaign" against tuberculosis and was then intensified when World War I came with the resultant underfeeding of millions and a whole generation of children with difficulties in building health with careful nutrition. It gave a strong impetus to the use of open-air treatment of anemia, rickets and scrofula. Meadows planned and equipped for air and sunbaths were reported to have become almost as common as swimming pools in the newer public parks of Germany. In children's camps, sun treatment was said to be universal. School authorities in Frankfurt, Germany, were described as pioneers in instituting sunbaths for children, a practice begun some 15 years earlier — around 1907. A result was that in the winter following their air and sun bath experience of the previous summer, the report said, "they are hardened; children who formerly were subject to colds are immune to such attacks." Artists and poets as well as health reformers and teachers had taken up the movement in Germany. Although the sunbath movement in Germany was started as a response to an increase in rickets in children, it was soon adopted for all children, healthy and unhealthy, as a prophylactic and treatment. In Lausanne, Switzerland, it was reported that physicians and teachers had called upon all parents to allow their children to spend their vacation on the shore of the lake clad only in bathing suits. To promote that idea a pamphlet had been produced, "To the Sun, to the Sun!"[18]

Still puzzled over how the sun worked its healing miracles, the *New Statesman* decided it was helpful to draw an analogy between humankind and plants. When the "human flower" was put in the sunlight, chemical processes began. As in the case of the plant, "Under the action of the light, pigment develops, and things yet not understood begin to happen."[19]

A 1923 article in *Scientific Monthly* argued that the rediscovery of the curative power of direct sunshine came by accident. In a hospital for children with rickets, it was explained, it was found that the child who had the luck to lie in a certain cot exposed to the rays of the sun recovered with amazing speed. Thorough experimentation, first on rats and later on children, proved that rickets could be cured either by sunshine or cod-liver oil. This reporter bemoaned the fact that people in the northern climes had gotten out of the habit of exposing their skins to sunshine — due to wearing thick clothing and staying in warm houses. Also bemoaned was the ordinary window glass found in homes, offices, and so on, because while it let through all the light that people could see it blocked out the invisible UV rays, the very rays that were said to be so beneficial. With respect to Rollier's method, the journalist said the aim was to get the skin tanned without being burned. "It seems that the curative effects do not come into play until the skin is well pigmented by exposure. No tan, no cure."[20]

After remarking specifically on the power of the sun to cure rickets and tuberculosis, in the *New York Times*, the editor of *The Medical Journal and Record* declared, "It is beginning to be generally believed that the

remedial and even curative properties of the sun are almost illimitable."
He added that the light of the sun was the most potent agent in the field
of preventive medicine while a lack of sunlight was responsible for various diseases and conditions of ill health, and the sun's rays, unimpeded by
the air pollution so common in London and other industrial cities, "exert
a remarkably effective healing power." Dr. Helen Mackay commented,
"Light is life, and lack of it causes ill health. The therapeutic virtues of sunlight can scarcely be overestimated."[21]

After extolling Rollier and his "miraculous" cures, a report in *Current Opinion* observed that a body of scientists at the National Institute
for Medical Research at Hampstead, England, had established the fact that
we lived, literally, by the chemical or actinic [UV] rays of the sun. It was
those rays that produced the summer tan and "[i]n some subtle fashion,
as yet imperfectly understood, they influence the nutrition of the body
and its resistance to disease." According to this report, a lack of sunlight
threw a heavy strain on the organs of digestion. That was because the violet and UV rays of the sun affected the body in such a manner that it
required less animal fat while it was being sufficiently irradiated. In the
absence of such rays, fats had to be consumed in larger quantities, and fats
were more difficult to digest in middle-aged or elderly people.[22]

When a reporter for the *New York Times* wrote about the Americans
who moved to spend the winter in Florida or California, he said they were
displaying an actinic hunger with a behavior almost as instinctive as that
of a migrating bird, and that a man "may be impelled by the desire for the
actinic rays screened out of Northern Winter by the etiolating clouds and
smoke." The aim of submitting people, ill and healthy, to the rays of the
sun, he argued, was to achieve "a widespread diminution of disease and
of great future improvement in the health, stature and beauty of the people of this country."[23]

Medical doctor Woods Hutchinson observed in 1925 that, of the good
results on TB patients, "we have long noted that patients gain most rapidly
and substantially when they acquire a good coat of tan." When it was discovered that results were not so good if patients sun-bathed in glassed-in
areas, such as rooms or porches, it was finally determined that ordinary
window glass filtered out the sun's UV rays. Besides praising the role of
the sun in curing TB, Hutchinson extolled the curative effect of sunlight
on children with rickets. Reportedly, a Russian scientist by the name of
Raczynski had shown, around 1915, that sunlight cured rickets. Then about
1920, explained Hutchinson, "Huloschinski caught and caged his sunlight
in the so-called mercury-vapor lamp so that he could turn it on whenever
he wanted it, regardless of the weather, and he triumphantly cured by its

use a number of cases of rickets." Thus, the sunlamp was born. As with the treatment of tuberculosis, it was said to be the UV part of the sun's rays that cured rickets. Administering cod-liver oil was another major treatment, and cure, for rickets.[24]

To prove UV rays cured rickets, Hutchinson added, researchers irradiated olive oil for several hours with UV light and then gave it in spoonful doses to children with rickets. They began to improve at once. Already in England, declared the physician, quartz lamps [sunlamps] were reportedly being installed in school buildings and in selected centers in the tenement districts where children could be given "their daily bath of ultra-violet rays; especially during the short foggy winter days when rickets flourishes and growth is stunted. Physicists are eagerly at work developing plates of quartz of sufficient size and thinness to be used as window glass."[25]

James A. Tobey, secretary of the National Health Council, flatly declared in 1925, "Today it has been definitely proved that the sun's rays will cure tuberculosis and rickets and are efficacious in the treatment of other diseases."[26]

Journalist Floyd Parsons, in a long 1925 article that focused on urging authorities to cut down smoke pollution in cities and towns—because such pollution blocked out the sun's rays—made some of the most exaggerated claims for the sun's rays. After noting that it was not understood why those who tanned most easily got the greatest benefit out of sunlight treatments, he went on to declare that sunlight enriched human blood in calcium, phosphorus, iron and probably iodine. As well, it increased the number of white blood cells and the number of platelets, "thereby rendering the individual more or less immune to disease." Parsons added, "The belief that the efficacy of sunlight is principally confined to ailments such as rickets and tuberculosis is wholly fallacious. The dermatologist has discovered the value of sunlight in the treatment of nearly all cutaneous affections. It is also an effective remedy in many cases of digestive disorders and rheumatic conditions."[27]

Parsons went on to argue that people who lived largely in the sunlight did not require as much food as those who spent their time in the shade and, "for this reason we must all recognize that light is a food substitute that can be made to afford material relief to our digestive mechanism." Additionally, he argued people would be better off going around bareheaded and wearing "sunshine clothing." According to his account, an investigation of cotton goods—some black and some white—proved conclusively that, through the black material, light would not cure rickets, but through the white clothing it would. Of greatest value of all, felt

Parsons, would be solariums at beaches, in homes, and on the top of some city buildings where people could expose their bodies to unobstructed sunshine. For this reporter it was obvious that the light of the sun was our benefactor although its heat could become our enemy. Official observations in several cities were said to have revealed that from 50 to 87.5 percent of the sun's power was prevented by smoke from reaching the congested parts of those cities, and one investigation disclosed that there was a 35 percent loss of sunshine in a residential suburban community situated eight miles from a large coal-burning city.[28]

The Pennsylvania State Department of Health had two state sanatoria for the treatment of TB; both had existed for years. Starting in about 1920, inspired by the Rollier method, they began applying heliotherapy to their child patients at those facilities. Climatic conditions did not allow the year-round use of the direct sunbath, so in the winter months the children were exposed to sunlamps. During the summer, children were kept outside in direct sunlight as much as possible, with the boys wearing only brief shorts and no tops. Girls, of course, wore tops and shorts. Such methods were still being used five years later, in 1925. By then hundreds of children had been given heliotherapy.[29]

Even miracles were attributed to the sun. In a highly exaggerated piece, the newspaper of record, the *New York Times*, reported that a sunbath treatment had saved the life of a 22-month-old child in London, England. From the time of his birth on Christmas Eve in 1923, the male baby lay perfectly still without uttering a cry and was described as "stone cold." Doctors declared he was suffering from a disease that prevented him from growing teeth and gave him the brain and arteries of a man of 80. Soon the case became famous within the medical community with the result that 24 eminent specialists held consultations about him. They decided to subject the infant to sunbaths and to place him mainly on a diet of juice, milk being forbidden. Supposedly the treatment was successful, with the baby beginning to wake up and to cry normally. In its headline about the case the *Times* was moved to enthuse, "Sun ray baths save baby."[30]

Professor D. T. Harris commented that it was the sun's infra-red rays [the heat rays] that were the potent rays in the causation of sunstroke, while the UV rays caused sunburn. After the sunburn abated, the majority of people developed pigment [tan], he explained. If then the same region of skin was exposed to UV light, it would be found that a burn did not appear on the pigmented skin but only on the neighboring non-pigmented skin. Harris also admitted that how the pigment worked in curing various ills was unknown. Still, he praised the sun for what it did in curing TB and rickets and for what it did in aiding the growth and development of young children. He, too, decried the presence of air pollution in so many cities and hoped that authorities would act to effect its speedy removal.[31]

Doctor Edwin E. Slosson, with the Science Service in Washington, D.C. remarked, as had so many others, that it had been known for years that UV rays, whether from sunlight or the mercury-quartz sunlamp, greatly benefited and often cured children struck by rickets or TB. "It is now found that light treatment not only betters their bones and improves their general health, but also brightens their brains and sweetens their dispositions." As an example, he cited a class of boys from the London slums who were taken to the garden of a private house on Clapham Common, where they studied and played all day long, attired in "very short shorts and no shirts." At the end of six weeks they were said to show an increase in their mental capacity and alertness as well as in their appetites.[32]

In another example given by Slosson, it was reported that a comparison of the results of mental tests made in the special schools for physically defective children in London with those made on the children who had taken the sunlight treatment at the Lord Mayor Treloar Cripples' Hospital at Alton showed a marked superiority for those who had the advantage of sunshine. A more "exact" test was reportedly given at Alton to a ward containing 20 young children, all afflicted with tuberculosis of the spine and rendered immobile in their beds. All received the same diet and treatment except that 10 of the children were given systematic treatment with artificial light. Henry Gauvain, superintendent of Treloar Hospital, wrote, with respect to that test, "While the physique of those receiving light treatment showed improvement as compared with the others, the effect on the mentality was even more definite. Those exposed to light were markedly happier, more vivacious, more alert, and, I may add, more mischievous. They would often laugh and sing and appeared to be overflowing with animal spirits, while their fellows remained silent."[33]

At the American Health Congress meeting in 1926 at Atlantic City, New Jersey, William J. Bell, Deputy Minister of Health for the province of Ontario, Canada, spoke of the power of the sun to cure TB, claiming it cured 89 of the first 100 patients with surgical TB he had treated. "It is reasonable to think that sunshine is just as essential for the development and health of a child as is food," he told the gathering. Dr. Frederick F. Tisdale of Toronto also addressed the meeting. He said mothers should be told of the importance of sunlight as a factor in the production of healthy infants. After praising the mercury vapor quartz lamp [the sunlamp that delivered artificial UV rays], Bell added that he thought it was unlikely such lamps would ever be in general use from a public health standpoint because of their expense. However, he did issue a caution against "the present-day indiscriminate use of these lamps in the treatment of almost every known pathological condition. This in time will minimize their real value and bring discredit to the medical profession."[34]

A year later Tisdale delivered a paper in Toronto before the Canadian Society for the Study of Diseases of Childhood. After giving a recap of an experiment he and Dr. Allen Browne had conducted over the prior eight months on sunlight, Tisdale asserted that research showed conclusively "that sunlight is an important influence in the promotion of health and the prevention of disease, particularly in early infancy."[35]

John W. M. Bunker, associate professor of physiology and biochemistry at Massachusetts Institute of Technology, observed in 1926 that the science of heliotherapy had developed in the short time of less than 25 years [dating its beginning to Rollier in 1903] but "we are convinced that sunlight and light from other sources may be effective in the treatment of certain diseases and that exposure to light of certain kinds is effective in preventing other diseases."[36]

R. I. Harris, writing in the *American Journal of Public Health*, noted the sun's value had been proven only in the case of rickets and of TB while other claims awaited investigation but nevertheless said, "Let us seize the evidence we have and preach the gospel of the outdoor life and sunshine in every community."[37]

An example of the Rollier method of treating children with TB, in the mid 1920s, was practiced at the J. N. Adam Memorial Hospital in Perrysburg, New York, near Buffalo. According to Robert Fitzgerald, also writing in the *American Journal of Public Health*, "In summer the children play and frolic over the extensive hay fields and woodlands. In winter, with only the protection of a loin cloth, they ski, coast and toboggan on the snow covered hills—their delicate, sick bodies in the meantime being rebuilt and hardened by exposure to the direct sunlight."[38]

Another hymn to sunlight came from Charles Sheard in an official publication of the American Medical Association (*Hygeia*—aimed at the lay reader). Sheard applauded the introduction and spread of the daylight saving time system because that extra hour of sunlight did the recipients "good, not only then and there, but their energy is stored and they build up resistance that helps tide over the untoward conditions induced by the indoor life of the long winter months of our north country."[39]

Another contributor to *Hygeia*, in 1927, was Benjamin Harrow, who urged the reader to "Meet Doctor Sunshine." Exposure of the skin to UV radiation, he said, increased the bactericidal power of the blood and thus produced an increased resistance of the body to disease. According to Harrow, the Rollier method had long since moved from only treatment to include prevention. Children with reduced powers of resistance brought on by various disorders, such as measles or whooping cough, and who were thus thought to be at greater risk to develop tuberculosis, were boarded at the Rollier facility in Switzerland. Such children continued their studies there, outdoors in the direct sun for two hours every day, wearing only loin cloth, linen hat and shoes. Other parts of the day were also spent outdoors, engaged in nature study and "Swedish drill."[40]

By 1927, Leysin, Switzerland, home to Rollier's clinic, contained a total of 38 sanitaria devoted to heliotherapy. Those facilities ranged from simple houses to luxurious establishments and contained, in total, more than 1,000 patients. Rollier's School in the Sun was held year round, with the children wearing the same clothes (shorts and a hat) with the exception that in winter they wore overshoes. Asked to explain how heliotherapy worked, he said the general sun bath, by dilating the capillaries, determined a flow of blood from the depths to the surface through the muscular layers; "it stimulates and regularizes the circulation better than the best massages, and admirably restores the musculature. The toxic action manifests itself also on the thoracic and abdominal organs. It revives the appetite, stimulates the digestive functions and gives new life to the vital forces."[41]

By 1927–1928, the huge volume of articles praising the sun as a healer, in uncritical and often highly exaggerated fashion, dramatically slowed down and then dried up. Apparently everything that could be said had been said, usually many times over. Never again would the sun be praised so exhaustively as a healer of almost any disease.

More perspective was brought to the issue and the occasional negative word was heard. Writing in the unlikely venue of *Popular Mechanics* in 1928, reporter Crag Dale cited Dr. A. C. Carlson, of the University of Chicago, who argued that overexposure to the sun's UV rays could have injurious effects. Carlson argued overexposure could work to lower the blood pressure and produce shock. Another researcher, Dr. W. T. Bovie of Northwestern University, believed too much exposure to the sun might be expected to dwarf an individual, literally. As evidence he cited the difference in height between the natives of the tropics and those of the temperate zones. More ominously, he added that all known pygmies in the world were black or brown, indicating generations of exposure to the sun's rays.[42]

Physician Edgar Mayer, writing in 1933 in The *American Journal of Nursing*, declared that sunbaths had a triple significance — as a healing agent in the cure of disease, as a preventive to disease by building up bodily resistance, and as a sheer pleasure-giving tonic that increased the feeling of well-being." Generally, he commended the fashion of getting a tan, provided tanning was indulged in with knowledge of the drawbacks as well as the benefits to be derived from it. He gave the usual warnings about avoiding sunburn and not lying in the sun in the hottest part of the day. Also, he made the distinction that employing sunbaths for the cure of diseases was a different matter altogether from a healthy person enjoying a sunbath. Mayer declared that little benefit was to be derived from sunbaths unless they resulted in a tanned skin. As to the UV rays' much heralded ability to cure TB, Mayer argued that sunlight was of value in the fight against TB only in the general sense of building up bodily resistance, and that only in one form of TB, fairly uncommon, were UV rays a decidedly curative value. Only three forms of treatment had proven their worth beyond dispute in treating TB, he said, and they were rest, food, and fresh air. "It is said that ultraviolet rays cure or at least have a decidedly beneficial effect on the common cold, rheumatism, neuralgia, sinus infection, anemia, various skin disease, falling hair, and so forth," he said. "Few of these claims are supported by sound evidence." In conclusion, Mayer asserted, "If man's diet is adequate he requires little sunlight, especially if he obtains sufficient fresh air and sleep. However, light energy in some diseases is definitely an agent of remedy."[43]

Henry Laurens, professor of physiology at the School of Medicine, Tulane University, argued in 1936 that sunlight was useful in the treatment of rickets and extrapulmonary TB. "But these facts do not justify the extravagant claims made for it as a vitally necessary curative and preventive agency." Heliotherapy, he observed, contained many other factors (fresh air, wind, temperature, humidity, altitude above sea level, and so on) as well as those of diet and occupation. It was all too easy to overlook this and attribute any observed improvement in patients exclusively to the sun. Sunlight, he believed, played a subordinate role in the regulation of the physical and chemical processes that made up the life of normal people, who could get along with little or practically no sunlight, provided their diet was adequate and they got plenty of fresh air, sleep and exercise. Laurens concluded, "Owing to the hypersensitivity of many infants and adults caution should be used in the use of sunlight, both natural and artificial. Over-indulgence, even in the normal, is foolhardy."[44]

Arguing along the same lines as Laurens was Allen S. Johnson in *Hygeia* in 1937. He, too, felt there was no question of the benefits of sunlight when used properly, and there was some evidence that it helped in curing rickets and certain types of TB of the skin or bone. "But neither

man-made nor natural sunlight actually possesses all the miraculous properties which have been attributed to it.... The evidence that either sunlight
or artificial ultraviolet light will cure the vast array of skin or systemic disorders treated by it is of the most scanty and equivocal character." Johnson remarked that it was not certain that sunlight was absolutely essential
to health, citing the Eskimos of northern Greenland who were exposed to
very little sunlight. Claims that exposure to UV rays by healthy people
increased or improved the tone of the tissues of the body as a whole, stimulated metabolism or tended to prevent colds, declared Johnson, had not
been proved.[45]

But the pervasive hype of the 1920s, especially, (but starting earlier
and more slowly) had the effect of reversing people's attitude toward the
sun. All those reports of miraculous cures from the sun's UV rays, for a
variety of diseases, and that the better the tan the better the health outcome, had the effect of turning suntanning into a huge fad and fashion.
It, too, started slowly (around 1908) and reached its peak in the 1920s. Not
surprisingly, the peak volume of articles on tanning followed, by a couple
of years, the peak volume of media articles about the sun as healer. While
the latter was most prevalent in the 1925–1928 period, tanning articles (the
style and fashion of it), reached their height between 1929 and 1930.

3

The Tanning Fashion
Takes Hold: 1920–1945

"Nothing is better for babies — or grown people either — than a coat of tan, we have it on high scientific authority."
Literary Digest, 1923

"The fact remains, with all its far-reaching implications, a tanned body is a healthy body."
Gulielma Alsop, M. D., 1926

"The 1929 girl must be tanned."
Vogue, 1929

"The tan ... is an integral part of smart costumes for morning, noon and night."
Mildred Adams, 1929

Along with the fashion of tanning came the bane of sunburn. A sunburn contracted on the beach at Atlantic City, New Jersey, in 1921 by Anna Doyle, 26, of Philadelphia was said to have been so severe as to put her life at risk. Doyle spent two days in Atlantic City during which time she spent most of her time lying on the beach in her bathing suit taking sun baths. Her burns were so extensive that she was sent to the hospital. In lying on the beach in the sun at Atlantic City, Doyle was simply doing what so many others in America were doing all over the country.[1]

An editorial in the *New York Times* described the Doyle case as a warning to the many people believed to have an exaggerated idea of the benefits of sunlight. Agreeing that people did well to spend a reasonable amount of time in the sun, the editor went on to caution, "Between tan and health there is no such immediate relation as is the popular assumption, and to come back from a vacation 'as brown as a berry' by no means proves that health has been improved by unaccustomed exposures and activities."[2]

New York City Health Commissioner Frank J. Monaghan issued a warning in July 1924 against the danger of sunburn. He said that at the seaside summer clinics, maintained by the Health Department of New York City, at Coney Island, Rockaway Beach, and Staten Island, hundreds of cases of sunburn received first aid treatment daily. The year 1924 was not the first year that New York had opened summer clinics at certain beaches to deal specifically with sunbathers, another example of the extent of the fad. Monaghan advised people that to avoid sunburn, they should rub exposed body parts with cold cream, cocoa butter, or zinc oxide. Some of the sunburn victims were children and infants.[3]

According to a news item, George Minard, 15, died in hospital in July 1925 as the result of a sunburn reaction that developed into Bright's disease. He went sunbathing at Orchard Beach one Thursday and became ill the following Monday. A physician declared that the sunburn he received had reacted, causing complications that made respiration difficult.[4]

When the popular magazine *Literary Digest* warned about the perils of being sunburned by the summer sun, in 1925, it agreed that UV rays "help cure many ills" but danger lay in overexposure. Tips to avoid a burn included the wearing of a hat and not falling asleep on the beach in direct sunlight. "Build up a coat of tan, if you can. This deposit of pigment will prevent the sun from burning your skin," ended the piece.[5]

In 1930, in one of a series of weekly health broadcasts over radio station WEAF, New York City Health Commissioner Wynne warned against haste in acquiring a tan but stressed the advantages of slowly increasing the amount of time the skin was exposed to the sun.[6]

Dr. Charles F. Pabst, chief dermatologist of the Greenpoint Hospital in Brooklyn, New York, looked at the economic costs of sunburn in 1930 and concluded that every year in America 200,000 working days were lost because of illness due to sunburn, which represented an annual total loss of $1.4 million. In the majority of cases, he felt, "the sunburn is deliberately and intentionally acquired." Arguing for safe and sane tanning, Pabst said it was dangerous to expose a body to direct sunlight during the summer months.[7]

A year later, Pabst issued the same warning about the perils of sunburn and cited the same figures on economic losses as he had in the past. In a prediction well off the mark, he said the fashion of tanning would soon wane, bringing down the economic loss numbers.[8]

Sunburn was enough of a problem that by the mid–1930s efforts were being made to develop some type of sunscreen — something specifically designed to prevent sunburn, as opposed to the various home remedies then in use that utilized products designed for other purposes in addition to sunscreens. A 1935 article advised people to use one or another of the following products before exposing their skin to the sun: olive oil, calamine lotion, yellow petroleum jelly, cold cream, cold cream with powder, and so forth.[9]

Later that same year, reporter Frederick Bigelow presented a list of active ingredients said to prevent sunburn: titanium oxide (two percent to 98 percent cream); salol, often used for rheumatism and neuralgia; a form of quinine; barium sulphate; aesculin (also spelled esculin), said to be one of the most commonly used ingredients in the "countless sunburn creams on the market" [apparently none of them worked at all]; and tannic acid. For use after suffering a sunburn, a lotion of titanium was recommended; or one of zinc oxide, or carron oil (a mixture of lime water and linseed oil).[10]

The first breakthrough, in terms of an effective sunburn lotion, or sunscreen, came around 1943 with the discovery that in humans there was a vitamin that not only caused sunburn but could also be used to prevent it. Dr. Stephen Rothman of the University of Chicago discovered Para-

SPLASH on Absorbine Jr. as soon as possible after exposure. It is cooling, soothing and comforting. No disagreeable odor, no stickiness, does not stain the skin. In severe cases pat the raw, blistered skin with Absorbine, Jr. diluted and soaked in absorbent cotton. It cleanses, and helps to restore the skin without leaving blemishes.

Keep Absorbine Jr. handy for small insect bites, ivy poisoning and sore muscles. It is an invaluable vacation aid.

At all druggists' $1.25. Hospital size, $2.50
Send for free trial bottle

W. F. YOUNG, Inc.   SPRINGFIELD, MASS.

for sunburn
—instantly soothes and comforts
apply

Absorbine Jr.

This ad in 1928 touted the benefits of a product, not designed for sunburn use, to be used, nevertheless, for that purpose. It was an example of marketers taking advantage of a growing trend.

aminobenzoic acid (Paba for short), a B vitamin that helped cause sunburn due to its ability to absorb UV rays of sunlight. In his experiments, Rothman proved Paba to be the sunburn culprit by first irradiating a solution of it with an ultraviolet medical lamp and then injecting some of the irradiated solution under the skin; inflamed spots of artificial sunburn

Sun-scorch—
how to cool it

NO one minds acquiring that healthy outdoor look—but nobody wants a fiery sun-scorch. That's painful—looks anything but alluring. To cool sun-scorch—smooth in Hinds Honey & Almond Cream. It will ease and relieve it—instantly. Make the skin feel soft and fresh again. Try it and see.

But do you know that Hinds Cream also *prevents* sun-scorch? Just pat it on, and powder, *before* going out into the sun. And your skin will be safe from violent sunburn. Because Hinds Cream, with powder over it, will protect the skin from the burning rays—prevent it from getting red and blistered—keep it lovely.

Would you like to try Hinds Cream in these two ways—to relieve sunburn and to prevent it? Then send for the sample bottle. The coupon below will bring it to you. Fill it in and mail today, while you think of it.

Made by A. S. Hinds Co., a division of Lehn & Fink Products Company. In Canada, A. S. Hinds Co. (Canada) Limited. Distributed by Lehn & Fink (Canada) Limited

HINDS
Honey & Almond
CREAM

Try HINDSCREAM *Prevents chapping, prevents windburn, makes powder cling to face, smooths "catchy" fingers, softens skin, protects skin, cleanses skin, softens cuticle, soothes skin, before and after shaving, protects against alkali, protects from hard water, for children's skin.*

Buy Hinds Cream in the 50c and $1 bottles too. You get more at less cost.

Lehn & Fink, Inc., Sole Distributors, Dept. 538, Bloomfield, N. J.

Send me a sample bottle of Hinds Honey and Almond Cream, the protecting cream for the skin.

Name ....

Address ....

This coupon not good after July, 1928

Another product that tried, in 1928, to take advantage of the growing trend in tanning. This ad went so far as to proclaim that the product prevented sunburn, an unlikely outcome.

promptly appeared. Other substances suspected of being responsible for sunburn were similarly irradiated and injected, but did not produce sunburn.

So, the Chicago researchers decided to use Paba's ability to absorb UV by placing it between sun and skin. Their tests indicated a salve containing Paba (a 10 to 15 percent ointment) provided the best protection. Unlike so many other products of the time that supposedly prevented sunburn (none did) the Paba-based lotion was stable, did not soil clothing, was colorless and odorless, did not irritate the skin, and, to an extent, was effective.[11]

A sunburn was once deliberately used by a man in 1943 in an unsuccessful effort to avoid the military draft. The unidentified man was arrested in June that year by the FBI, accused of draft delinquency and held on a criminal complaint. According to FBI spokesman E. E. Conroy, the sunburn was designed to get the prospective inductee a brief deferment, and it did. However, the five days gained did not bring him to his 38th birthday [the draft cut-off age], so he took a short "vacation," then notified his local draft board that he was 38 years old and they could not have him. Then came the FBI.[12]

Writing on the advantages of tanning in 1923, the *Literary Digest* observed, "The white skin automatically protects itself against the injurious action of the sun's rays by developing a layer of dark pigment." UV rays were described as having a shorter wavelength than the violet rays, which were the shortest wavelength rays that could be seen. Ordinary sunshine contained only about one percent UV rays; a little more if the air was dry, a little less if it was damp. Of the rest of the solar radiation, about 19 percent was in the form of visible light and around 80 percent was in the form of heat or infrared rays. UV rays were acknowledged to be fatal to the living cells of the body, while the long-wave rays were not, but did not penetrate as deeply into the skin. Still, said the account, what was needed in the skin was some sort of contrivance that would take those UV rays and transform them to the "harmless" heat waves. "Well, we have such a contrivance in tan. It seems that the ultra-violet and violet rays may be positively beneficial when properly transformed by a coat of tan." Concluded the article, "Nothing is better for babies—or grown people either—than a coat of tan, we have it on high scientific authority."[13]

So popular and fashionable had tans become by this time that famed author D. H. Lawrence included references to tanning in his short story, "Sun," copyrighted in 1922. Part of the plot concerned a woman who had been told by her doctor to take sun baths for some unnamed ailment. To that end she traveled from New York to a sunnier climate. This woman

also urged her young son to play in the sun. "She could feel the sun penetrating into her bones," wrote Lawrence. "She had told Marinina [a ser-
vant] who went shopping for her in the village, that the doctor had ordered
sun-baths [in the real world doctors were doing just that with real
patients]." Lawrence also wrote "So she remembered that the Greeks had
said a white, unsunned body was fishy and unhealthy," and "The child
and she were now both tanned with a rosy-golden tan all over."[14]

Writing in 1922 Doctor Lulu Hunt Peters observed that "every summer a large per cent of our population may be seen on the beaches going
through their annual sun-worship. They lie around, clothed in various
states of abbreviation, getting the brand of their god, the sun, upon them,
and being sun-kist." On gradual exposure to the sun, she explained, the
pigment in the skin was formed, the skin became darkened or tanned "and
this protects the skin and underlying tissues from the burning of the sun
and allows only its beneficial rays to penetrate."[15]

A 1923 article in the *Los Angeles Times* declared that open-air complexions were all the rage. "Gone is the languid beauty of the winter time,
with her trailing black draperies, her white face and carmined lips,"
explained the story. "Sports clothes are upon us, and with the tennis frock,
the bathing suit, or the white serge tailleur goes a complexion of richest
Arabian tint."[16]

More evidence for the pervasiveness of tanning appeared in an ad in
the *Los Angeles Times* in 1926, for a book titled, *How to Take a Sun Bath*,
by Professor Paul C. Bragg, Chief Clinician of the Health Center and
reportedly nationally known physical culture expert. Bragg's book on the
science of sun bathing gave rules and advice on how to get and keep a tan.
Cost of the book was 50 cents post-paid. According to the ad, "Prof. Bragg
has taught thousands how to banish disease and bring back glowing vigorous health by sun bathing and proper living."[17]

Gulielma F. Alsop, college physician at Barnard College, argued in
1926 that sunlight was "absolutely necessary to the creation of a beautiful
skin" and that professional boxers had discovered "the power of the tanned
skin to resist bruises." She explained that in the famous fight between Jack
Dempsey and Georges Carpentier, Dempsey's victory "was partly due to
his elastic tanned skin which Carpentier's blows did not harm." Boxers
then, she declared, devoted two or three months of their training to tanning in the open, clad only in trunks so that the entire upper torso became
deeply tanned. "Tanned individuals possess a far greater resistance to all
infections than pallid people," Alsop stated. "The fact remains, with all its
far-reaching implications, a tanned body is a healthy body."[18]

Dealing with the fashionable aspects of tanning was a 1928 article in the *New York Times*, which wrote about the Monday morning sunburn found on office workers in July and August in particular. "The season is here when New York's office boys and girls take on the color of a sunrise in the Alps, while the chorus girls wear their tanning décolletés almost as if they were the badge of their profession," wrote the journalist. Allowing that bathing suits had become skimpier, the reporter explained, "Youth likes its tan too well, and bathing suits are put on more frequently than not for the purpose of getting a sun bath, not for an ocean bath." Although the sunburn was becoming more common, along with its associated costs, the benefits of UV exposure were substantial and artificial sunlight treatment, from sunlamps, was being increasingly used by physicians, according to Dr. George W. Mellon of the New York Skin and Cancer Hospital, who found "its effects are undeniably beneficial."[19]

Fashion magazine *Vogue* said in a lead article, "Whether or not to sunburn [suntan] is a question that many women are asking themselves and their beauty specialists." Much less equivocal was that magazine's pronouncement a year later, "The 1929 girl must be tanned."[20]

Dr. James Walton of the New York State Department of Health gave a radio talk on the dangers of sunburn, in 1928. He gave the by then usual advice to wear a hat, stay out of the summer sun between 10 A.M. and 3 P.M., and so on, "if you are seeking the tan that has become so desirable in recent years." He closed his talk by saying, "Enjoy your vacations; develop any tan from light yellow to deep bronze; but, if you value your comfort or your health, avoid sunburns."[21]

Another 1928 article in the *New York Times* commented on tans of various shades seen on people all over the streets of New York. At makeup counters the new tints being sought faddishly by women were said to be sunburn and suntan. For those who did not want to follow the rules of gradual exposure yet did not want to get burned, a way around the problem had been found and "No harem favorite ever anointed herself with oil more faithfully than does the flapper of 1928." Olive oil and any other pure vegetable oil were then used by many sunbathers because they supposedly prevented sunburns yet still allowed the wearer to tan.[22]

A year later it was observed that "backless" garments were the fashion rage because they allowed more skin to be exposed for tanning. Fashion designers were making undergarments without a back to conform to the backless dress that was so much in demand. Those costumes, backless almost to the belt line at the back, were being made for sports, beach sunning or for the most formal evening gown. According to a news item, "Each of these kinds of dress now has the same exposure, which the fashion is to make use of to display an Oriental complexion [that is, a tanned one]."[23]

Just one week later the *New York Times Magazine* described in detail the tan and fashion connection as the so-called health benefits of the practice gave way to concerns that were mainly only stylish ones. As interpreters of the meaning and value of tanning, the medical establishment was beginning to lose out to the fashion industry. "The vogue for suntanned complexions seems to be growing steadily instead of diminishing for if it were smart for women to have copper-tinted skin during the Winter, it is even more so now that Summer is here," went the story. "Even the fashion plates show the trend, and advertisements have a tendency to feature slender, haughty women of dusky hues, usually clad in white satin dresses, the better to show off their healthy color." According to this account, not more than 20 years earlier bathers frequented the beaches wearing high-necked, long-sleeved bathing suits and wearing hats with chiffon veils to protect the face. But by 1929, even legs were often tanned, making the wearing of stockings optional, "while bathing suits are so designed as to prevent that bugbear of a few years ago— a ring of brown ending several inches above the cut of an evening dress." If the beach was not an option as a place to go to acquire a tan, the reporter advised using a sunlamp or that there were many beauty parlor preparations to help in the acquisition of "the chic shade. There are liquid powders, lotions that are guaranteed waterproof, and salves and powders for the blonde as well as for the brunette." In conclusion the journalist remarked, "To burn or not to burn is a question to be decided by the individual, but acquiring a becoming sun tan and being able to wear the new colors is a temptation to most of the fair sex."[24]

At the same time the above article appeared, one was published in *The Nation*, wherein Stuart Chase admitted he had made his debut in the society of sun worshippers (which he defined as men who spent endless time lying in the sun and tanning whenever possible, even in winter) almost 20 years earlier. "Nobody had ever heard of ultra-violet in those days," he explained. "Few of us arrived [to lie in the sun] because of a doctor's order.... We talked sagely of therapeutic effects" but did not understand them. However, "by and large we knew, with a profundity which mocks science, that what we were doing was good for our bodies and good for our souls." With the cult of sun-worshipping expanding rapidly, Chase felt pseudoscience had muscled its way in with the result that quacks and charlatans were all hard at work trying to make money from the tanning fad, advertising sunlamps that actually produced no UV rays, for example, and trying to sell special window glass hyped as admitting UV rays when it did not. Solariums were opened in cities where the air pollution was so bad that UV rays did not penetrate in sufficient strength to be of value. "Face preparations are sold guaranteed to give that real Palm Beach effect," he added. "Cure for all known disease is promised when as a matter of fact ultra-violet rays have no effect on most diseases, and actually compound the evils of some diseases by stimulating cell growth."[25]

An editorial in the *New York Times* that commented on Chase's article on the joys of sun-worship offered the opinion that "The sun heals. The sun ministers to random ills of the human body. And the current fashion of sun-tan shades of face powder and sun suits, and the scourge of ultra-violet ray machines, silently attest to the therapeutics of the sun."[26]

A flood of articles on the fashion of tanning were published in 1929 and 1930, the two years that represented the peak of media attention devoted to the fad. Suntanning, by then, was a pervasive and accepted part of American culture. Writing in the *New York Times* in 1929, Mildred Adams declared the sun had claimed a new host of 20th century devotees and "has become the god of debutantes and stenographers, bank clerks and the garment industry." In that cult "the worshippers lie for hours prone before the majesty of the sun. They wear garments specially designed to bare to his rays as much of their bodies as their consciences or the police will permit." And if a person could not get to the beach, Adams also mentioned that sunlamps were available. Noting the fad was rooted in medical opinion, she wondered how the craze of tanning had spread as far as it had. In answer she said, "Idealists would like to believe that the people, investigating the medical doctrine and accepting it as sober fact, went deliberately forth to get what was good for them, and took to sun baths with an avidity they had never shown for spinach, sleep, or orthopedic shoes."

Adams also commented that observers of feminism linked the fad with the whole trend toward sports for women, freedom of movement and the casting off of hampering clothes, while cynics argued it was the result of the force of commerce concentrating on a new fad and using medical phrases as a camouflage to sell expensive equipment such as sunlamps and to sell new sets of clothes. Nevertheless, the tan was very fashionable then, in 1929, and "The tan that it imparts to its devotees is an integral part of smart costumes for morning, noon and night." To be in fashion, she emphasized, "One must be tanned, naturally if possible, or if the skin protests too much, artificially. There are lotions that call up the walnut stain of gypsy kidnapping tales, there are creams and powders warranted to keep one tanned even under the splash of salt water." Adams thought the backless dress fashion had started in the summer of 1926 with the tennis outfit and rapidly spread to dresses for other occasions. Tanned faces and arms were everywhere in New York in 1929; she felt "the mode has

now reached its height." Admitting it was on women that this style had
the most noticeable effect, Adams argued, though, that men were also
affected, that bankers as well as debutantes sought to exchange their pallor for the fashionable color under the glow of artificial sunlight. One of
New York's more fashionable men's clubs was said to have an entire room
full of sunlamps.[27]

James J. Walsh, in *The Commonweal*, remarked that various health
officials across America (including Dr. Shirley Wynne, Commissioner of
Health of New York City) issued annual warnings in the summer to take
care in sun bathing so as to avoid sunburn, and of the potential health
dangers that could result from a severe burn. That had to be done, thought
Walsh, because "We have heard so much in recent years of the wonderful
health-giving effects of sunlight" that there was a risk people would forget about the dangers of sunburn. "Unfortunately a great many people at
the present time are quite convinced that a thoroughgoing coat of tan is
a definite index of the greatest benefit to health," said Walsh, and that it
was not unusual to see people lying out in the sun for long periods of time.
People used to seek the shade, as a rule, he said, "but now, after having
heard so much about the benefit of the sun's rays, many choose the open.
They seem to think that every possible evidence they can secure of the
action of the sunlight upon their skins is definite proof of the accumula-
tion of solar energies in their bodies. Coats of tan have become so popular recently that enterprising manufacturers of cosmetics have invented a
number of skin applications that simulate tanning."[28]

With regard to tan and health, Walsh was a skeptic, arguing that no
one believed that because of their highly pigmented skin blacks were much
more healthy than whites. On the contrary, he felt, they were less healthy
than whites with a comparable background. While their pigmentation protected them from sunstroke and other evil effects of the sun, it did not
increase their immunity to disease. Walsh worried that when a white person acquired a deeper and deeper tan, the further beneficial action of the
sun on that person was very largely prevented, due to the sun blocking
out more and more UV rays as the tan deepened. As evidence for that idea,
Walsh said black children were more likely to suffer from nutritional diseases, especially rickets, because their highly pigmented skin shut out so
much of the sun's rays. His confusing contention seemed to be that a tan
was positive and health-giving, but only up to a point. That as a tan got
darker, it conferred less and less benefit until one reached the level of pigmentation found in blacks, at which point the tan acted in a negative,
health-taking way. Concluded Walsh, "The present fad for acquiring a coat
of tan, either by the direct action of sunlight or by artificial means, is

almost inevitably certain to prevent the very valuable action of the sun in health-giving ways thereafter."[29]

Human skin produced melanin, the pigment that "blackened Negroes and tanned white people, remarked reporter E. E. Free in 1929. He went on to add, "for once the lords of fashion and learning agree, for doctors hail the present sun-tan fad as healthful...." Of the cosmetics that simulated tans, said Free, few even deceived the casual eye; and none, of course, produced the physiological response of the real tan. It was somewhere in a baby's skin, argued Free, for example, that certain kinds of UV rays found chemicals from which to manufacture vitamin D, a lack of which caused rickets.[30]

Around the same time, in London, England, George Lansbury, Commissioner of Works in the Labour Government, addressed a meeting of women in London and said, "People in the next generation, I think, will wear far less clothes than now." He was referring to the value of sunbathing and the opportunities afforded for that activity in the public parks, which came under his jurisdiction. "When I spent a fortnight at the seaside this year I saw number of children running about almost naked, enjoying the sun's rays," he elaborated, "and I was very much struck with the improvement in their condition within a few days." Lansbury went on to tell his audience he hoped his department would have some sort of organized sunbathing for children in the public parks by the following summer.[31]

Delegates to the annual convention of the Illuminating Engineering Society were told in September 1929 that too much tan was a bad thing because it served to shut out the sunlight and barred the sun's "curative" rays from entering the body. That is, this was another criticism in which people were urged to acquire a mild coat of tan, since it was beneficial, but that a deep and dark tan actually had an injurious effect. Henry Phelps Gage of the Corning, New York, glassworks, who led a discussion on the curative effects of sunlight, condemned the vogue for heavy coats of tan, arguing the amount of sunshine required to prevent or cure rickets and other diseases was less than was necessary to cause sunburn or tanning. "One's body must not acquire a coppery veneer to derive the full benefit of sunlight," Gage continued. "In fact, the curative qualities of sunlight decrease with each additional coat of tan." At the same time this group was said to be working and researching so future generations could avoid "sunlight starvation" (due to a murky atmosphere, indoor jobs, and so on).[32]

Writing in the *Saturday Evening Post* at the end of 1929, Floyd Parsons described experiments conducted at the Massachusetts Agricultural College. Researchers reportedly compared the development of vegetables

grown under ordinary window glass, which shut out UV rays, with that
of similar vegetables grown under glass that permitted the passage of a
greater percentage of UV rays. Radishes were said to be 69 percent heavier if grown under the special glass while heads of lettuce were 76 percent
heavier, after 38 days. Two groups of 12 pullets were separated for 16 weeks.
The first flock produced 124 eggs while the other flock (treated the same
as the first group except they were subjected to 10 minutes of UV rays per
day) produced 497 eggs. And the eggs of the second group contained more
lime and calcium, making them a more nutritious food for human consumption. "A healthy skin, moderately tanned by ultra-violet light," said
Parsons, "presents the likelihood of vigor and energy as the result of a
properly functioning adrenal gland." Athletic coaches at several large uni-
versities supposedly had taken to having their athletes do sunbaths, natural ones when possible and artificial ones in winter. "Records of muscular
tests conducted on different groups of athletes have shown that those pigmented by irradiation display 20 percent more energy and persistence than
the young men not given light treatments," went the story.[33]

Parsons declared that another survey disclosed an increase of nearly
100 percent in the intelligence of school children who were kept out in the
sun for a week, although he provided no details. According to his account,
foods of many kinds were being bathed in artificial radiation from high-
powered electric sunlamps. Such exposures supposedly "vitalized" yeast,
commercial casein, and lanolin and grain products. "Let no one think that
this growing appreciation of the value of sunlight is merely a fad," said
Parsons, with regard to the growing movement to more sun. "The new
knowledge being piled up concerning the benefits of bodily exposure to
various bands of rays is founded in truth. The arbiters of fashion in clothes
will be compelled to shape their ideas on style in accordance with the dictates of health." He saw a time when authorities would banish smog and
air pollution — to admit more sunlight — and a time when science would
increase the amount and quality of UV rays that people were daily exposed
to — such as by the perfection of a window glass that admitted more UV
radiation and was also affordable. "It all represents merely the beginning
of a great scientific adventure that will doubtless bring disclosure of
unmeasured value to the well-being of mankind," he enthused. "More and
better light, both natural and artificial, means increased happiness,
improved health, larger profits and greater prosperity."[34]

After extolling the virtues of sunbathing for all the usual reasons, in
his article in *Sunset Magazine* in the summer of 1930, journalist Gerald
O'Gara revealed that when he had recently gone to his doctor he had been
asked about his skin pigmentation. That physician explained that pig-

mentation, or degree of tan, was usually a pretty fair index to health because it revealed how much sunshine a person had been absorbing. O'Gara added that his doctor gave him a prescription for the best summer tonic of 1930. "R. Ultra-violet rays. Dose: A little every day," wrote the doctor. "As a practical matter we know that sunbathing soothes the nerves, tones up the system generally, and enables us to get more joy out of life." Asked when the best time of day was for a sunbath O'Gara's doctor replied, "Between 11 and 1 o'clock. The sun's rays are most potent then." O'Gara suggested that home sunrooms and solariums be constructed for family use, provided quartz glass was used.[35]

Moral sensibilities were sometimes enraged by the practice of sunbathing. A police patrolman was permanently assigned to the town park in Rye, New York, in 1930 to prevent its being used for sunbathing by women from the beach, following complaints of "shocking" conditions made to park commissioners by Warren J. Martin, town superintendent. Martin said that after taking a swim, many women made a practice of reclining on the green lawn of the park to become tanned. Rye Mayor Livingston Platt, after remarking that "women nowadays seem to have lost all sense of proportion," ordered Police Chief William H. Balls to station a man at the park to stop the practice.[36]

A further testimony to the fad and fashion of the suntan came from journalist Alma Whitaker in the *Los Angeles Times* in July 1930, when she reported on the status of the tan among Hollywood's female actors. Joan Crawford was said to have banished makeup altogether and sported "a lovely natural brown skin," while Norma Shearer wanted a tan but she was one of those people who only freckled. Grace Moore was "sumptuously brown"; Bessie Love disliked a tan but Mary Doran "flaunts her deep tan," as did Greta Garbo "who exposes her face and arms, hatless and sleeveless for tennis, her pet recreation." Billie Dove and Lilyan Tashman had competed with each other for most extensive tan the previous year and were doing the same that year, "their backs and arms being even more golden brown than their faces." Janet Gayner and Maureen O'Sullivan were both well tanned; Lois Moran "loves a tan the year round ... a smooth light tint." Marjorie White was said to dread a tan and took every precaution to avoid a hint of it while Marguerite Churchill had a "deep becoming tan," and Fifi Dorsay "flaunts a stunning tan this year." Irene Rich had acquired "a nice gentle conservative tan while Zelma O'Neall wore "a mighty tan." Clara Bow and Kay Francis each had "a deep brown complexion these days" while Nancy Carroll and Ruth Chatterton each had a lighter tan. Louise Fazenda said she liked lots of tan but could not find the time to acquire one, as she was a hard-working girl.[37]

According to Whitaker, Hollywood personalities against a tan included Jean Arthur, Mary Brian, June Collyer, Marlene Dietrich, Jeannette Macdonald and Fay Wray, all of who agreed with Bessie Love and Marjorie White on the subject. Natalie Moorehead and Evelyn Knapp both scorned the idea of ruining their fair skin with a tan. On the other hand, Irene Delroy and Winnie Lightner both loved to tan. In this survey, said Whitaker, "the tans have it by a large majority. They say it makes them feel husky, self-confident, jolly and athletic. They also insist that it is very good for their skin, especially as most of them eschew make-up, except lipstick, outside of working hours."[38]

In the summer of 1930, Dr. Arnold H. Kegel, Health Commissioner of Chicago, asked for the establishment of solariums at all beaches, one for each sex. He explained that a solarium "is nothing but a stretch of sand with a high board fence around it."[39]

During that same summer, it was reported that sports had become a prominent feature of life in the Soviet Union and that sun worshippers were also "legion." In Moscow people took sunbaths on balconies, in yards or on roofs, while along the Moscow River many sunbathed in the nude. Those Russians fortunate enough to spend their vacations in the Crimea or on the Black Sea got the deepest tans of all, "to the great envy of their friends."[40]

Leonard Falkner, a journalist reporting in *American Magazine* in 1930, declared that America's foremost dermatologists agreed that the sunbath was "wonderful medicine." Having heard that too much suntan would in time wrinkle the skin, Falkner consulted a dermatologist at the New York Skin and Cancer Hospital. "Wrinkle the skin?" laughed the dermatologist. "Not sun tan. If it did we'd be a nation of wrinkled faces by this time. The sun tan fad has been with us for five years, at least. And I haven't noticed any boys or girls getting prematurely old."[41]

An editorial writer for the *New York Times*, after observing that the suntan fad had not disappeared as some observers had speculated, commented that the beaches continued to be "public rotisseries" cluttered with "oiled bodies roasting to a turn."[42]

An editorial in *The Commonweal* in 1932 observed that bathing suits were held together by the slenderest of threads and all sorts of innovations were replacing the familiar arm-straps so that the women, when they appeared in evening dress "shall not present variegated patterns of brown and white...." It used to be, said the editor, that a family would retire to the shade of a tree and stay there for their outdoor activities, but "Now the fashion seems to be to conduct everything in the pitiless glare of the sun."[43]

A new fashion in Manhattan in 1932 was reported to be people getting sunbaths on the roofs of the many apartment buildings in the city. That is, people who lived in buildings were using their own roofs more often to save money on trips to the beach — it was the Depression. But also reported was that some commercial roof centers had been started, offering deck chairs, dancing, card playing, and so on, for a fee.[44]

Discussing the philosophy of tanning in 1932, an editorial in *The New Statesman and Nation* remarked on how selective tanning was for those involved, with participants wanting to give more and more time to the practice. "All the sights and wonders of the world, save the sight and wonder of brown skin, mean as little to them as to a blind man." He added that he believed everything he had read about the curative properties of sunlight and therefore, taken in moderation like a bottle of medicine, "it is one of the best of all medicines. But these people I saw sun-bathing were like perfectly healthy people drinking bottles of medicine all day long." He worried about such excesses and "whether the European brain can survive so much sunlight." Was it not only after he had lost his brown skin that the European undertook his greatest achievements such as building temples and cities, writing great novels and painting great pictures, he wondered. "After all, our own ancestors went through a long process of bleaching, and how excellent were the results may be seen in Europe today. Civilisation spread as men learned to take shelter from the sun," he noted. "My convictions are fluid in regard to sun-bathing, but I hold that we ought to proceed cautiously in the matter and not plunge recklessly back into a brown-skinned civilisation from which we may never be able to emerge again," the editor concluded. "We must always remember that it is to a bleached and gouty race that we owe the position in which we are in 1932. No brown-skinned generation could have brought us to this."[45]

When Dr. Charles F. Pabst, chief dermatologist at the Greenpoint Hospital in Brooklyn, gave his annual radio warning reminder in 1935 against over-exposure to the summer sun's rays, he added the additional caveat that "Alcohol and sunlight do not mix." He advised vacationers at the beach not to drink highballs or strong liquor while exposed to the sun, although he did not explain why. Especially warned to be careful were blondes and redheads but "the olive-skinned brunettes are heliophiles, who can acquire safely a deep mahogany tan in small doses," he stated. "They may wear the modern, backless bathing suit, which may be of the fishnet variety with meshes as coarse as the law permits."[46]

John W. Harrington was another who described the increasing popularity of sunbathing on the rooftops of Manhattan apartment buildings and commercial buildings. Hundreds of Manhattan apartment houses were said to have been altered to appeal to sun worshippers. Health clubs housed on the tops of skyscrapers had sunlamps inside for use on inclement days.[47]

At the American Progressive Chiropractic Association's annual convention in Los Angeles in 1937 (more than 500 delegates representing 39 states were in attendance), Dr. Hanus Von Yahnah told delegates that California led the nation in traffic accidents and deaths because the glandular functions of its citizens were disturbed by too much sunbathing. "Violet rays penetrating the skin result in abnormality, either under-functioning or over-functioning of the glandular system," he explained.[48]

Life magazine featured the fashion of tanning in a July 1941 issue, in which it said, "On days when the sun shines hottest, when every sane man and beast tries to hide in the shade, seaside resorts present the amazing spectacle of young vacationers sprawled out in the blazing sun." The account continued, "All of them are hard at work at the job of acquiring a deep suntan. No matter how great the heat and discomfort, a good tan is a vacation must. In the young mind, male or female, the success of a vacation is measured in terms of the degree of tan acquired." However, all 10 photos with the article were of young women tanning. Mentioned within the article was the story of a fad within a fad. Sun-tattooing involved placing cut-outs of initials, the U.S. flag, an American eagle, and so forth, on the body and then removing it after the surrounding area had tanned. One photo showed a woman with an aluminum-coated cardboard screen in the sand beside her to reflect the sun's rays to parts of the body where the deepest tan was desired. When that bather was tanning her back, her face got an extra dose of the sun. Reflector tanning has remained part of tanning culture up to the present.[49]

The vogue for tanning also extended to children and even babies, with the medical establishment and the media urging parents to expose their children to UV rays. Given that much of the early so-called evidence that touted the sun as healer involved cures for children suffering from TB and rickets, the movement to tan healthy as well as sick children was not surprising.

Doctor Lulu Hunt Peters, after listing the virtues of the sun in 1922, and some cautions, such as don't stay out in the sun too long at first, declared, "Meanwhile, heeding my cautions, have your babies join the sun worshippers."[50]

A year later an article in the *Literary Digest* noted that the first few years of life were the hardest for babies, with a death rate, during the first 12 months of life, as high as the rate for 75 year olds, but "Sunshine is the preventive and cure." If the weather was inclement, parents were urged to expose their babies to artificial UV light from sunlamps.[51]

Burn, baby, burn? This 1923 photograph showed child minders exposing their charges to the late summer sun at the seaside somewhere in America. Note that all but one child were hatless. These minders were following the latest medical advice of the time — doctors overwhelmingly urged people to get lots of sun exposure, advice that extended to babies as young as a month old.

Doctor C. W. Saleeby declared in 1924 that the beach was very good for children because sunlight "is the first, best, cheapest and most honest of antiseptics." Colds and other infections were not to be feared when children played on the beach. He felt the antiseptic sunlight killed infectious germs, such as the ones children in city schools perpetually infected each other with, and enriched the blood of those exposed to the sun with elements such as lime, phosphorous and iron.[52]

When she was director of child hygiene at the U.S. Children's Bureau in 1925, Doctor Martha M. Eliot stated that the sun was a good baby doctor and that parents should let the sun have a chance at their child. Her slogan was "more sunlight for babies." She elaborated, "In the campaign for better babies and healthier children, more stress must be laid upon sunlight. The baby or little child who has been kept out-of-doors and tanned by the sun is strikingly healthy and vigorous in contrast to the pale, flabby baby or child who has been kept indoors." Eliot's recommendation was to expose the baby to the sun gradually until he got a one-hour sunbath each morning and each afternoon (she did advise parents to avoid exposure between 10:00 A.M. and 3:00 P.M. in July and August). Concluded Eliot, "Sun-baths in the direct sunlight are the simplest method of giving the baby enough ultra-violet light. Sun-baths should be begun when the baby is about three or four weeks old.... A slight reddening of the skin each day will gradually tan the baby."[53]

Writing in the *American Journal of Public Health* in 1926, Doctor Frederick F. Tisdale, attending physician at the Hospital for Sick Children at Toronto said, "from the evidence at hand it is extremely doubtful that we can get too much ultra-violet radiation in sunlight." He urged that mothers be told of the importance of sunlight as a factor in the production of healthy infants and children. "We have found that the best results are obtained by telling mothers that they must get their children sunburnt." Whenever possible, even in the middle of winter, he asserted, "the infant should be taken out on bright days for a time between the hours of 11 A.M. and 2 P.M. and the sun allowed to shine directly on its face." And, "The amount of tanning or sunburn may be taken as a rough estimate of the effectiveness of the treatment."[54]

Sir Truby King, in Sydney Australia, advocated an hour a day in the sunlight for infants, as part of Australia's school curriculum. He claimed it would eliminate tuberculosis. Recently, King had been knighted for his work in reducing infant mortality.[55]

When reporter Gerald O'Gara had received his own prescription for a sunbath from his doctor, he asked about sunbaths for children. The physician's response was, "Infants entirely unclothed can be beneficially exposed to the sun when they are a few weeks old."[56]

Edgar Mayer, a medical doctor writing in *The American Journal of Nursing*, said, "Sunlight is of great importance to infants.... Therefore, every mother should make it her duty to have her child derive all benefit from sunlight under proper methods of exposure. When the infant is a few weeks old, he should be put out-of-doors in the sunlight, for about a half hour at first, and then gradually increasing the time until he may be kept in the sunlight two or three hours daily."[57]

Tanning became so popular that an entire industry evolved — sunlamps — to cater to the desire to tan when the weather was not right for outdoor sunbathing. Also, several attempts were made to introduce UV rays into offices and workplaces, through special glass, for example. All such attempts failed but they illustrated the degree of interest in the fashion.

4

Sunlamps, New Window Glass, and Industrial Tanning: 1920–1945

"Eventually I expect to see sunlamps used for lighting in place of the modern bulbs."
Leonard Falkner, 1930

"The lamps now commercially available for providing ultra-violet rays at home are reported to be as effective, perhaps even more effective, than the sunlight itself."
Henry Hubbard, 1931

"In the future ... we shall have ultra-violet light rays pouring down on us as we sleep, producing the effect of reposing on a sunlit meadow in a tropical land."
Dr. M. Luckiesh, Lighting Institute
of the General Electric Company, 1931

The craze for tanning, full blown by the early 1920s, had several offshoots connected with it besides the obvious one whereby people exposed themselves outdoors to the direct sun in the sunbathing ritual. One was a fad for sunlamps that delivered artificial UV rays so the tanning process could continue unhindered by weather. Another was an attempt by various industrial and commercial concerns to somehow expose their workers to more UV rays. Those firms thought that perhaps workers exposed to more UV radiation would be ill, and therefore absent, less often, that when such absences did occur they would be of a shorter duration. These companies also believed that a workforce would become more energetic by such exposure and be more productive. Third, research efforts were made to produce glass used in ordinary windows that admitted more

UV rays, since ordinary window glass blocked UV rays. Quartz glass admitted more such light and did exist then, but it was prohibitively expensive.

At a meeting of the health section of the 13th annual safety congress of the National Safety Council held in Louisville, Kentucky, in 1924, Dr. A. J. Pacini of Chicago told delegates that during the previous two years 60,000 cases of hay fever, bronchial asthma, rickets, fractures, wounds and industrial injuries had been cured by American physicians and surgeons with the "new instruments" [sunlamps] that furnished light and heat "many times more intense" than that from natural sunlight. Pacini had formerly been chief of the X-ray section of the United States Public Health Service. The sunlamp was said to accomplish in 15 seconds what natural sunlight required two days to complete. According to Pacini the human body had to receive heat, light and UV rays to "effect a balancing of the functions of the organs, thus bringing about a normal condition."[1]

Members of the U.S. House of Representatives in Washington, D.C. joined the fad of tanning by artificial sunlight early in 1929 when several sunlamps, of a type recently pronounced by the U.S. Bureau of Standards

Ads from 1928 and 1929 touting the wonders of sunlight in general and Alpine Sun Lamps in particular for adults and children. Note that the ads show goggles on all the lamp users.

to be among the best, were installed in the House Office building. It was explained that a ruddy complexion was the first result of exposure to the sunlamps, followed by gradual tanning if the exposure was continued.[2]

Dr. Donald A. Stockbarger, assistant professor of physics at MIT and a pioneer in the development of artificial sunlight machines, published an article at the end of the 1920s warning physicians and the public that sunbathing under such machines could be a serious menace to health. Stockbarger advised against the indiscriminate use of sunlamps while pointing out that scientists did not yet know the exact nature of the ultimate effect of the artificial UV rays "with which many doctors and thousands of patients are now bathing themselves and others." He also declared that direct sunlight itself still held many secrets science did not then understand, and that while plenty of exposure to sunshine was probably a good thing, too much exposure might not be such a good thing.[3]

Correcting what was said to have been a misconception that made it appear the U.S. Public Health Service had condemned the use of lamps emitting UV rays, in a radio broadcast, the department announced in 1930, "such lamps have unquestionably been shown to be of great value when used under certain conditions." However, the statement reiterated a warning that the personal selection of any one of the three then common types of sunlamps, "which are used to aid in correcting widely varying conditions, should only be made after consulting with a physician, and that there should be competent medical supervision of the sunlamp usage."[4]

Another 1930 article espoused the virtues and curative value of the sun's rays, natural and artificial, adding, "Day-long sunshine is the best doctor." For this reporter the fact that six of Toronto's hospitals had an "extensive number of UV ray lamps meant that no other endorsement was necessary." He concluded, "There is no question that, in putting the daily sun-bath within the reach of everyone [through the use of sunlamps], science has made a great forward step in safeguarding the health of young and old alike."[5]

In an editorial in a 1930 issue of *Hygeia*, the American Medical Association's main publication directed at lay readers, it was noted that the American people were given to fads and crazes. Just ending then, for example, was the vogue for the shaker, or automatic exercise machine. "Perhaps the most striking demonstration of mass interest in a health device has been the promulgation of apparatus for providing artificial sunlight," commented the editor. However, he added, "Again and again it has been emphasized that the ultraviolet rays of the sun have the specific power to create vitamin D and that beyond this effect they seem to be of little service in promoting the health and growth of the human being." While vitamin D may have been of special importance for the mobilization of calcium and while calcium metabolism was related to the course of various disorders, he said, it was next to impossible for the average adult to know whether or not his calcium metabolism was progressing properly and whether or not he needed extra UV rays, vitamin D or calcium. In the editor's view, rickets was not a problem in England until window glass was introduced there in the 16th century — ancient man lived mostly outdoors and rickets was not a great problem. But since the advent of window glass, rickets had been prevalent. Still, "This is no warrant, however, for overexposure of adults to artificial sources of ultraviolet rays in the home nor is it any indication that the amount of sunlight available in most communities is not sufficient for most practical purposes." Also, he believed there was far more to the value of sunlight in the open air than could be accomplished by the use of an artificial source of UV in the home — such as the exercise, fresh air, breezes, and the stimulation of pleasant companionship.[6]

Reporter Leonard Falkner asked an unnamed doctor if the benefits of sunlamps were comparable with those from the rays of the sun. Supposedly the answer was yes and that the sunlamps were a "wonderful invention" but they had to be used carefully under the supervision of a physician. Added the doctor, "In time they may even be an improvement on sunlight, since they can filter out certain unimportant rays and they can regulate the length of the rays. Eventually I expect to see sunlamps used for lighting in place of the modern bulbs."[7]

Uncritically praising the UV rays in general in a 1931 piece was journalist Henry Hubbard, who remarked, "We are just learning to appreciate the fact that sunburn and tan are indications of inward as well as outward health." He reported that the UV deficiency of the winter sun was compensated by high-power UV generators such as quartz, mercury, and carbon arc lamps. Tungsten filaments, as well, were then available in UV transmitting bulbs and would, thought Hubbard, have wide application "for human and animal growth, vitality and resistance to disease. He also believed that radically new scientific developments in the use of UV rays to increase the nutritive and health-giving properties of foods could have far-reaching effect also in food preservation. "The lamps now commercially available for producing ultra-violet rays at home are reported to be as effective, perhaps even more effective, than the sunlight itself," proclaimed Hubbard.[8]

During a controversy in Chicago in 1932 about how little clothing could be worn on the city's beaches, whether a fence should be constructed to block the sight of the immodestly clad, and so on, Mayor Cermak posed

Ads for two different makes of sunlamps, even for use in the bathroom. In these 1929 ads, users were not wearing goggles.

in goggles, shirt and trousers, basking under a sunlamp and endorsed the sun itself as being just as good.[9]

Dr. Edgar Mayer explained in 1933 that various kinds of UV lamps were being offered on the market. And, "Some of these sold for a few dollars, and the so-called 'ultraviolet generators' are generally worthless as they do not transmit sufficient [UV rays] to have any beneficial effect on the body." Mayer also mentioned special window glass then on the market with pure fused quartz freely transmitting UV rays, but "it is extremely expensive." More moderately priced types of glass were being made, he added, that transmitted a "moderate percentage" of UV, one called Vita-glass. Sunlamps enjoyed their greatest popularity in America from 1929 to 1934, roughly. After that they quickly faded into the background and were rarely mentioned, although they did not disappear. They were rarely mentioned until about 1978 when they returned with a vengeance, in the form of tanning salons.[10]

Writing in the *New York Times Magazine* in 1927, journalist Walde-mar Kaempffert commented on the spreading belief in UV rays as a panacea and of a number of attempts, some under way and some planned, for a more industrially minded application of UV rays. Kaempffert argued, "There is a definite relation between light and health and consequently between light and productivity which has made its appeal to manufactur-ing companies." Because of that, architects were said to have taken to designing office buildings and other commercial structures with more glass windows. Architect Hugh Ferris proposed that skyscrapers, apartment houses, hotels, and virtually any human habitation be built not only with more glass but with glass through which UV radiation of the sun could pass. Since UV rays did not pass through ordinary glass, noted the reporter, "So far as ultra-violet radiation is concerned our houses and office build-ings are all dungeons." The only transparent substance through which the rays could pass was said to be quartz, but it was difficult and expensive to make windowpanes out of quartz—$100 a square foot for a pane [to be practical the price would have to have been pennies per square foot]. Pro-fessor Daniel Berthelot believed UV rays aided digestion and speculated that "perhaps physicians of the second half of this century will prescribe instead of the classic pill of pepsin a dose of ultra-violet rays introduced into the stomach, thus to avoid the period of indigestion." F. E. Lamplough of Cambridge, England, had developed a glass substitute so rich in quartz that it transmitted from 50 to 65 percent of available UV rays [a pure quartz pane transmitted close to 100 percent] but it was still too expen-sive. Lamplough's glass cost approximately $2 a square foot.[11]

In a school in Southwick, England, Dr. J. Bell Ferguson, a medical health officer, had one room glassed with Lamplough's glass; another room of the same size and exposure was left with ordinary glass. At the end of nine months, reportedly, the children who had studied under Lamplough's glass had gained an average of 3.25 pounds more in weight and six-tenths of an inch more in height than the others. Dr. W. T. Bovie, professor of biophysics at Harvard University, was said to have raised two flocks of chickens in a greenhouse, conditions equal for the two groups in all ways except one flock was exposed for 15 minutes a day to the UV rays of a

Still more manufacturers advertise their lamps, in 1929 (left) and 1931. The Campbell model claimed a few minutes under its rays gave a tonic, invigorating effect while the GE copy pitched use in the gloomy winter time, even in the bathroom.

quartz mercury-vapor lamp. "The results were startling. All the chickens that had been treated with ultra-violet rays lived, except a few killed by rats, but about 75 percent of those raised under glass died from 'weak legs,' a disease called 'rickets' when it affects babies," enthused Kaempffert. "Moreover, the ultra-violet chickens were livelier, larger and more vigorous than the survivors of the competitive group." Bovie claimed that some

97 percent of all babies in Northern U.S. cites were "more or less" afflicted with rickets and suggested it was not inconceivable in the future that we could light our restaurants with sources of UV light, so that while eating foods rich in phosphorous and calcium "we could partake of light energy that would enable us to utilize those salts in a normal manner."

Noted by the reporter was the fact that cod liver oil was effective also in treating rickets. But, according to Dr. Alfred F. Hess of the College of Physicians and Surgeons its effectiveness was due entirely to the absorption of UV radiation by the microscopic plants on which the cod fed. Dr. Hess and Professor Steenbock of the University of Wisconsin reportedly found that UV rays could activate food such as bread, oatmeal, corn, flour, milk, and vegetable oils, thus enabling those items to cure rickets. Stimulated by Hess's work, Dr. J. Stuart Colwell of London advocated the radiation of cows by UV lamps during the winter months so that their milk would acquire ricket-curing properties. "Summer milk is better for babies than Winter milk," argued Colwell, "because cows receive the benefit of more sunlight in Summer."[12]

An editorial in the *New York Times* in 1927 told of a woman in the suburbs who planned to build a glass house. "Nowadays the tendency is to make the sun do duty to the utmost as a sanitary agent and physician," remarked the editor. "In town, we must look to the new kinds of glass which transmit the health-giving rays of the sun much better than plain window-glass. This new product is being installed in many hospitals and in homes, particularly where there are children."[13]

When the National Conference on Housing in America met in 1929, one item on its agenda was to find a means for mitigating the smoke pollution nuisance, described as one of the greatest blots on modern civilization. Blame for the clouds of smoke that shrouded the cities and cut off a large percentage of the available sunshine was placed by several speakers on householders as well as on industrial concerns. It was agreed that bituminous coal was, and would continue to be, the basic medium for the production of heat and power but that proper use of it would cut down the smoke problem by half. Wayne D. Heydecker, field secretary of the Regional Plan of New York City, reported to the conference that after exhaustive studies on the effects of sunlight on health, a recommendation was made for the building of houses that would allow 15 percent more window area for the total floor area of the rooms served. At the conference Professor Donald Stockbarger of the Department of Physics at MIT expressed the belief that the "ultra-violet home" was at hand. In his paper he pointed out that ordinary window glass did not admit UV, but science, by developing different types of glass, "which permit the health-giving rays of the ultra-violet family to enter homes" has assured the human family of better health, especially in Winter months.[14]

Encouraged by the results achieved in 1929 in, supposedly, practically eliminating colds among students, Dr. Dean F. Smiley, medical adviser at Cornell University, announced in 1930 that a further extension of that work was being implemented with the establishment of cold prevention classes. During the previous year, the UV ray solarium that had been in operation at Cornell was credited with effecting a 40 percent reduction in the number of colds among those taking the treatment. Treatment provided in the 1930 cold prevention classes included weekly UV ray "light baths," alkalinization, instruction with regard to diet and ventilation and, in selected cases, a special study of the nose and throat and the use of a catarrhal vaccine, explained Smiley.[15]

For the three-year period from 1929 to 1932, the Cornell University Nursery School (Ithaca, New York) conducted an experiment in which the afternoon group of three year olds spent part of their school time indoors under UV rays, while the morning pupils received no such exposure. The experiment was done in the hope that sunlamps might provide a substitute

Two 1932 ads that were quite wordy as they sought to explain in detail the wonders of UV light indoors. The home sunlamps enjoyed high popularity in the 1920s and well into the 1930s.

for the missing sunlight during a Northern U.S. winter, and "Ideally, this constant exposure to the ultra-violet lamps would give freedom from colds, stimulate appetite, cause gains in weight and strength and ward off anemia — all the beneficent effect of Summer." Children exposed to UV lamps wore only cotton trunks, shoes and rolled-down socks. Six or seven sunlamps were placed along the walls of the two playrooms with the temperature starting at 70 degrees F., and rising to "Summer heat." Those UV rays were said to be tempered so the children would not tan but get just under the tanning dose. Exposure began gradually and worked up to a duration of one hour. Yet no conclusion was drawn from the study.[16]

An ad from 1946. By that time the craze for sunlamps was over.

Dr. M. Luckiesh, director of the Lighting Institute of the General Electric Company (Cleveland), gave a 1931 lecture before members of the American Society of Mechanical Engineers, the American Institute of Electrical Engineers, and the New York Electrical Society. During that lecture he predicted, "In the future we shall sleep in beds shaped like covered wagons and instead of pajamas we shall have ultra-violet light rays pouring down on us as we sleep, producing the effect of reposing on a sunlit meadow in a tropical land. The benefit to our health should be incalculable."[17]

Ultra-violet ray lamps were placed in the billing department of the Philadelphia Company (in Pittsburgh) to test their effect on 50 female employees. Reportedly, the experiment was to demonstrate whether or not the rays would improve the health of the women and, as a corollary, increase their efficiency. With a start date of October 1, the experiment was due to run for five months. As a control group, the company had another department where 50 female workers labored under the same conditions as those in the billing department, but, of course, without the UV rays. At the end of the five months, the intent was to compare the health and efficiency of the two groups. Said Dr. W. M. Holtz, in charge of the Philadelphia Company's medical department,

"We selected girls for the health test because females in general have more of the body exposed than males." No report on the outcome of that experiment seemed to have been published.[18]

During a session of the American Congress of Physical Therapy, Dr. Frank T. Woodbury, attending specialist at the U.S. Veteran's Bureau in New York City, warned that the sunlamp was a physician's tool and could not be used safely by the untrained, a situation he described as "like letting the baby play with the medicine chest." Doctor F. Howard Humphris of London, England, declared that UV treatment would "do more than any other physiotherapeutic agent to maintain and restore normal physical conditions." He added that the four principal means of maintaining youth were achieved via the use of natural and artificial sunlight, baths and bathing, exercise and massage, and electricity. As evidence of the efficacy of artificial sunlight treatment, Humphris cited experiments conducted by the managements of the Drury Lane Theatre in London, and the Mansfield Colliery. No details were provided, but Humphris said that in both instances it had been demonstrated to his satisfaction that routine exposure to ultraviolet radiation benefited those who took the treatments.[19]

5

Early Warnings: 1920–1945

"[It is a] well-known fact that cancer of the skin is more frequent among those exposed to excessive sunlight."
New York Academy of Medicine, 1929

"Sunlight, like most things that are good for us, if indulged in to excess may be harmful — even to the point of causing cancer."
Dr. George C. Andrews, 1941

While the vast majority of articles written about the sun and its role as healer, health-giver, curer and preventive in the years up to 1945 were lavish in their uncritical praise, a few early warnings were issued from the medical community that exposure to the sun could have negative effects. They were very few and far between and were best described as the typical lone voices in the wilderness. Such warnings were, of course, ignored. So far away from mainstream medical opinion were those "heresies" and warnings, that no one even bothered to acknowledge them to the extent of refuting them. Any such contentions were too far in the minority, too silly, to be engaged at any level.

Physician H. H. Hazen and Registered Nurse Florence Biase co-authored a 1933 piece in the *American Journal of Nursing* in which they discussed some things they felt had been overlooked "in the present craze for sun-baths and coats of summer tan." One of those items was their belief that Caucasian skin exposed continuously to the sun would result in the skin becoming dry and wrinkled. The fad for open-necked dresses had resulted in what they called "automobile neck," a prematurely aged upper chest and throat. Hazen and Biase reported the farmer, the sailor, and the modern golfer developed browning, wrinkling, atrophy, and later horny growths and "superficial" cancers— with the latter being a condition that had years earlier been described by another researcher as "sailor's skin." The skin of the face became dry and wrinkled and keratoses developed. "It is well known that the farmers of the sunny mid-western states are especially prone to these keratoses that so frequently end in skin cancer." At the best, they argued, skin that was habitually exposed to the drying action of the sun aged much more than skin that was not so unduly exposed. They felt it was certain that if women realized that excessive sunlight on the face would cause them to look aged, years ahead of time, the fad of suntanning would be less popular. "That the skin of the neck of the farmer and anyone else daily exposed to the sun's rays becomes thick, brown, and wrinkled is a fact apparent to all of us," they added. "The frequency of horny, thickening keratoses and cancers in these areas is less well appreciated."[1]

A decade later journalist Martha Parker declared the sun in too large doses was a beauty foe to be reckoned with and that beauty experts warned that the sun dried the skin, and hastened the wrinkles associated with aging.[2]

One of the earlier medical warnings about the sun and cancer was given in 1911 by Dr. A. E. Tozzer, then engaged in cancer research at the Harvard University Medical School. Specifically, he saw a danger to future generations from the sun's UV, or actinic, rays. Cancer, he said, "starts from a bad case of sunburn where the skin is peeling, fails to react and becomes atrophied. From the mere irritation in the beginning the skin grows thin and parchmentlike. Blotches of a brownish hue, like large freckles appear, and from these cancer starts."[3]

At the start of 1929 the New York Academy of Medicine reported that skin cancer occurred most often among persons exposed to excessive sunlight, and experiments with UV radiation confirmed the suspicions of scientists that in certain cases sunlamps then so popular for home use could have dangerous results. The information bureau of the Academy of Medicine warned against the indiscriminate use of UV radiation lamps by the public. Joining the Academy in its warning announcement was the Medical Society of the County of New York. It was a warning issued in connection with the "experimental confirmation of the well-known fact that cancer of the skin is more frequent among those exposed to excessive sunlight." One scientific discovery made in 1928 was that, reportedly, in certain cases UV rays increased, rather than decreased, the effectiveness of the agent producing cancer. It was in that connection that the "well-known fact" was cited and warnings about sunlamps issued.[4]

Before criticizing the practice of tanning in 1930, Dr. W. A. Evans of Chicago acknowledged the good points of the fad — that tanning helped to combat pneumonia, colds, and consumption, prevented and cured rickets, and stabilized the nerves. However, he declared that a healthy person did himself no good by exposing himself to direct sunlight to an extreme extent. "In some respects it harms him or may do so," he explained. "A thoroughly tanned skin will never get back to prize-winning condition. No woman ever tanned her skin to a mahogany brown, and later became known for a peachblow complexion." Evans also observed that tanned skins were "somewhat prone to develop skin cancer."[5]

Professor Hubert Jausion of the Val de Grace hospital in Paris warned sunbathers in 1933 about the dangers of immoderate exposure of the skin to sunshine. An overdose, he said, could result in a kind of skin cancer that was frequently found among farm workers and fishermen. Some 14 percent of the skin cancer cases treated in the hospital in Marseilles, France, were said to have been traced to sunburn.[6]

Medical doctor Karl Zwick agreed with the warning from Jausion and added, "The casual relationship between the cancer occurring in outdoor workers and the exposure of these workers to the sun is so well established that dermatologists ... have coined for this variety or form of skin cancer the term 'sunlight cancer.'" He also believed that sunlamps could be as dangerous as the sun itself.[7]

Dr. James Ewing of New York City told the International Cancer Congress at Madrid, Spain, also in 1933, that sunlight was one of the principal causes of carcinoma. Ewing thought the steady growth in cancer cases was due in part to "exaggerated sun worship."[8]

Writing in the American Medical Association's publication for the lay reader in 1942, *Hygeia*, journalist Paul Bechet said the dangers from sunbathing were then known to medical personnel but remained unknown to most laymen. According to Bechet, as early as 1896 physicians described "sailor's skin," a condition observed in sailors, policemen, farmers, and others who were constantly exposed to sunlight. It was a condition characterized by brownish, scaly, dry patches on the face, shot through with dilated small blood vessels "and occasionally exhibiting the raised, pearly bordered, ulcerating lesions of typical skin cancer. That skin cancer on the exposed areas of the face can be aggravated by excessive sunlight is well attested." Bechet noted that skin cancer was much more common in blondes and redheads than in brunettes, and extremely rare in blacks, and speculated that skin pigmentation was perhaps a protective mechanism as the "natural inhabitants" of tropical zones were all dark-skinned. One investigator reportedly found that 62 percent of his skin cancer cases occurred in blondes, 31 percent in the red- or auburn-haired, and only seven percent in dark-skinned people. Another researcher, living in Australia, commented on the great frequency of skin cancer on that continent as compared with England. He ascribed that to the fact that the number of days of sunshine in England was half that in Australia while the ultraviolet ray content of the sunlight in Australia was far greater than it was in England. By then skin cancers had been produced in rats by many different researchers by means of prolonged exposure to UV ray sunlamps.[9]

At a 1941 forum on "Sunlight and Cancer," held in New York City and organized by the American Society for the Control of Cancer as part of the general education program of the Society, Dr. George C. Andrews declared the so-called "smoker's cancer" of the lower lip, which was found frequently in agricultural laborers was not due to smoking, as had been believed in the past. Rather, it was the result of a chronic inflammation of the lower lip from habitual sunburn. Doctor Frank Adair, chairman of the executive committee of the society, said the question of whether sunlight was an important factor in the cause of skin cancer, which in 1939 caused 3,494 deaths in the U.S., was very important. "One-third of all skin cancers occur on the nose, and this may be at least partly due to the large amount of sunlight the nose receives," said Andrews. "Sunlight, like most things that are good for us, if indulged in to excess may be harmful — even to the point of causing cancer."[10]

During that forum Dr. Arthur Purdy Stout pointed out that skin cancer was eight times as frequent among men of the U.S. Navy as among the general population. He also believed its high incidence in Australia indicated that it might result from exposure to the sun's rays. He wondered if there was any danger that the incidence of skin cancer might increase due to the tanning fad but concluded, "My personal opinion is that those who tan readily probably receive sufficient protection from this pigmentation to prevent serious skin damage." A research fellow at the National Cancer Institute, Dr. Harold Blum, told the forum that the demonstration that skin cancer could be induced in rats and mice by exposure to UV light was additional evidence against the sun, and that all available evidence constituted a warning against excessive exposure to sunlight. However, added Blum, "At the same time it does not justify fear of moderate exposure."[11]

Taking a slightly different position, in 1940, was Dr. Sigismund Peller of the Johns Hopkins School of Hygiene. Although he agreed that exposure to sunlight during childhood and adolescence could result in cancer of the lip or skin, he also argued that it helped to prevent death from other cancers. According to his theory, the development of the "easily curable" skin or lip cancers protected against the development of cancer in parts of the body that were less accessible for treatment and were therefore more likely to be fatal. Dr. Frank L. Apperly, of the Medical College of Virginia, in a report to the American Association of Pathologists and Bacteriologists (working independently from Peller) also argued that evidence existed that showed exposure to sunlight did produce cancer immunity in some cases. Therefore, "Preventing cancer by sunlight may be possible if scientists can learn more about how the sun's rays affect the body." But Apperly was not one who believed it was necessary to have skin cancer in order to become immune to other forms of cancer. In his opinion, the sun's rays had two separate effects. One was that they produced some sort of selective immunity to cancer in general and, in those localities where the mean temperature was less than about 42 degrees Fahrenheit, even to skin cancer. Secondly, at mean temperatures above 42 degrees F, "sun rays produced more cancer on those parts of the skin exposed to them, in spite of a generally raised immunity."[12]

By around 1945 articles about the sun's effects and suntanning were still overwhelmingly positive. The completely uncritical glow had worn off to a slight extent but not enough to alarm the public or to cause it to alter its behavior. While health warnings tying the sun to cancer had been issued every now and then for decades they were very much in a minority position. And, in any event, they were ignored. The fashion of tanning was well entrenched and would remain so for a long time to come. Still, a new phase began sometime after World War II. It began with a few articles, grew slowly, and turned into a flood from around 1980 onward. The days of the sun as healer were over; enter the era of the sun as killer.

6

The Sun as Killer:
1946–2004

"Deciding to stay out of the sun after reaching the age of 40 to 50 is a decision made too late, for the damage has been done."

Consumers' Research Magazine, 1980

"Even one day's exposure [to the sun] can cause damage."

Dr. Fred Urbach, 1983

"Fry Now Pay Later."

American Cancer Society, 1985

"Suntans can kill you."

Dr. David Reuben, 1990

In the years prior to 1946, the sun was overwhelmingly portrayed as the health-giving healer, capable of performing miracles through the contact of its rays with the skin. As time passed the claims for the sun as healer grew more and more exaggerated and over-the-top. Reporters and journalists who felt the need to write another article about the sun's healing rays seemed to also feel the need to insert new and/or more highly exaggerated claims into the story, as a way to make their article stand out from a slew of similar pieces. If that period was marked by outrageous claims and excesses in favor of the sun — and it was — the post-war period was marked by a reverse trend in which the sun was portrayed as killer. That trend moved very slowly over the 1950s through the 1970s but then picked up speed rapidly in the 1980s; a trend that has continued to the present. As time passed, the claims for the sun as killer grew more and more exaggerated and outlandish. Many articles had not a single good word to say for it. An increasing number of diseases were attributed to the sun, and the habit of bathing in its rays or even being caught coincidentally for a short time in those rays, from a general erosion of the immune system to an increased incidence of cancers in general, to gallstones. The practice of tanning, in some quarters, was equated with the practice of smoking. A fear of the sun came to rule the land, and it has remained.

Writing in the *New York Times Magazine* in 1950, reporter Ruth Adler discussed the spread of tanning fashion and sunbathing but went on to declare that "People who overdo it, though, soon feel the sun's wrath. Old Sol, the doctors say, can cause skin cancer, stomach ulcers, kidney strain, toxemia, and shock, and encourage downy hair growth on women's legs and arms." She added that women eventually discovered "that overdoses of tan, year after year, rob the skin of natural oils, leave it dry and coarse, a fertile field for the wrinkle's plow." Adler's article was more negative in its attack on the sun than most of the time, but was an omen of things to come.[1]

Around the same time journalist Bernadine Bailey observed that doctors "are now sounding a solemn warning to all sunbathers: don't overdo it, for too much sunshine increases the likelihood of cancer of the skin." However, she also acknowledged the supposed good points of the sun, pointing out the sun's rays killed surface bacteria and tended to clear up acne. As well, she mentioned what she felt was the most striking benefit of exposure to the sun — the triggering of the formation in the body of Vitamin D, which protected against rickets. "As yet, there is no consistent proof that sunshine will help to cure the common cold or other respiratory infections," added Bailey.[2]

Two years later, Veronica Lucey Conley wrote, in the American Medical Association's chief publication for the lay reader, *Today's Health* (the renamed *Hygeia*), that when a comparison was made between the actual benefits of persistent exposure to the sun with the inherent dangers, "the evidence weights heavily toward the latter. There appears to be some relationships between the sun's rays and malignancies of the skin." Conley also argued that sun "has some role in other skin diseases either as the causative agent or as an aggravating factor," although she did not name those conditions. In her view the benefits of repeated sunning were not well defined, aside from preventing rickets in children.[3]

At an American Medical Association meeting in Dallas at the end of 1959, Doctor John M. Knox, a dermatology professor at Baylor University's College of Medicine, warned his audience that he, along with other skin specialists in the Southwest, were seeing more and more harmful effects from exposure to the sun. Skin cancer from exposure of the face, neck and hands to the sun was, he told his audience, first described by Germany's Paul G. Unna in 1894. A dozen years after that, William Dubreuilh made an observational refinement in the Bordeaux vineyards: women got skin cancer on the parts of their faces left exposed by their scarves, while men got it on the back of the neck. In the United States, continued Knox, 91 percent of all skin cancers were found on the hands, face and neck; two percent occurred on parts of the body occasionally exposed to the sun; and 6.5 percent of all cases were found on sites of the body never ordinarily exposed to the sun. He felt an individual's risk of harmful consequences from sun exposure, ranging from sunburn to cancer, was in an inverse ratio to the density of the screen built into his own skin, the amount of pigment in the epidermis. That is, blacks had higher tolerances (and greater protection from sun damage) increasing with the darkness of the skin. It was time, concluded Knox, for the medical profession to begin an education campaign on the harmful effects of excess exposure to the sun, and to advocate the use of sunscreens to ward off both cancer and the premature aging of the skin.[4]

In 1963 *Time* magazine observed, with respect to tanning, "This rite of summer is warming, relaxing and so socially desirable that few sun worshippers heed the constant words of caution from doctors." That was a reference to a warning of a few years earlier from the American Medical Association's Committee on Cosmetics on the sun's damaging effects. "There is undeniable evidence that the effects of the sun are cumulative and at some point irreversible," added the piece. "The evidence is clear that chronic exposure to sunlight can be one of the major factors in the production of precancerous and cancerous conditions of the skin."[5]

Scientist Harold F. Blum, with the National Cancer Institute in Bethesda, Maryland, said in 1964 that the theory that sunlight caused skin cancer dated back to the turn of the century. And that it was generally accepted in the scientific community that people most exposed to sunlight, whether because of occupation or geographical location, were more likely to develop that type of cancer. Blacks, who did not easily sunburn, declared Blum, experienced only a small incidence of skin cancer that could be attributed to sunlight. Since 1928, when cancers were first produced with ultraviolet light in laboratory animals, it had been possible, explained the researcher, to support some of those claims with greater assurance. The type of radiation that caused skin cancer was said to be the same type of radiation that produced sunburn and destructive processes in living organisms in general.[6]

Exaggerated articles that intensified the idea that the sun was a Great Satan began to appear much more frequently around 1980. One of the lead-off articles was from *Consumers' Research Magazine* under the headline

"Sunshine: Hazardous to Your Health." It was a long piece devoted entirely to the supposed bad effects of the sun and, like many that would follow in its wake, this one had not so much as a single good word to say on behalf of the sun. Researchers, readers were informed, had found that Tucson, Arizona (a location with many bright sunny days), had one of the highest incidences of skin cancer in the world. Doctor Jo Ann Hansen, of the Cancer Center Division at the University of Arizona Health Science Center, said, "Any place you've got a lot of sunshine you've got a lot of skin cancer." Another dermatologist, Dr. Robert Friedman, referred to the myth of the healthy tan as a symbol of health and sexual potency "as being ridiculous" and remarked that it was going to take a long time to re-educate people. According to this account more than 300,000 cases of skin cancer (with 7,000 deaths per year), typically caused by overexposure to UV radiation, were recorded annually. Gloomily the piece declared, "Deciding to stay out of the sun after reaching the age of 40 to 50 is a decision made too late, for the damage has been done." Even long-term smokers were encouraged to quit the habit, no matter what their age, as there was always a benefit, no matter how late in life a person changed his lifestyle. However, this article denied sunbathers even faint hope. It urged people to stay out of the sun completely, if at all possible. Herein the sun was portrayed as a relentless and remorseless enemy with there being no talk about how to tan sensibly; complete abstinence was necessary. For people who had to be out in the sun, such as farmers and fishermen, the advice was to use plenty of sunscreen, wear wide-brimmed hats and long-sleeved shirts.[7]

Another extremely negative view of the sun, almost as bad as the one above, came a year later from the pen of Jane Ogle in the *New York Times Magazine*. One difference was that some hope was held out for those who gave up the tanning habit. But a new health worry was added. Ogle observed that sunscreens were one of the most important cosmetics on the market then because most of the changes that one associated with aging — wrinkles, sagging, excessive dryness, broken blood vessels, blotchiness, transparent skin — "are caused not by some inevitable deterioration over the years but by chronic sun damage." Yet she went on to say that many doctors and researchers believed those so-called symptoms of aging could be prevented by using an effective sunscreen with unfailing regularity whenever one was out in the sun for any length of time. Ogle also argued it was never too early to begin such a skin-care program, and never too late. "The damage can be arrested, whether one is 20, 40 or 60-plus. There is now even some evidence that it may be partially reversible if sufficient care is taken to guard against further injury," she explained. According to Dr. John H. Epstein, of the University of California at San Francisco, if the skin absorbed enough UV radiation to produce and maintain a tan, enough energy had been absorbed to produce cellular damage. Aside from aging, reported Ogle, UV radiation — UVB for the most part — was implicated in squamous-cell and basal-cell cancers (very non-lethal forms of skin cancer) and the far more dangerous skin cancer, malignant melanoma. (At this time a distinction was beginning to be made in stories on UV radiation. There were two types of UV rays, UVA and UVB radiation. It was a difference that would become more important over time.) Then Ogle added a new worry by declaring, in addition to the dangers she had already listed, "A particularly insidious effect of UV radiation, damage to the immune system, the body's natural mechanism of self-defense, is of growing concern to dermatologists...." However, her account was more than a little vague as to just what were the bad effects from this upsetting of the immune system.[8]

Joining the scare bandwagon was reporter Matt Clark, who declared in *Newsweek* in 1982 that some 400,000 new skin cancer cases would be diagnosed in the U.S. that year "and almost all of them can be blamed on overexposure to the sun." Although Clark mentioned the role of the sun in producing wrinkles and aging skin, he concentrated on the cancer connection, differentiating basal and squamous. He also said that melanoma had been linked to exposure to sunlight but, unlike Ogle, Clark declared its cause probably involved a number of other factors, including heredity. According to recent research, reported Clark, it was suggested that UV radiation also contributed to a breakdown of the body's immune system, which in turn, encouraged the growth of cancer in general.[9]

One year later, Claudia Wallis stated in *Time*, after sounding the usual warnings, that the incidence of the most lethal form of skin cancer, malignant melanoma, "though less directly linked to sunshine" than squamous- or basal-cell carcinomas, had jumped tenfold in the previous 20 years. After mentioning that malignant melanoma struck 15,000 Americans each year, killing 45 percent of them, she hedged her bet a little more when she declared that with respect to melanoma "its relationship to the sun remains unclear." Some 300 dermatologists and others gathered that year in Manhattan to discuss the situation at what was called the first World Congress on Cancers of the Skin. Dermatologist Dr. Fred Urbach of Temple University in Philadelphia led the fear promoters by warning, "Even one day's exposure can cause damage." Also reported at the medical gathering was that the most insidious rays of the sun were the short wave-length UVB rays but new research had shown that even the longer wave-length UVA rays could promote skin cancer. Said Harvard biologist Madhu Pathak, "Both UVA and UVB are carcinogenic." A number of doctors at the conference urged year-round use of sunscreens (some of which were said to then be formulated to block UVA and UVB rays). But the most urgent and unanimous recommendation at the conference was to protect the skin of young children. Although skin cancer might not show up until the age of 50, the initial damage was done in early childhood, stated dermatologist Isaac Willis of Morehouse School of Medicine in Atlanta. About 80 percent of skin cancers caused by the sun were said to be basal-cell, the most common and curable form of cancer in the U.S.[10]

In 1983 the Skin Cancer Foundation predicted that one out of every seven Americans would suffer from some sort of skin cancer during their lifetimes yet, to most people, lamented journalist Bernice Kanner, "bronze skin signals health and success."[11]

Jane Brody reported in 1985 that, according to doctors, the incidence of malignant melanoma was then rising faster than any other cancer in the U.S., except for lung cancer in women. There were then some 50 sunscreen preparations on the market. "Although this cancer was long thought to be unrelated to sun exposure, it is now known that the burning rays from that star play a major role in many, if not most, melanoma cases," she declared. "Individuals who suffered severe sunburns in their younger years, and anyone with a family history of the disease, seem to be at particular risk." Ogle and Clark had each reported in the early 1980s that a link between melanoma and sun exposure was very weak or had not been shown. If new research over the intervening few years had established such a link, Brody failed to report it. With respect to basal-cell and squamous-cell cancers, she said the sun's responsibility "is unquestioned." There the damage was said to be gradual and cumulative, the result of years of repeatedly exposing vulnerable skin to the sun. Brody then mentioned the aging of the skin caused by the sun and "the UVB, the burning rays, are the primary cause of sunburn and skin cancer," while the UVA rays "can aggravate the damaging effects of UVB...." For people who tanned easily, she said, "their tan will act as a sunscreen, too. While it will not block the aging effects of sunlight, it can help prevent cancer-causing damage." Which, of course, contradicted and confused her earlier arguments.[12]

As summer began in 1985 the American Cancer Society launched a new campaign, "Fry Now Pay Later," to educate the public about the link between suntanning and skin cancer. The medical community was said to be especially concerned about the renewed popularity of tanning salons (the tanning parlor industry started around 1978). At the same time, the American Medical Association released a report that warned against the hazard of high intensity UV radiation used in tanning salons. Even the new tanning beds that purported to use only UVA in their lamps were not safe.

According to Atlanta dermatologist Dr. Isaac Willis, UVA aged the skin prematurely and studies suggested UVA might act as a cancer "promoter" by inhibiting enzymes that could otherwise repair cells damaged by UVB. Nonetheless, in this *Newsweek* article from Jean Seligman, UVA was not seen as especially dangerous. It was said that 90 percent of all skin cancers were due to sun exposure. Temple University dermatologist Dr. Frederick Urbach argued that it took 30 to 40 years of exposure before a person got skin cancer. That year an estimated 500,000 new cases of basal-cell and squamous-cell cancers were expected to be diagnosed, up from 300,000 in the middle 1970s. Even more disturbing to the medical community was the rapid increase in malignant melanoma, a deadly cancer of the skin cells that manufactured the pigment melanin, which produced a tan. For the previous three decades the worldwide melanoma rate, said Seligman, had doubled every 10 years; 22,000 cases were expected to be diagnosed in America in 1985, along with 5,500 deaths. While the other skin cancers seemed to result from years of cumulative sun exposure, declared the reporter, dermatologists believed that melanoma was more likely related to severe sunburn, either in childhood or adulthood. Signs that the American love affair with tanning was starting to wane appeared to be in evidence. With respect to teenagers, Dr. Dore Gilbert, a Newport Beach, California, dermatologist, asserted, "Kids today are learning to apply sunscreens when they go outside as a matter of course, just as they've learned to lock their seat belts when they get into a car."[13]

Canada's major news magazine, *Maclean's*, joined the attack with a huge article on how excruciatingly bad the sun was. With nary a good word for the sun, Mary McIver's piece lumped tanning with smoking and concentrated on raising the terrors of melanoma. The latter was indeed a deadly cancer with a high kill rate while squamous and basal cancers were, relatively, very non-lethal, less so than any other type of cancer. According to McIver, the rate of cancer incidence and cancer death rates in Canada had remained stable in recent years; the two major exceptions during the previous 17 years being lung cancer and melanoma rates. "As a result, such homely but prudent courses of action as shunning cigarettes— and suntans— remain essential weapons in the continuing war against the disease." McIver argued that medical experts had known since the 1950s that overexposure to the sun caused skin cancer but because it was one of the most curable forms of the disease, "it provoked relatively little concern." Estimates were that 40,000 cases of skin cancer would be diagnosed in Canada that year and that 2,200 of them would be melanoma. Some 500 would die that year from melanoma. In the 1930s the incidence of melanoma among Canadians was reported as one in 10,000; in 1988 it was expected that one Canadian in 135 would develop melanoma in his or her lifetime. Some medical experts attributed the phenomenon, in part, to the thinning of the earth's protective ozone layer but this issue was subject to debate amongst dermatologists. Basal-cell cancer would affect one in seven Canadians over a lifetime with the rate for squamous-cell given as one in 50. Vancouver dermatologist Dr. Alastair Carruthers argued there was evidence that melanoma was not so much provoked by the cumulative effects of sun exposure as it was by the short, intense bouts that led to bad sunburns. People who worked indoors but who spent their weekends and holidays burning and peeling were more susceptible to melanoma, thought Carruthers, than those who worked outdoors and were routinely exposed to the sun. Following the one-time-only-will-kill-you school of thought, McIver issued a warning, "As well, doctors say, even one serious, blistering sunburn suffered in childhood or adolescence can often lead to melanoma."[14]

American physician William Bennett added his weight to the anti-sun forces in his 1989 piece in *Vogue* magazine wherein he argued that Americans were beginning to heed the warnings of dermatologists that bright sunlight aged the skin and raised the risk of skin cancer. Bennett added a new worry when he observed that the sun was also under suspicion for causing acute discomfort to the eyes and permanent damage to the lens and retina. Still, this doctor did have a good word for the sun. He argued that the majority of adults, especially older women, would probably benefit from a little unprotected sun exposure — about 15 minutes — two or three times a week. The reason, he said, was vitamin D; a substance that was crucial for the health of bones. While vitamin D was readily available — mainly in fortified milk — Bennett thought most adults did not consume enough milk and for them sunlight was a significant source of vitamin D. It was the UVB wavelength of light that was required to make vitamin D, he added, the same wavelength that caused sunburn, wrinkles, and skin cancer, and the same wavelength blocked by sunscreen. At the end of 1988, a research group led by Dr. Lois Y. Matsuoka of Jefferson Medical College in Philadelphia reported that the average vitamin D level in 20 regular users of Paba, one of the more common sunscreens, was less than half the level in non-users. In two Paba users the level was low enough to be called a deficiency. All things considered, according to Dr. Michael D. Holick, professor of medicine at Brown University's Skin and Bone Research Laboratory, adult women would benefit by spending short periods of time in midday sunlight before applying a sunscreen. Exposing the skin of the face, arms and hands was said to be sufficient. Nevertheless, Holick added, "Aggressively tanned skin, however, is anything but healthy." He felt the role of sunlight in causing melanoma was less clear than it was in the case of basal- and squamous-cell carcinomas but he believed the number of sunburns one had, especially at an earlier age, increased the risk of melanoma, although total exposure might also play a role. However, he added that some research indicated that people who lived in constantly sunny environments and maintained a fairly steady tan had a lowered risk of developing melanoma, even though they still suffered other forms of skin damage and skin cancer.[15]

At the same time Cheryl A. Sweet reported, in the *FDA Consumer*, that during 1988 melanoma was diagnosed in one out of every 128 Americans and killed nearly 6,000, a 93-percent increase in the number of cases since 1980.[16]

The American Medical Association's Council on Scientific Affairs issued a warning in the summer of 1989 in its *Journal* that getting a tan raised the risk of skin cancer, wrinkles, eye damage, and changes in the skin's immune system. No health benefits were known from cosmetic tanning, continued the warning, except that "tanned skin, may have positive psychological value by creating an enhanced image of personal worth." Lamented by the report was the fact that despite the hazards, many people could not be dissuaded from sunbathing or using artificial tanning devices. For people who insisted on tanning, the American Medical Association gave the following guidelines: stay out of the sun between 10:00 A.M. and 2:00 P.M.; wear a hat and protective clothing; beware of surfaces like sand, snow, ice and concrete that reflect sunlight, wear a sunscreen with an SPF of 15 or higher; keep babies out of the sun as much as possible; apply sunscreens to older children who are to be outdoors for long periods; avoid tanning machines. If tanning machines were used, consumers were urged to limit their exposures to 30 to 50 half-hour sessions a year or less, to use a device with a timer, to wear protective goggles, and to make sure an attendant was nearby in case of an emergency.[17]

David Reuben was a medical doctor and very well known pop psychology writer of the day when he penned an extreme, hysterical, anti-sun article in 1990 for *Reader's Digest* under the ominous title, "Suntans can kill you." Some 600,000 Americans would get skin cancer that year, and more than 8,000 would die, he warned. "Sun exposure, it turns out, is far more dangerous than even the experts supposed," counseled Reuben, and "exposing their bodies to the sun is one of the riskiest things Americans do." Based on his opinion, leading medical experts agreed that there was absolutely no safe way to tan. "That's it. The scientists who know more about human skin than anyone else confirm that all suntanning is dangerous—no exceptions." As a precaution to protect oneself from the sun, Reuben urged the use of a high SPF sunscreen, "Twelve months a year, whenever you go out — whether for a ten-minute stroll or a long afternoon of gardening ... even on cloudy days...." The idea that someone going for a 15-minute walk at 8:30 A.M. in the winter on a cloudy day in, say, Seattle, needed sun protection was, of course, ludicrous. But it was indicative of the I-can-scare-you-more-than-anyone-else-can style of anti-sun journalism so prevalent at the time.[18]

Writing in the federal government publication *FDA Consumer* in 1991, Alexandra Greeley cautioned, "Even tanning slowly and carefully is dangerous." According to the American Cancer Society, more than 600,000 people were diagnosed in the U.S. with basal cell and squamous-cell carcinomas in 1990, up from 400,000 in 1980, while 35,000 more were diagnosed with melanoma in 1990, double the number from a decade earlier. As to what caused the increase in melanoma, Dr. Paul Bergstresser, chairman of the department of dermatology at the University of Texas Southwestern Medical Center in Dallas, said it was associated with sun exposure, but the link to sunlight was not as logical as for other forms of skin cancer. Patients with melanomas were more common in southern latitudes that experienced more sun exposure, but melanomas could appear on body sites that were protected from the sun. Those people with the highest sunlight exposure appeared to have a lower frequency of melanomas than those who got sunlight more episodically," Bergstresser added. Greeley commented that not all melanomas seemed to be related to sun exposure. Harvard University associate professor of dermatology Dr. Arthur Sober felt the cause of melanomas in general was still a controversial topic. Dr. Sydney Hurwitz, clinical professor of dermatology and pediatrics at the Yale University School of Medicine, argued that most skin cancers began in childhood. And the greatest exposure — 50 to 80 percent of a person's lifetime exposure — to the sun occurred during childhood, by the age of 18. Studies showed that a history of painful or blistering sunburn during the first 10 to 20 years of life doubled the risk of skin cancer, added Greeley. Bergstresser issued the following warning; "Less sun is better. No sun is best of all."[19]

After Naomi Freudlich issued the usual warnings and advice in her 1991 article in *Business Week*, she added that one dermatologist at Beth Israel Hospital in Boston said there was little evidence to support reports that a few bad sunburns as a child put an adult at serious risk for skin cancer. According to Dr. Perry Robins, a skin surgeon at the New York University Medical Center and president of the Skin Cancer Foundation, by the age of 55, the likelihood of getting skin cancer rose to 27,000 cases per 100,000 people for those men who had spent a lot of unprotected time in the sun. But for those who had avoided the sun, only 1,614 per 100,000 suffered that fate.[20]

Early in 1992 an article appeared in the *New York Times* that reported on a new study that suggested people who sunbathed a lot might have a significantly greater chance of developing gallstones than people who stayed away from the sun. Researcher Dr. Stan Pavel, a biochemist and dermatologist at University Hospital in Leiden, The Netherlands, compared 206 white people, examining their attitudes toward sunbathing and the incidence of gallstones among them. He found that people who reported enjoying sunbathing ran twice the risk of developing gallstones as the general population. For people prone to burning after sunbathing, primarily those with red hair and very pale skin, the risk was twenty times as great.[21]

Journalist Katarzyna Wandycz indirectly commented on the prevalence of anti-sun articles in the media when she started her 1993 piece by saying "Summer is here, and with it the predictable flood of articles about the dangers of too much sun and the benefits of protective sunscreens. Does anyone need another such article? If you're a male over 40, the answer is: probably yes." Mostly the article was a scare piece about the increasing rates of melanoma diagnoses, an increase reported to be about 30 percent faster for men than for women, according to the National Cancer Institute. Also, it was a danger that grew with age. Although women tended to develop melanoma more often than men, until their mid 40s, by their late 60s men developed twice as many cases of melanoma as did women. Melanoma accounted for 75 percent of the 9,100 deaths per year in America from skin cancer. Reasons for the difference were unclear but some felt it was because men did not use enough sunscreens.[22]

When reporter Susan Brink did her scare article about tanning in 1996, she briefly mentioned aging skin effects but concentrated on the cancer connection, mostly on melanoma. Although the piece gave several case histories, with all the victims being young, male and female, it did not mention that sunscreen did not protect from melanoma nor was there any evidence it decreased the likelihood of contracting the disease. Nor did it mention the link between sun exposure and melanomas was cloudy at best. That year, in America, there were expected to be 800,000 basal-cell carcinoma diagnoses, 100,000 squamous-cell cases, and 38,300 melanoma diagnoses (half of them in people under 50); 7,300 were expected to die in the U.S. in 1996 from melanoma. Since the 1930s the diagnosis of malignant melanoma was said to have risen 1,800 percent, to become the most frequent cancer in women aged 25 to 29, second only to breast cancer in women aged 30 to 34.

Brink mentioned that new lines of clothing said to block out almost all UV rays had come on the market. A line cleared by the FDA called Solumbra, which included articles from leggings and safari shirts to toddler coveralls, had an SPF of 30 or more. Some dermatologist reportedly thought of such clothing as "extreme and unrealistic" for most people and said that normal summer-weight clothing with a tight weave provided adequate protection.[23]

When Mary Tannen wrote her anti-tanning article in 1997, she mentioned that it took 25 years for smoking to go "from cool to depraved" and wondered "Will it take that long for tan to go from chic to outré?"[24]

Newsweek declared, in 1999, that more than 44,000 Americans were expected to be diagnosed with melanoma that year and about 7,300 would die. Although melanomas accounted for only four percent of all skin cancers, they caused six out of every seven skin cancer deaths. Risk factors for melanoma were reported to be; fair skin, light eyes and hair, having a large number of moles, a family history of melanoma, "and bad sunburn as a child." Among the usual pieces of advice offered to deal with the sun was a strong suggestion to avoid direct sun between the hours of 10:00 A.M. and 4:00 P.M. (10:00 A.M. to 2:00 P.M. had been more or less standard) as people were pushed to adopt a more Dracula-like existence.[25]

A perhaps logical outcome to the anti-sun hysteria occurred in 2002 when Eve Hibbits, of Brilliant, Ohio, was jailed for allowing her three children to get severely sunburned at a county fair. She faced three felony counts of endangerment of her two-year-old daughter and 10-month-old twin sons. Sheriff Fred Abdalla of Jefferson County in eastern Ohio explained, "As soon as I looked at them I could tell. It looked like the children had been dipped in red paint. It was 95 degrees and they were literally baking." The sheriff said he had no choice but to arrest her at the Jefferson County Fair. Keith Murdock, a spokesman for Trinity Medical Center, a hospital in Steubenville, Ohio, said the sunburn was not particularly severe. The children were treated with cold compresses and released the same day. "We treated the minors for second-degree sunburn," said Murdock. "Most people who get sunburned get second-degree sunburn. It means any sunburn that is beginning to blister. They were blistering."[26]

Hibbits was released from jail, after she had spent about a week there, and the felony counts were suddenly dropped. Prosecutor Brian Felmet explained that the children were not as severely injured as officials had thought, prompting him to drop the charges of child endangerment. While hospital officials had originally said second-degree burns, they later reclassified the children as having lesser, first-degree burns. However, Hibbits was still charged with a misdemeanor count of child endangerment, which carried a maximum penalty of six months in jail and a $1,000 fine. She pled not guilty and was released on her own recognizance. Nothing more was reported on the case.[27]

Reporting in the *New York Times* in 2002, Howard Markel went so far as to say a few good words about the sun. Specifically, he mentioned that several scientists had put forward a theory that people who did not get enough sunlight and had diets low in vitamin D could be at higher risk of developing colon, prostate, rectal, ovarian and breast cancer. Over the previous 20 years or so, they said, laboratory evidence had suggested that vitamin D might block the growth of malignant tumors. Wondering how much sun was too much or too little, Markel answered his own question by concluding that no one knew for sure, pointing to the often contradictory barrage of medical studies and advice in the media. Just wondering how much sun was too much or too little was a novel idea then since most anti-sun scare stories never entertained such a concept; only zero exposure, abstinence, would do. Also, Markel did not say a word about using sunscreens, another example of heresy. While he did advise some exposure to the sun, he advised that 10 minutes or less was probably safe for other than the fair-skinned, who should still avoid the sun completely.[28]

In 2004 the American Cancer Society estimated that more than one million non-melanoma skin cancers and 55,100 melanoma carcinomas would be diagnosed as new cases in America that year. According to the organization, 7,910 Americans would die of melanoma in 2004, 5,050 of whom would be men. Basal cell carcinoma accounted for about 75 percent of all new cases of skin cancer; squamous cell carcinoma, about 20 percent; melanoma caused 79 percent of all skin cancer deaths.[29]

Given the enormous number of attacks on the sun and tanning, it was not surprising that one of the responses was the growth of a whole new industry, sunscreens (or suntan lotions as they were usually called in their early years). Prior to World War II, the use of sunscreens had been almost nil, with the few exceptions being homemade preparations, or the use of items such as oils originally created for other purposes. The sunscreen industry grew slowly through the 1940s to the 1970s, then increased dramatically from about 1980 onward. That pattern mirrored the development in the quantity and quality of the scare stories about the sun.

7

Sunscreens: 1946–1979

"Protective claims [by sun care lotions] without basis were extravagant; consequently the entire product class ... was endowed with a tenacious reputation of fraud and in some degree, although no longer warranted, the stigma still persists."

L. Stambovsky, 1968

As reporter Bernice Kanner observed, in 1983, suntan lotions, or the sunscreen business, did not even exist before the 1940s. Benjamin Green, a pharmacist who lived in Miami Beach, brought out the first commercial suntan product in 1944, after cooking up various cocoa-butter–based potions on his wife's stove and testing them on his own bald head. When one of them allowed a suntan but not a burn, he launched it on the market as Coppertone Suntan Cream. A year later, in 1945, he added a suntan oil to the product line. Promotion of that early Coppertone line took place under the slogan "Don't Be a Paleface." Among the first users of suntan products were World War II servicemen in the South Pacific.[1]

Other researchers were active around the same time. In the General Electric lab in Cleveland in 1946, the company's lighting expert, Dr. Matthew Luckiesh, said he had developed a special petroleum compound to prevent sunburn. That GE research was undertaken in 1942 at the request of the U.S. Army Air Force, then badly in need of a protective compound for fliers forced down at sea and exposed for long periods to blazing tropical sun. According to Luckiesh, the best answer was a dark red veterinary petrolatum; the jelly was once used to treat horse "collar gall" and other animal ailments. For human beings that petrolatum alone gave ample protection from the fiercest sunlight, did not rub off, and even with constant use did not irritate the skin. Although it was very effective, it never caught on with people because it looked bad, smelled bad, and made a mess of clothing.[2]

By the end of the 1940s, there were enough sunscreens on the market that consumer magazines began to evaluate them. In its June 1949 review article, *Consumers' Research Bulletin* began by noting, about suntanning, the "present vogue is not so healthy a practice as its devotees are wont to think." For some years the magazine said it had warned that too much UV from the sun might be a predisposing cause of cancer. It pointed out it was well known that both skin and lip cancer were more prevalent among fishermen, farmers, and Navy personnel than among other occupations. Women were said to be discovering too, from sad experience, that acquiring a heavy coat of tan, year after year, took a toll in robbing the skin of its natural oils, leaving the tissues dry, roughened, coarsened, and ripe for lines and wrinkles. Mentioned was the pioneering work of Luckiesh in developing his petrolatum —claimed here to protect the skin from the strongest sunshine for 20 hours— but, "it is obvious, however, that such a material will hardly be accepted on an appearance basis at a fashionable beach or swimming pool, or even on the golf course."

For its evaluation, Consumers' Research purchased samples of eight well-known brands of suntan lotions and tested their effectiveness in preventing sunburn and/or promoting suntan. According to the article, UV rays of a wavelength of about 2967 Angstrom units were of greatest importance in producing sunburn. Seven of the eight tested lotions blocked those wavelengths. For the production of a good tan with a minimum amount of sunburn, it was required that light energy shorter than 3200 Angstrom units be reduced to a minimum. Ultraviolet energy of longer wavelength was said to be quite effective in the production of a tan, for example, 3342 and 3650 Angstrom units. One lotion tested was Dorothy Gray Sunburn Cream. Consumer's Research called it an excellent sunburn preventive, because it admitted zero percent of light energy with a wavelength of 2967 Angstrom units; but also described it as not good for tanning, because it admitted only six to 12 percent of the longer wavelengths mentioned. Helena Rubenstein Suntan Oil transmitted zero percent at 2967 units, four percent at 3130 (Dorothy Gray admitted zero at that wavelength) "but efficiently transmitted ultraviolet energy effective in producing tanning," admitting 91 percent and 95 percent of the light energy at wavelengths of 3342 and 3650 Angstrom units, respectively. Thus, Helena Rubenstein Suntan Oil was rated as "one of the most effective in promoting a tan."[3]

Consumer Reports (from the Consumers Union — CU — organization) evaluated such preparations in July 1950, with the comment that to that point sunburn preventive preparations had their greatest acceptance along the North Atlantic Coast, in the Great Lakes area, around Los Angeles, and in the winter resorts. For its evaluation CU tested 46 brands of preparations; 14 of the 46 provided reliable protection against burning with the rest producing uncertain results. However, 17 of those remaining 32 did give protection to some of the people on whom they were tried; the other 15 were of help to very few people. Those tested preparations came in three forms; creams, lotions, and clear liquids (both alcohol and oil-base types). Each of the three rated most effective was a cream, while eight of the 10 brands at the bottom of the ratings were oils. Used as volunteers in the test were 34 women and 14 men. The backs of those volunteers were marked off into rectangles of one to two square inches and a different preparation applied to each rectangle. All of the 46 preparations were tried on every person. Instead of lying in the sun, the volunteers sat before batteries of four sunlamps. Product price was found to be unrelated to product effectiveness. One of the cheapest (Noxzema's Greaseless Suntan Lotion, at 15 cents an ounce) was rated as giving effective protection while the most expensive product in the entire sample (Sun Bronze by Charles of the Ritz, at $1.05 an ounce) gave "uncertain protection." CU placed the products into three categories: effective protection (14 brands ranging in price from 15 cents to 60 cents per ounce); uncertain protection (17 brands, 20 cents to $1.05); and poor protection (15 brands, 13 cents to 45 cents).[4]

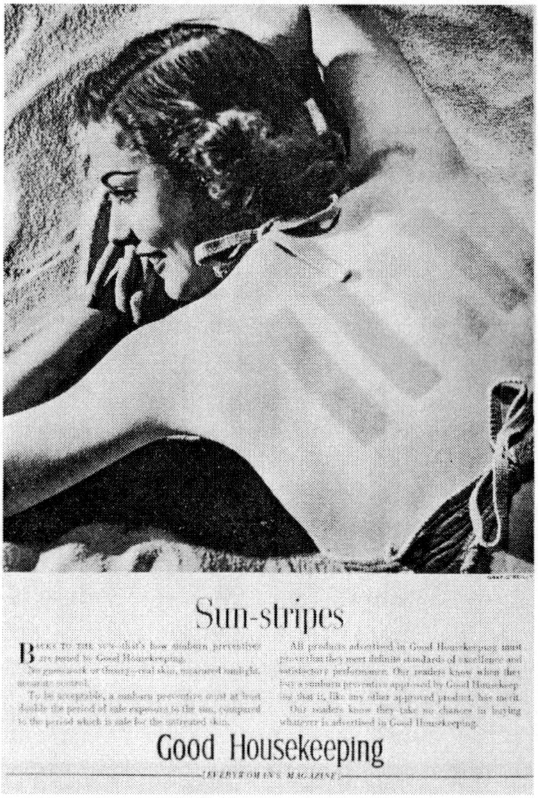

Good Housekeeping outlines in 1936 how it evaluated sunburn preventatives, at a time when there were very few around.

Consumers' Research

returned with another evaluation article in 1954. With respect to all the preparations then on the market, Consumers' Research observed that those customarily advertised as sunburn preventives contained a sunscreen substance or chemical. Since they were defined by the provisions of the Federal Food, Drug, and Cosmetic Act as drugs, they were required to declare their essential ingredients on the label. Other preparations that only claimed to act as an aid in acquiring a tan were regarded as cosmetics and were not required to list their ingredients on the label, although they sometimes contained a sunscreen and could be effective in preventing sunburn. The ultraviolet energy most effective in causing sunburn was said to be in the spectral region, between 2950A and 3150A. Twelve brands were rated in this evaluation, five creams and seven lotions. In the recommended category were three creams (33 cents to 38 cents per ounce); in the intermediate category were four lotions (18 cents to 25 cents); in the not recommended category were two creams (21 cents, 50 cents) and three lotions (17 cents to 27 cents). To rate the preparations, Consumers' Research submitted its randomly purchased samples to an independent laboratory for determination of their ultraviolet transmittance curves.[5]

Journalist John Abele reported, in 1957, that sales of suntan lotions and preparations were expected to reach $10 million for protective preparations (excluding products designed to ease a sunburn, for example) that year; compared with 1956 sales of about $9.2 million. Volume for 1956 was about twice the amount sold in 1951. Trade sources expected further strong sales increases as they estimated the products were then reaching only some 20 percent of their market. "Years ago, light-skinned peoples placed a premium on paleness," noted Abele. "The Gibson Girl with parasol aloft was a symbol of this. Within the last thirty years or so, however, the suntanned look has become increasingly desirable, whether as a sign of health, an accompaniment to summer fashions or as tacit proof of a good vacation." According to Abele, the basic job of a suntan lotion or preparation was to screen out the burning rays of the sun and admit the tanning rays. Even then the suntan market was described as a highly competitive one with "hundreds of preparations" battling for the public's dollars. Among the leaders were Tartan (produced by McKesson & Robbins); Skol (J. B. Williams); Sea & Ski (the Rolley division of Botany Mills); Bronztan (Shulton); and Coppertone (Douglas Laboratories). Cosmetic houses such as Revlon, Elizabeth Arden, Helena Rubenstein, Avon Products, and Dorothy Gray also sold suntan lotions. Distribution of those products from wholesalers to retailers followed the northward course of the sun, reaching a peak in late April and early May. Most of the retail selling of the preparations was concentrated between Memorial Day and Independence Day.[6]

Skol ads from 1939 and 1941. A foreign import, Skol was on the market in America before the first domestic brands were available.

Consumers' Research purchased 12 nationally distributed brands of sunscreen in 1958 for another evaluation and, as in the past, submitted them to a laboratory for determination of their ultraviolet transmittance curves. One of the lab evaluators was Dr. Matthew Luckiesh, who added that the extremely short-wave UV energy in sunlight (2950A–3150A) was most effective in producing sunburn and less effective in producing an eventual tan than ultraviolet energy of somewhat longer wavelengths. Therefore, he said, "the major result of a satisfactory sunscreen lotion or cream should be to absorb much of the short-wave energy." Luckiesh felt an effective sunscreen should admit no more than one percent of the light energy in the spectral range from 2900 to 3100 Angstroms. Of the 12 items evaluated, five fell into the recommended category (all had a transmittance of less than one percent in the 2900 to 3100 Angstrom units range); five fell into the intermediate category (more than one percent but less than 3.5 percent); and two brands appeared in the not recommended category (a transmittance of more than 3.5 percent).[7]

Burn remedies and tanning lotions began to arrive in greater numbers in the 1940s, and beyond. These ads for Unguentine, to be used after a sunburn, appeared in 1941 (left) and 1949.

When *Consumer Reports* evaluated suntan preparations in 1961, they tested 31 of the most popular brands on 37 volunteers. Their tests and ratings were based on the idea that the more completely the product stopped UV, the better. It was not necessary to tan through a film of the preparation; it was better to expose the skin enough to set up a tanning reaction before applying a sunscreen, and then get as full protection as possible. Also noted was the "quirk" in the law whereby products claiming to prevent sunburn were classified as drugs and therefore required to list all active ingredients on the label, while those that only claimed to aid the tanning process were classed as cosmetics and did not have to disclose their ingredients on the label. On that basis, Consumers Union believed that a number of the brands it tested to be in violation of that law. In this evaluation piece CU placed the 31 tested brands in four categories: acceptable–moderately high protection (nine brands); acceptable — moderate protection (15); acceptable — slight protection (five); acceptable — very slight protection (two).[8]

Annual sales of suntan preparations were about $20 million in 1963, with Coppertone and Sea & Ski dominating the market, and Shulton's Bronztan a distant third. Both Coppertone and Sea & Ski were introduced a decade or more earlier, while Bronztan first reached the market in 1955. While precise market shares were unclear, one business service estimated the two top makers accounted for about two-thirds of the market. Coppertone (then a subsidiary of Plough, Inc.) was expected to spend $2.5 million on advertising its sunscreens in 1963, while Sea & Ski was expected to spend about $1 million. Coppertone claimed it outsold all other suntan products combined in 1962, and cited an independent business source that put its market share at 56 percent. Product lines for that firm included Coppertone brand suntan lotion in oil, cream, and spray form; Shade for children with sensitive skin, Noskote and Lipkote for sensitive-area protection; Royal Blend, a combination suntan and beauty preparation introduced in 1963; and QT, a quick-tanning product. Sea & Ski asserted it shared 80 percent of the total market with Coppertone, with its share being some two-thirds of Coppertone's. Products in its line included a new Sea & Ski "oil-less" oil, Sun 'n Fun cream; Tanfastic dark tanning oil; and Snootie, a product designed for sensitive-area protection. Shulton's Bronztan had an estimated 10 percent of the total market with its Bronztan clear lotion and cream; Sun/Stop, and After-Flow, a post-exposure lotion.[9]

Time magazine pointed to store shelves crammed with dozens of suntan lotions and creams in 1963 as evidence that people were willing to risk sunburn's dangers in the hopes of getting a tan. It allowed the dark red veterinary petroleum jelly was the most effective sunscreen of all but acknowledged its characteristics made its public acceptance impossible. Also, drug companies were then investigating lotions made with benzophenone compounds, said to be 10 to 50 times more effective than existing sunscreen agents.[10]

Writing in the trade publication *Drug & Cosmetic Industry* in 1968, industry executive L. Stambovsky remarked that the annual sales volume of the industry had reached around $46 million. Within the past three decades, he continued, "sunbathing has assumed the scope, intensity, and devotion of a religion. Among all races, all social levels, and all ages, wherever the sun shines with sufficient warmth, millions of people court solar radiation with fanatical enthusiasm." He felt that "since a deep tan is indubitably flattering to everyone, male or female, young or old," that cosmetic enhancement had overcome warnings against the hazards of exposure to sunlight and helped fuel the growth of the suntan preparation industry. With respect to the early years of suntan lotions, Stambovsky admitted, "Protective claims without basis were extravagant; consequently the entire product class (known as suntan lotions or sunburn preventives) was endowed with a tenacious reputation of fraud and in some degree, although no longer warranted, this stigma still persists."[11]

Many ill-fated adventures in the early years of the suntan lotion industry were listed by Stambovsky. One took place several decades earlier when a well-known ethical drug firm marketed a suntan lotion using hydroquinone as the screening agent. Some 10 years before the advent of that preparation, Stambovsky had examined hydroquinone as a candidate for sun screening and found three critical defects; 1) absorption of UV rays in the burning range was "totally inadequate"; 2) the absorption curve fell off sharply in a matter of minutes during exposure to those rays; 3) chemical deterioration of the product took place after more than one season on the retailer's shelf. "Notwithstanding these faults, for more than a decade this company persisted, aggressively and expensively, in promoting this product," he added. Finally, the product was quietly removed from the market. Another early lotion he said had attained sizable volume and was able to maintain its position of strong sales by massive advertising rather than by therapeutic performance. Its protection was accomplished by tannic acid, but Stambovsky declared it had two inherent defects: 1) it did not absorb enough of the UV rays to function as a protective; 2) that absorption rate, weak as it was, deteriorated so rapidly in sunlight that after a few minutes, absorption was practically nil. Other similar failures over the past 5 to 20 years were also outlined by the executive.[12]

Stambovsky related that there were several new preparations being formulated with digalloyl trioleate — a synonym for tannic acid — as the

Another early arrival on the scene was Gaby. This copy was from 1941 (left) and 1945.

active ingredient. "In view of the historical incompetence of tannic acid and the failures in which it has been instrumental, to resort to this compound or modifications thereof seems to me to reflect a profound ignorance of basic commercial and scientific facts of suntan formulation," concluded a cynical Stambovsky. He believed the burning and major tan-

ning rays of sunlight extended from about 2950 Angstrom units to 3150
Angstrom units, and that while radiation from 3150 to about 4200
Angstrom units was not erythemogenic (sunburn producing), there were
zones of that spectral region at about 3400, 3800, and 4000 Angstroms,
and probably other nearby wavelengths, up to the ultraviolet limit that produced tan. Overall, Stambovsky declared, "It is hoped that the concrete
illustrations will be sufficient to convince those interested that the suntan
industry has been, and to some degree still is, influenced by unqualified
experts and authorities."[13]

A piece in *Today's Health* in 1970 divided the preparations into classes:
sunscreens, which permitted tanning and gave minimum protection; sun
blocks, which prevented tanning and gave intermediate to good protection; and physical barriers, such as red veterinary petrolatum. In total it
mentioned 28 brands. Those who insisted on tanning were urged to use
a sunscreen, and a more general warning was given: "The beneficial effects
of the sun are almost nil and you should consider the adverse effects before
joining the sun cult this summer."[14]

Two more suntan lotions in an increasingly crowded market; Sutra (1947) and Tartan (1950).

Writing around the same time, reporter James Forkan said there were about 18 suntan potions then on the market with Coppertone (and the other suntan product lines from that maker) claiming around 70 percent of total industry sales. Sales for the industry had jumped from $20 million in 1963 to more than $40 million in 1970, according to Forkan.[15]

In a 1971 evaluation of the products, Consumers Union commented that promotion for most suntan products tried to convey the impression that the product would enable the user to get a better tan than he would by using a competitive product or by using none at all, "better" being implied by such descriptors as "deep," "bronze," and "even." The fact is, though, pointed out CU, that none of the preparations could help a person tan any faster than he would otherwise, nor could any suntan potion affect the final shade of the tan or its evenness. "But, alas, the hopes of sun-worshippers die hard, even in the face of the physiological facts," lamented CU. For this evaluation CU studied 33 popular suntan preparations and rated them solely according to their sunscreening ability. Those products came in six forms: creams, lotions, gels, butters, clear liquids, and aerosol foams. CU produced five rating categories: acceptable — very good (very high protection against sunburn, three brands); acceptable — good (high protection, four brands); acceptable — fair (moderate to high protection, four brands); acceptable — poor (low to moderate, 18 brands — including seven of eight from market leaders Coppertone and Sea & Ski); conditionally acceptable — poor (poor protection, four brands — all the aerosols were conditional, on not being subjected to high temperatures).[16]

By 1975 the suntan preparation market was worth some $85 million per year, according to business reporter Lorraine Baltera. That year also saw the beginnings of a shift in the lotions to high protection levels as well as the start of a coding system. Baltera thought it was due to a growing customer concern over the relationship between skin cancer and sun exposure that a new impetus had been given to an emerging category of sun care products. Those new entries based their market position on high protection and total sun-blocking benefits. However, went the account, "high-screen products are still a new trend that will not reach full impact for at least another summer." Several marketers were said to be then starting to shift their advertising and marketing strategies from products that "tan you" to products that "protect you from sunburn."[17]

The FDA was then exploring the feasibility of requiring suntan products to be numbered on a scale of one to six, according to sunscreen efficiency, a system then in effect in European markets, explained Baltera. [This, of course, was the forerunner of our current system of giving an SPF — sun protection factor — number to such products.] American marketers had already begun to differentiate between products at varying levels of sun protection with their own (voluntary) color systems. Coppertone had a color-coded tanning guide at the point of purchase; Lanvin-Charles of the Ritz had also color-coded its Bain de Soleil line "to help the consumer correctly identify suntan levels by their level of protection." Other marketers who had not yet adopted the strictly voluntary color-coding system indicated they would take a wait-and-see attitude until a universal color-coding system was developed and enforced. They argued that if each company had its own color-coding system, the end result would be nothing but confusion for the consumer. Marketers reportedly did not oppose the FDA idea. As of 1975, reported Baltera, Coppertone had a 55 percent market share; Sea & Ski was second at 18 percent for its product line; Bain de Soleil at five percent; Tanya (Bristol-Myers), five percent; and Pfizer's Swedish Tanning Secret at five percent. The latter three products battled for third place in the market. Coppertone's main advertising theme then was "Whatever your kind of skin, there's a Coppertone for you," while Sea & Ski's main slogan was "Nobody's equal under the sun, so Sea & Ski has a tan for everyone."[18]

CU evaluated sunscreens

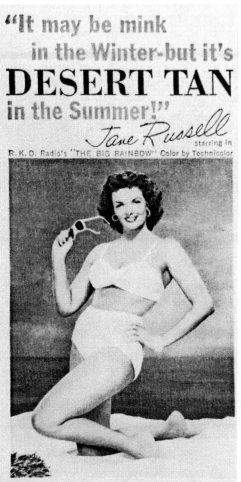

Capture a tan ... instead of a sunburn ... with the protection of fragrant, rich-in-lanolin DESERT TAN. Smooths on easily, absorbs completely. Perfect for all out-door living. Choose your DESERT TAN as you like it ... cream, liquid or new aerosol spray!

© 1954, D. T., Inc., Hempstead, N. Y.

Actor Jane Russell appeared in this endorsement ad in 1954 for yet another brand of suntan lotion, Desert Tan.

again in 1975, the first *Consumer Reports* update since 1970. Noting that medical people had continued to sound warnings about sun exposure throughout that period, CU went on to assert that experts generally agreed that 90 percent or more of all cases of skin cancer were caused by excessive exposure to the sun. Cited was Dr. Malcolm M. Lane Brown as having said that a person spending longer than 30 minutes a day in the brightest sunlight ran an increased risk of skin cancer. According to CU it was known that UV wavelength from 295 to 310 nanometers (a new terminology, equivalent to 2950 to 3100 Angstrom units) was responsible for burning the skin of most individuals. In their tests, preparations that blocked at least 99 percent of those harmful rays were given an "A" recommended rating (maximum burn protection, eight brands); those that blocked between 90 and 99 percent were rated "B" intermediate (moderate burn protection, four brands); and those that blocked less than 90 percent of the rays were given a "C" not recommended rating (minimal burn protection, 14 brands). [Note that until then, *Consumer Reports* had always found every sunscreen they tested to be "acceptable," albeit not equal, with a wide range of acceptability.] A second objective of many who used sun preparations—after burn prevention—thought CU, was to obtain the best possible tan. "Since tanning rays for most people are those of wavelengths from 320 to 400 nanometers (3200 to 4000 Angstrom units), we also evaluated the efficiency of the thin films in blocking these rays," added the article. However, those results were not presented in a particularly scientific way, with tanning ability mentioned only in the notes and only for 10 of the 26 brands. Evaluation in that area concluded that one brand allowed tanning, two allowed moderate tanning, two allowed appreciable tanning, one allowed minimal tanning, one allowed maximum tanning, and three brands blocked an appreciable amount of tanning rays.[19]

By 1977 more companies that manufactured sun preparations were coding their products with numbers or symbols to indicate how much sun screening could be expected from each preparation; to simplify which skin should use which product. Companies such as Arden, Revlon, and Coppertone were all using codes consisting of numbers while Estee Lauder used symbols. All of this was still voluntary. As far as the FDA was concerned, a sun product was classified as an OTC (over-the-counter) drug or cosmetic according to what the manufacturer claimed for it. If a maker sold it as a tanning product, then it was a cosmetic; if it was sold to prevent sunburn, it was a drug. According to journalist Angela Taylor, Paba was still considered the best sunscreen agent, its use as a sun blocker having been discussed in medical journals as far back as the late 1940s. However, Taylor did admit that the only absolute sun block was zinc oxide, the white substance lifeguards often wore on their noses. Because of esthetics, zinc oxide was rarely used by the general population.[20]

By 1978 the U.S. sun care product market had increased to a value of $120 million annually. Many of the products liked to emphasize both tan-

The age of specialization began to creep into the sun care industry with, for example, Sun-Fluff (1954) that was said to condition skin while helping to tan it, and the same firm's Skolex (1954), which was said to completely prevent sunburn.

ning and protection in their marketing and advertising campaigns. Breaking down that market, business writer Pat Sloan reported that "conventional" tanning products accounted for 35 percent of the total, "high tanning" products took 25 percent, sunscreens were at 25 percent, after-exposure products took five percent, and products that claimed to produce a tan without the sun or any UV exposure accounted for 10 percent of the total. Coppertone was still thought to be the industry leader, with an estimated 35 percent share of the market. Sea & Ski still claimed to be number two, but an increasing number of market observers no longer believed that claim, putting the firm's share at between seven and 14 percent. As recently as two years earlier, the market shares of Coppertone and Sea & Ski had been estimated at 55 percent and 18 percent, respectively. Such a dramatic change in the industry was felt to have been driven by segmenting of the market as consumers worried more about sun effects.[21]

One of the most famous advertising trademarks, not only in sun care product copy but throughout all marketplaces, was Little Miss Coppertone, showing a pigtailed, wide-eyed little girl whose panties had been pulled down by a mischievous puppy, revealing her suntan line. Jackie Callaway of Caldwell, Idaho, declared, in 1979, the trademark was a copy of a photo of her taken by her father in 1941, and she was seeking royalties on what she considered the unauthorized use of her body by Coppertone. She said her father took the by then famous photo in San Diego when she was two and her last name was Wills. Reportedly the photo won second prize in a contest sponsored by *Popular Photography* magazine and later the father sold it for $25 to a Canadian calendar company. Callaway did not know how Coppertone (part of Plough, Inc.) obtained the photograph. Plough denied that Callaway was Little Miss Coppertone.[22]

A change in the suntan industry took place at the end of the 1970s. After a long period of inaction, the FDA stepped in and mandated a coding system for the sun care products. Increasingly strident scare stories had alarmed the general public to worry more and more about the effects of sun exposure. As a result all sun care product manufacturers changed their advertising and marketing strategies. They emphasized even more the sun-screening or sun blocking aspects of their products, and emphasized tanning aspects even less.

8

Sunscreens: 1980–2004

"There is not enough ultraviolet light on earth to warrant an SPF over 15..."

Heinz Etermann, FDA, 1988.

"...fear is a powerful selling tool. The come-on now [for sunscreens] is to push increasingly potent, expensive and specialized goop, since marketers are having a harder time selling more of it."

Toddi Gutner, *Forbes*, 1992

"The details of the sunlight-cancer connection are unclear.... For one thing, it turns out to be hard to show that people who wear a lot of sunscreen have a lower cancer rate than other people with similar sun exposure."

Consumer Reports, 1998

Both Consumers' Research and CU looked, once again, at the sun care industry in the spring of 1980. By this time the FDA's system was in place, whereby sunscreens were labeled with a factor telling how much protection a person got by using the item; SPF (sun protection factor) 2–4 for people who seldom burned and who tanned well; SPF 4–6 for people who needed extra protection from sunburn; SPF 8–15 for maximum protection with little tanning; SPF over 15, for people who always burned in the sun. The system was in place in monograph form; still, it would be some time before it passed through the entire regulatory rule-making procedures. "Drug store operators have confirmed the fact that tanning folk know that too much sun is bad for them but for the most part they do not seem to care," worried Consumers' Research. "They tend to buy deep-tan lotions and oils with minimal sunscreen ingredients, and also those that are useless for the purpose, but are still best sellers, namely cocoa butter and baby oil." This organization's attitude was best summed up in the title it chose for its article, "Sunshine: Hazardous to Your Health."[1]

Somewhat less foreboding was the CU article in which it was observed that the short ultraviolet rays (UVB, about 0.2 percent of the sun's radiant energy reaching the earth) were responsible for burning while longer wavelength ultraviolet rays (UVA) were tanning only, more or less, and did not burn. UVB rays would also produce a tan. According to CU, for those who could develop one, a tan provided a good barrier against sunburn, and the safest and quickest way to tan was by gradually increasing exposure over several days or weeks, aided by the use of a good sunscreen. Non-melanoma skin cancers were said to be the most common of all forms of cancer, constituting one-third of all cancers in the U.S. Some 300,000 new cases were diagnosed each year in America but they accounted for less than 0.1 percent of all cancer deaths. CU admitted that the evidence linking melanomas to sun exposure was not strong but argued that most experts believed that there was a connection, perhaps indirectly. Indicating how much marketing of these products had changed was that in its evaluation only one of the 24 preparations tested was touted as a "tanning" lotion. Most of the others put themselves forward as sunscreens, sun blocks, or sun filters.[2]

The passing from the marketplace "of tanning elixirs that promised what only your own body could deliver" could be credited to the U.S. Food and Drug Administration, thought *Consumer Reports*. Since at least 1973, manufacturers had been on notice that the FDA was considering new regulations for OTC sunscreen items. The FDA was interested not only in eliminating advertising myth and legend, but also in promoting public awareness of the real purposes of sunscreens. According to CU, painless exposure to the sun often produced a tan, "itself a kind of living sunscreen" and that the quickest route to a tan entailed a daily UV exposure of about double one's minimal erythema dose — that is, the exposure time that kept the skin in a state of painless redness and the pigment cells at a maximum production of melanin. About 14 days was the FDA's estimate as to how long it took for most white people to develop a full tan. Lotions could not hasten the development of a tan but sunscreen products "do allow you to safely extend your time in the sun without resorting to such encumbrances as wide-brimmed hats and parasols," explained CU. To that date 21 chemicals had been declared as safe and effective by the FDA in protecting against sunburn. In explaining the SPF system, it was noted that if a person's minimal erythema dose was 30 minutes and he applied a sunscreen with an SPF of 3, he could assume the time it took for his skin to redden slightly was three times as long, or about 90 minutes.[3]

All but five of CU's rated products had SPFs of eight or greater; seven had SPFs of 15 or more. Although manufacturers were not yet required to print the SPF number on the label, most firms had anticipated proposed regulations by doing so. The FDA wanted the products designated by SPF ranges, with the lowest number in the range appearing as the number on the label. Thus, an SPF of 8 would be the designation of all sunscreens with SPFs of from 8 to 14. CU's recommendations were that lotions with SPFs of 15 and up should be the products of choice for people who either never could acquire a "protective tan" or who preferred not to. Products in the 8–14 SPF range were said to be about right for those who wanted to stay out in the sun for a fairly long time, turn a little pink, and then develop a tan over a period of days. Products in the SPF range of 15 and more were described as "too tan-inhibiting most of the time." Within each ratings group (done by SPF range) CU found little difference between products and advised that cost be the chief guide. In the ratings group SPF 8–14, the cost "per dollop" ranged from about five cents to 25 cents.[4]

Strong growth of about 13 percent caused the sun care market to reach a volume of around $225 million in 1981, with sunscreen products making up one-third of that total. From 1980 to 1981, sunscreen products experienced a 15 percent growth rate while tanning products refused to fade away, growing by 12 percent. Coppertone maintained its leadership position with 39 to 41 percent of the total sun care market. However, it placed only third in the sunscreen market with a 16 percent share of that submarket. Overall, its nearest competitor was Hawaiian Tropic with a 23 percent share.[5]

Writing in *Forbes* in 1982, business reporter Barbara Rudolph discussed the FDA coding at length. Four years earlier, she wrote, spurred by reports that too much sun could cause cancer, the FDA advised manufacturers of sun care products to number their lotions according to the quantity of sunblock ingredients they contained. "Gone are the days of simply promoting a deep dark tan," she explained. "Now you have to see good health, too." That meant firms like Schering-Plough and Johnson & Johnson started aggressively selling sunscreens and sun blocks. Such products were then the fastest growing sector of the business. "It's a rare case where government regulation actually helped business," concluded Rudolph. "Sales of the traditional products, the lotions and oils that contain virtually no sunblock protection, are flat."[6]

However, Rudolph did recount that those regulations did not come about because the FDA was vigorous and proactive in recognizing a problem and then moving to hopefully safeguard the public. "Look closely, in fact, and you'll see that the FDA had a lot of help drafting its new rules," she declared. "Schering-Plough, which makes Coppertone and Tropical Blend and has enjoyed around a 45% market share for years, bombarded the government with studies claiming that their sunblock products might help prevent skin cancer." That company joined with its competitors in fighting for some carefully selecting wording, and had their way. Sunscreen packages asserted that "with liberal and regular use over the years," tanning preparations "may help reduce the chance of skin cancer." One sunscreen marketer exclaimed, "Being able to say this is a pretty neat thing." In Rudolph's opinion that was an understatement because: "The industry now offers many different versions of what used to be one product. There's a special lotion available for every tan and a grading system that measures protection...." To Rudolph it all meant that people were less likely to go out and buy just one bottle of lotion when they were led to believe they really needed two or three, to have proper control over their tan. Alan Sadovnick, a marketer at Carter Wallace's Sea & Ski division, for example, saw a repeat in the tanning business of what had happened in the coffee industry. "There's an equivalent of freeze-dried, instant, ground and decaffeinated." Selling season for the products was very short in the U.S., running from Memorial Day to Labor Day, with consumers buying an average of only two bottles a year, and those were usually purchased early in the summer.[7]

Hawaiian Tropic remained second overall, with Rudolph estimating its market share at 20 percent. In 1967, Ron Rice was a 27-year-old high school chemistry teacher who also worked part time as a lifeguard in Daytona Beach, Florida. He decided he could make a suntan oil as good as anything on the market. He got a large trash can and borrowed $500 to buy chemicals, oils and bottles. Soon Hawaiian Tropic emerged, and quickly became popular. Rice's winning idea was said to have been to make a lotion that smelled like coconut (it did contain coconut oil). By 1982 his privately owned company earned more than $50 million annually in sales.[8]

Journalist Bernice Kanner argued in 1983 that our craving for deep, luxurious tans had been at least furthered, if not exactly engineered, by the suntan product industry. Manufacturers, she continued, were behind much of the interest in protection from the sun, too— they were major supporters of the Skin Cancer Foundation. She noted that the FDA announcing a numbering system for measuring the effectiveness of oils and lotions, in 1978, gave the business a boost. Also recommended by the FDA was that sunscreen products bear warnings about exposure to the sun and carry a statement saying, "liberal use of this product may reduce the chance of premature aging of the skin and skin cancer." It all worked out well for the industry, observed Kanner, as in the five years that followed, industry sales increased 50 percent.[9]

When the trade publication *Progressive Grocer* conducted a survey, it found that 42.7 percent of all shoppers questioned used suntan products. A few years earlier, *American Girl* magazine found that 87 percent of its youthful readership used the product. According to Kanner, Schering Plough Corp. had 29 sun care products, including the Coppertone line, and held 45 percent of the total market. In 1980 sunscreens with an SPF of five or more accounted for 25 percent of the overall market. By the end of 1982 their share stood at 39 percent. Kanner believed that gain was due to the success of the FDA's coding system more than to company advertising. Marketers of sunscreens relied largely on what they called "ethical advertising," whereby they would concentrate on dermatologists, talk to them about the SPF numbers "and blanket them with samples to give to their patients," according to Karen Reilly, product manager for Allergan's Eclipse line. As to why the bikinied beauty was almost ubiquitous in suntan lotion advertising, Chuck Levy, an executive with Warwick Advertising (Coppertone's agency), said, "To sell a good-looking tan, you've got to show the end benefit — as much of it as possible. There are few items you can put people in that show it better than a bikini. And because so much suntan-product advertising is image advertising, you've got to suggest the beach and good times."[10]

The total U.S. sun care market reached a volume of about $270 million annually in 1985; the American cosmetics industry then had a volume of around $2 billion a year. Plough, Inc.'s Coppertone line reportedly stood at a 30 to 35 percent market share, down from about 40 percent three years earlier. For at least 10 years, at that time, companies such as Coty, Estee Lauder, and Elizabeth Arden had included sunscreens in everything from lipstick to face colors. Until 1985 that added ingredient had been positioned in marketing as an added product benefit rather than as the main sales pitch. But that year Avon Products' Avon division reformulated four moisturizers with what it called the Age Protection System. Lisa Siegel, Avon senior product manager for skin care, confirmed the significance of that reformulation to the arrival of toothpaste with fluoride. As Avon saw it, with respect to using these reformulated items, explained Siegel, "it's really as important as brushing your teeth every morning with a fluoride toothpaste." Prevention of premature aging, she emphasized, was mandatory. UVB blockers were then common in almost all sun care products but some were including UVA blockers as well. Business reporter Pat Sloan explained that while damage from UVA radiation was not as immediately noticeable as that from UVB rays, "the risks of premature aging and skin cancer from these rays are just as great, if not greater, than those from UVB exposure." French cosmetics firm Lancome introduced Conquete du Soleil,

a sun "strategy" that "promotes a healthy glowing tan — minus the hazards of UVA and UVB sun damage," according to company promotional
material. Mostly, though, the companies refrained from talking about UVA
and UVB specifically in their ad material.[11]

A year later journalist Lisa Belkin reported in the *New York Times* on
the large number of products then available in the sun care industry. It
was, said Belkin, an indication of how producers were searching for tricks
to distinguish their offerings from all the others in a field that had suddenly grown crowded. Effectively, there was no difference in the new products. Said Joseph Gubernick, senior vice president of technology for Estee
Lauder, which owned Estee Lauder, Clinique, and Aramis and Prescrip-
tives cosmetics and had brought out three new sun care lines in the previous two years, "They all work, and they all work well; a sunscreen is a
sunscreen is a sunscreen." By then the U.S. sun care industry was valued
at $300 million annually. Sales of suntan products had been flat between
1980 and 1985 while sales of sunscreens and sunblocks had increased 70
percent. Belkin thought a lot of that growth was related to the FDA SPF
numbers. "Though the proposed numbers have not yet become law, they
have apparently helped win the confidence of the public. Sunscreens thus
now seem to carry a scientific cachet. Where they were once pitched as the
route to a deep, dark tan, they are now promoted as protection from the
ravages of the sun."[12]

Though the word cancer did not appear on product packages, Belkin
believed prevention of that disease was implied by those products. Commented David Garlin, president of Cosmotech, a chemical consulting firm
to the cosmetics industry, "Cancer is not a good marketing strategy. When
you talk about 'sun protection,' it's not a scare word and people still know
what you mean." Manufacturers hoped to use the new image of sunscreens
as health products to increase sales even further. The goal, declared Pamela
Fields, vice president of marketing for Biotherm, was to make a sunscreen
something "you put on every morning when you put on makeup or brush
your teeth."

While the government's SPF numbers opened up new opportunities
for the marketing of sun care products they also set new limits. Because
the numbers defined the sun protection a product provided, companies
could not claim that their sunscreens were more effective than was a com-
petitor's. If two bottles "have the same number, they're the same," said
Michael Benson, a pharmacist who reviewed sun products for the FDA.
An example of similar products marketed as though they were different
could be found in the sun protection sticks sold by Biotherm and Lancome.
Both companies were owned by Cosmair, Inc., and the two products "are,

in fact, the same," admitted A. John Penicnak, senior vice president of research and development for Cosmair. Marketing directors for the two lines said that because each was aimed at a different type of consumer — Lancome for the "more glamorous" woman, Biotherm for the "more out-doorsy" one — each was selling well. Clinique repackaged its "Body Scrub" as "Suntan Polisher" in response to growing consumer interest in sun products, according to Iris Model, director of education for the firm. "They are the same," she said of the two formulas, "but now the name really iden-tifies what the product is there for. You can use it to enhance a tan." To try and differentiate their products some companies were using higher SPF numbers. In response to that tactic the FDA warned firms that use of SPF numbers higher than 15 may violate the proposed regulations. Numbers of 20 and 23 were "gilding the lily," said Heinz Etermann, director of the FDA's Division of Colors and Cosmetics. There were only a certain num-ber of hours when the sun was a concern, he said, and too much protec-tion, though not harmful, was superfluous.[13]

More good things happened to the industry to potentially increase sales, thanks to the government and other outside sources. During the summer of 1986 three sun-drenched cities, Atlanta, Tucson, and Birm-ingham (Alabama) were using a daily sunburn index (forerunner of today's widely reported daily UV index in newspapers and on radio and televi-sion weather reports). It was similar to the pollution indexes reported in some cities and was designed to keep people informed of the sun's inten-sity each day. In Atlanta the sunburn index was presented as the time it would take the skin of the average untanned person to turn red (an indi-cation of sun damage) on a particular day; in Birmingham, the readings were divided into four categories; low, medium, high, and dangerous. The program began in Atlanta in 1982, after a National Cancer Institute survey showed that Atlanta had the highest rate of skin cancer of eight cities. It was a system that relied on an ultraviolet meter developed by the National Oceanographic and Atmospheric Administration (NOAA). Readings were taken daily between Memorial Day and Labor Day and made available to local media through the NOAA weather wire.[14]

A 1986 study of sunscreen users had doctors in Sweden asking 50 peo-ple to apply five different sunscreens. They found that, in general, people applied only half as much as was needed to acquire the degree of protec-tion (SPF number) stated on the label. So the protective effect was only half of what it should have been. "The amount applied seems to be as important as the SPF of the product, probably even more so for products with a high SPF..." concluded the physicians who conducted the research.[15]

One company did go so far as to introduce a sun care product with the word "cancer" in its name. Called Skin Cancer Garde (made by Eclipse laboratories of Greenwich, Connecticut) its 1987 ad copy carried an over-size Surgeon General–type warning from the Skin Cancer Foundation stressing that repeated overexposure of unprotected skin to the sun could cause "premature aging and skin cancer, including malignant melanoma." That sun care industry then was worth $400 million a year with Plough continuing to hold the number one spot, with a 38 percent share. When the FDA issued its preliminary monograph on sun product coding in 1978, it acknowledged an SPF scale ranging from two to 15. Yet by 1987 some such products carried SPFs of as high as 36. Skin Cancer Garde had a label SPF of 36. Even Plough's Coppertone division and Tanning Research Laboratories' Hawaiian Tropic, two firms that had been aligned more strongly in the past with tanning than with protection, had added what Sloan described as "sky-high" SPFs. Coppertone was selling one item with an SPF of 25 while Tanning Research had marketed one with an SPF of 22. Because SPFs above 15 were not in the FDA monograph — which had still not been completed — some sun care marketers worried that the government and the industry could be headed for another confrontation. To that point, the FDA had not taken any steps to stop the trend toward higher SPFs, even though it saw no need for them. According to Heinz Etermann, the FDA's director of cosmetics technology, "There is not enough ultraviolet light on earth to warrant an SPF over 15.... But no action has been taken on these products because they are not unsafe."[16]

A tendency on the part of the industry to develop bizarre spin-off items reached a new height in the late 1980s with the introduction of tan accelerators as the latest fad in sun care products. Several major cosmetics companies — including Avon, Estee Lauder, Germaine Monteil, Lancome, Lancaster, and Revlon — sold tan accelerators, also called tan deepeners or pre-tan conditioners. In March of 1988 Estee Lauder replaced its Golden Sun Pre-Tan Accelerator (it had to be used once a day for three consecutive days before exposure to the sun) with another product, the Overnight Pre-Tan Accelerator; Lauder claimed it was faster and more effective. Unlike tanning creams that colored the skin (and supposedly imparted a tan without UV exposure), tan accelerators were supposed to work with sunlight. "It's a good idea," said Dr. Norman Levine, an associate professor and the chief of dermatology at the University of Arizona. "But it doesn't seem to work." A study published in the *Journal of the American Academy of Dermatology* in April 1987 looked at the effects of Lauder's Golden Sun Pre-Tan Accelerator and Coppertone's Natural Tan Accelerator. Researchers (all from the Cleveland Clinic Foundation in Ohio and led by Dr. Christine Jaworsky) found that despite claims by the manufacturers, those products did not increase skin pigmentation in the absence of ultraviolet light, nor did they enhance tanning in the presence of ultraviolet light.[17]

Commenting on the bewildering array of sun care products available to consumers in the summer of 1988, *Newsweek* observed that people could buy products with SPFs as high as 39 and "The range of choices is so daunting that a sun worshipper could end up spending more time at the drugstore than on the beach." It called SPF the "sun-profit factor." Companies were simply cashing in on an increased public awareness of the risks of skin cancer, argued the piece, as marketers shifted their promotional emphasis to "ultra-sunscreens." Lotions with SPFs of six and higher then made up nearly half of all industry sales, up from 35 percent three years earlier. Said financial analyst Ronald Stern of First Boston Corporation, "People are scared by skin cancer and companies have utilized that [fear]. Now, every company wants to have an SPF number for every potential customer." With respect to whether the high-end SPF formulas were more effective, the article observed that manufacturers said the lotions had been scientifically tested and had proven merit. However, dermatologists were reported to be skeptical. Dr. Mark Lebwohl, clinical director of dermatology at Mount Sinai Medical Center in New York City, believed an SPF 15 lotion applied frequently and in proper amounts was adequate protection for most people. "SPFs are tested in a sweatless, dry environment," he explained. "Using a sunblock with a 33 SPF doesn't necessarily mean that you can stay in the sun 33 times longer. By the time that block of time is up, you've probably sweat it off."[18]

Until about 1986 the highest SPF available was 20. Then in 1987 Eclipse Laboratories unveiled Cancer Garde with an SPF of 36. A year later Westwood came out with Pre Sun, a product with a label SPF of 39. On the sidelines the FDA continued to wonder whether to endorse SPFs more than 15. When that government agency introduced an SPF numbering system running from 2 to 15 in its 1978 monograph, technology rendered products with higher SPF numbers as next to impossible to create.[19]

Reporter Robert Brody stated that sunscreens and sunblocks accounted for about 35 percent of the $350 million annual market for sun care products in 1988, up from about 25 percent in 1980, far outpacing tanning agents. Steven Manenti, president of Eclipse Laboratories, maker of Cancer Garde sunscreen, said, "Ours will be a tanless society by the end of this century." Said Dr. G. Thomas Jansen, president of the American Academy of Dermatology, "If people continue to wear high-SPF sunscreens—and to take other precautions—we expect to see a demonstrable decrease in the incidence of skin cancer in the next 20 years." Some seven of every 10 adults and teens used sun care products but the American Academy of Dermatology also found that one-third of all adults worked on a tan, one-quarter took no precaution in the sun, and fewer than half applied sun-screens. More than 50 companies produced products for the sun care industry.[20]

According to Brody the cosmetics companies had largely avoided the sun care market until around a decade earlier, but by 1988 such products represented about 10 to 15 percent of sales for major cosmetics firms, at least twice the level of five years earlier. Many were kept out of the mar-ket by the seasonal nature of the product. Estee Lauder and Revlon were the cosmetic firms that broke through first. From the start, cosmetic firms appealed to well-to-do, beauty-conscious buyers. A typical sunscreen from Avon or Clinique could then run from $12 to $15, about twice the cost of a mass-market item. Also, cosmetics companies created a strategy to con-vince consumers to protect themselves from the sun year round, both indoors and outdoors.[21]

Business journalist Pat Sloan reported those upscale department store brands of sun care products accounted for about $100 million of the $500 million total annual market. Coppertone remained number one with an estimated 25 percent share of the $400 million mass-market segment. Sec-ond place was held by Tanning Research Laboratories (marketer of Hawai-ian Tropic and other brands; third place went to Procter & Gamble's Bain de Soleil). In 1987 products with SPFs of 25 and higher represented only six percent of the market; by 1988 they comprised 20 percent. Some mar-keters had reportedly gone so far as to drop product items with SPFs below 10.[22]

During 1988 there were 400,000 new cases of basal-cell cancer diag-nosed in America, as well as 100,000 new cases of squamous-cell cancer. Writing in the FDA Consumer in 1989, Cheryl Sweet argued that while sunscreens traditionally had been aimed at filtering out only UVB radia-tion, future products were expected to offer greater protection against UVA rays as well. UVB rays caused burning, tanning, and increased can-cer risks, explained Sweet, while UVA radiation penetrated more slowly and deeply into the skin, causing changes in blood vessels, creating the sags and bags associated with premature aging, and adding to the cancer risk of UVB rays. Research on mice had shown that animals exposed to both UVA and UVB had a much higher incidence of skin cancer than those exposed just to UVB light. Sweet recorded that sunscreens with an SPF as high as 50 were on the market, although an SPF of 15 remained the high-est number endorsed by the FDA. That agency was still evaluating whether to endorse higher SPF. Said Jeanne Rippere, a microbiologist with the

FDA's over-the-counter drug evaluation division, "I think there's possibly some justification for SPFs up to 30. For someone with very fair skin, a 15 might not be enough. But I think you get a diminishing return when you get to higher numbers. SPFs of 49 or 50 are absurd, in my view."[23]

Later in 1989, Dero Saunders, in *Forbes*, said that existing sunscreens were effective against UVB, assuming an SPF of 15 or more, but the new worry was UVA because "there is clinical evidence that it accentuates many UVB-caused conditions," and could be dangerous in its own right. "Clearly there is a commercial opportunity here." Already that year a new sunscreen by Hoffmann-La Roche (Photoplex) had gone on the market after the FDA approved its new UVA blocker butyl methoxydibenzoylmethane. Sunscreens containing it had been available in Europe and elsewhere for a few years. Hoffmann began marketing that compound in 1982. Herbert Laboratories (owned by Allergan, Inc.) made Photoplex in the U.S., and added a standard UVB screen to it. Some dermatologists were then advising the use of two sunscreens, Photoplex and a UVB screen.[24]

Early in 1990 the FDA sent "feedback" letters to Schering-Plough's Memphis-based HealthCare Products Division, Westwood Pharmaceuticals in Buffalo, and to Mary Kay Cosmetics in Dallas. While not regulatory actions, the letters "sternly" reminded the companies that claims they and other manufacturers had made on behalf of their products, that they blocked UVA rays, were "unsubstantiated." Reporter Joan Hamilton noted that most sunscreens blocked UVB, shorter wavelength radiation that caused sunburn and some skin cancers. But the longer UVA rays, once thought to be safe, were surrounded by a growing body of evidence that showed they "contribute to aging, cancer, and cataracts," according to FDA scientist Jeanne Rippere. While full screening from UVA was then felt to be desirable, that protection was difficult to measure and the FDA had not yet established a standard. To that date the only product to win FDA approval for its UVA screening ability was Photoplex, yet sunbathers could go to any retailer and find many brands of sunscreen that claimed in their packaging and/or marketing to offer "broad spectrum" or "UV-A protection."[25]

It was a situation that made Herbert Laboratories president A. Thomas Bender furious. "We paid our dues," he fumed, referring to a three-year FDA review process that added $1 million to the development costs. He said he would press the FDA to crack down on his unapproved rivals. "These companies," he said, "just changed their marketing." Hamilton remarked that most of those other companies admitted they had not added any new ingredients to their products. "They've simply added the claim based on their own measure of UV-A protection." William E. Gilbertson, director of the FDA's division of over-the-counter drug evaluation noted

that many of those claims could be "misleading and confusing." In his letter to Schering-Plough Corp., he singled out its Share brand, which could
"lead consumers to believe that they are obtaining a greater degree of UV-
A protection than they actually are." Scientists worried that people were
buying very high SPF products that blocked only UVB rays and then stayed
out in the sun far too long.[26]

Consumer Reports returned with an evaluation of sunscreens in 1991.
In discussing skin cancer statistics, it pointed out that the depleted ozone
layer could also be partly to blame. That thinning ozone layer, predicted
the U.S. Environmental Protection Agency, could lead to 200,000 additional skin cancer deaths in the U.S. over the next 50 years, an increase of
50 percent, from the current 8,000 deaths per year to 12,000. CU then
added that picking a sunscreen was then a difficult and complicated business, going into a long discussion, presenting pictures of skin types, as well
as presenting a discussion on MED (minimum erythema dose). With
respect to UVA radiation, CU believed exposure to UVA increased the
chance that exposure to UVB would cause skin cancer. For all those reasons the promise of UVA protection, argued the article, had become one
of the hottest selling points for sunscreens that summer. "But many products that claim to block UVA haven't conclusively proved that they do...."
UVB radiation was in the 280–320 nanometer range (one nanometer was
equal to one-millionth of a millimeter) while UVA was in the 320–400
nanometer range. Substantial protection against the full UVA spectrum was
provided only in sunscreens containing one of only two ingredients, Photoplex or Parsol 1789. Yet many other makers claimed UVA protection for
their sunscreens even though the items did not contain one of those two
ingredients approved by the FDA for UVA blocking. CU ignored such
claims in preparing its ratings. A survey of its readers revealed that more
than 99 percent knew the risks of sun exposure — but only 66 percent used
sunscreens. Of that group, 47 percent used the screens in spring and summer, while just 10 percent used sunscreens year round. More than half of
the sunscreen users began using a higher SPF, and more than 80 percent
of people with young children put sunscreen on them. CU rated 21 products for adults (with a price range from 80 cents an ounce to $4.28).[27]

A 1991 article in the Drug & Cosmetic Industry trade publication
remarked that for the marketers of sunscreens, the previous two decades
"have been replete with natural blessings" that had all served to sharpen
consumer awareness about the hazards of the sun. Blessings included: 1)
growing proof of erosion of the earth's ozone layer; 2) warmer temperature cycles from the Greenhouse Effect on the climate; and 3) observations
by dermatologists of the growing number of skin cancer cases, 600,000 new

cases a year, with 90 percent of them reported to be caused by sun exposure. Combined with a campaign by dermatologists to make tanning less fashionable because of its inherent hazards, those environment and health factors had combined to emphasize the importance of sunscreens in daily use, for children as well as adults, and as a component of makeup for women and skin toners for men. Total market for sunscreens (defined as items above SPF 4) in the U.S. and suntan products (all others) was estimated at $410 million for 1990.[28]

Little Miss Coppertone became an issue again in 1991. For 40 years (to that date), the Coppertone ad billboard with the little girl having her bottom exposed by her puppy had been a fixture in Miami, with the 50-foot-wide billboard fixed to the side of the Parkleigh Hotel. It admonished, "Don't be a paleface" and "Tan, don't burn." Jokingly the sign soon became known as "Moon over Miami." Then Coppertone's corporate owner Schering-Plough (Plough acquired Coppertone in 1957) declared that, as part of an overhaul of its advertising strategy, it was considering removing the sign. The billboard's pro-tan message was said to be no longer consistent with Coppertone's new focus on sunscreens. Also, a company spokesman said "different sensitivities" made it unwise to push a slogan containing the politically incorrect word "paleface." Not to mention that the baring of a little girl's bottom was also not politically correct. Nevertheless, word the sign was to be dumped ignited such civic pride and produced such a flood of complaints that Plough reversed its decision. Yet just days after that reversal, the Parkleigh announced plans to tear down the entire building to make room for a car park. Among the groups that had stepped forward to save the sign was the local historical society.[29]

Artist Joyce Ballantyne, who sketched the logo using her three-year-old daughter Cheri as a model and a neighbor's dog, said the fuss over the billboard surprised her. Then 72, she called it "much ado about nothing" but allowed that she understood why people cared about preserving images they considered pop art. "It has to do with vacations and summertime and associates itself with a good time," she added. Preservationists, who did not usually fight for billboards, said the image of the dog pulling on the bathing suit of the girl with a pigtail was a piece of Americana and should be saved. "It brings back so many wonderful memories that are part of what we've all grown up with," said Louise Yarbrough, executive director of the Dade Heritage Trust. "It's part of this city. We feel strongly it should stay here." Prior to reversing its decision Schering-Plough spokesman Doug Petrus said, with respect to the two slogans on the billboard, "Neither statement is in vogue with current thinking about damage that can be caused by overexposure to the sun."[30]

Writing in 1992 in *Forbes* magazine (a publication that happily proclaimed itself to be a capitalist tool), Toddi Gutner produced a very cynical piece on the sunscreen industry. According to the story, the sun care products industry had grown from $280 million annually in 1985 to $530 million in 1991, but lately sales growth had been slowing as sunbathers reached the saturation point for "protective goop." But as scare stories about ozone holes and cancer cases made the rounds, sunscreen marketers were being reminded, if they had ever forgotten, "that fear is a powerful selling tool. The come-on now is to push increasingly potent, expensive and specialized goop, since marketers are having a harder time selling more of it."[31]

Ten years earlier, reported Gutner, 65 percent of all sunscreens sold had SPF values of only two to eight. By 1992, 60 percent of sunscreens sold had an SPF of 15 or higher. Dr. Darrell Rigel, a clinical assistant professor of dermatology at New York University, called it "SPF inflation." Gutner added, "Along with SPF inflation comes price inflation." Schering-Plough had 40 percent of the market with its Coppertone, Water Babies and Shade brands. Its sunscreens sold for up to $4.99 for four ounces of SPF 4, $6.79 for SPF 8, and $7.99 for SPF 15. "Companies are pushing the cancer fear," said Gabriella Zuckerman, a cosmetics industry consultant. "Now they can sell a $3 product for $8." Gutner felt SPF inflation owed as much to marketing as it did to medicine. An SPF of 15 blocked out 93 percent of the sun's UVB rays, while a 34 SPF sunscreen blocked just four percent more, and an SPF 50 offered only six percent more protection than did an SPF of 15. "When pressed, dermatologists will admit that there's little need for most people to go beyond SPF 15," concluded Gutner.[32]

The push for new marketing gambits continued unabated. Pat Sloan reported in 1993 that some companies were going so far as to position sun care as all-year protective skincare for even routine activities such as gardening and jogging. Russ Elliott, vice president of advertising and marketing communications at Schering-Plough's HealthCare Products, remarked, "People no longer lie in the sun; they're active in the sun. The emphasis is on skincare in the sun." Lancome introduced an all-year "sun treatment" line in department stores that year while Estee Lauder was touting its new Advanced Suncare line, a technology that the company said provided children and adults with comprehensive coverage against "aging UVA rays, burning UVB rays and penetrating infrared rays. The products are formulated without harsh chemical sunscreens." Plough introduced a new Coppertone Kids line, as a bridge product between Water Babies and regular Coppertone. It was a product that targeted the 8–12 age group.[33]

Analysts Kline & Company reported the 1992 market for sun care at

$520 million (retail volume) while Salomon Brothers put it at $575 million. Both acknowledged that self-tanning products (involving no UV exposure) had grown more sharply than regular sunscreens, and then accounted for 15 percent of sun product sales. In statistical limbo (and not counted as part of the total sun care industry) were sunscreen-enhanced makeups, moisturizers, and so on, which remained in the makeup or skin care categories, but no market researcher had estimated the sales of those products as distinct from their non–sunscreen-enhanced competition. The *Wall Street Journal* provided a third estimate. For the year ending May 31, 1993, said the newspaper, the sun care market in supermarkets, drugstores and mass-merchandise outlets was $334.9 million with Schering-Plough brands (Coppertone, Tropical Blend, Shade) at a 33.9 percent share, Procter & Gamble's Bain de Soleil second at 11 percent, and Tanning Research Labs' Hawaiian Tropic third with 10 percent. Not included in the *Wall Street Journal*'s totals were upscale outlets such as department stores, where Estee Lauder sun care products, and those of many other makers, were found. Yet another source estimated Lauder's annual sales of sun care products at $36 million (wholesale volume). Increasingly the makers were positioning their products as physical — as opposed to chemical — barriers and thus advertising themselves as supposedly "Chemical-free" sunblockers. Titanium oxide and micro fine zinc oxide were two of the blockers that had found their way into many formulations that hyped themselves as "natural" products. From the *Wall Street Journal* piece it was clear that "marketers are charging more for their improved formula products, both in mass and prestige outlets.[34]

Later in 1993 the results of a study done by Australian researchers was released, which purported to show that people who used sunscreen before going outside cut their chance of developing the first signs of skin cancer. Said Dr. Darrell Rigel, of New York University Medical School, of that study, "It's a very important paper. It's the first time we have been able to definitely show that sunscreen lowers the risk of getting skin cancer later in life." According to the *New York Times*, the study was conducted on 588 men and women who were randomly assigned to use either a sunscreen with an SPF of 17 or a look-a-like lotion without any blocker. The experiment was run from September 1991 through March 1992, one Australian summer. Before and after the study the subjects were checked for solar keratoses, small, wart-like growths that resulted from "overexposure to the sun." Those growths were said to be forerunners of squamous-cell skin cancer, "a common, usually harmless form of skin cancer." Researchers (led by Dr. Sandra C. Thompson, University of Melbourne) found that the sunscreen users averaged a net loss of about one keratosis; those in the comparison group gained one. Authors of the study said keratoses "may disappear spontaneously, particularly in people who reduce their exposure to sunlight." Statistics given at the end of the article were that every year about 700,000 Americans were diagnosed with squamous-cell or basal-cell carcinomas. Both were easily treatable. "About 32,000 get melanoma, which spreads quickly and is deadly unless recognized early. Over the last 20 years, the incidence of melanoma has increased about 4 percent a year." Despite the fact that the article did not mention melanoma at all (save for the above quote) the title of the piece was "Sunscreen lowers risk of melanoma," a false and misleading statement. Even Rigel's conclusion was not based on the facts of the study. All that could be said of the research was that perhaps it altered the appearance of keratoses, something that may or may not have been a forerunner of squamous-cell cancer. In fact, nothing could be directly concluded from that study about any type of skin cancer.[35]

Donald A. Davis was a reporter who happily announced, in the pages of the trade publication *Drug & Cosmetic Industry* late in 1993, that in recent times sunscreens had been a veritable mother lode for their marketers. "They have been able to reap the benefits of products regarded by the public as cosmetics, with advertising featuring bronzed bikini-clad beauties and adorable tanned moppets, at the same time they enjoy the blessings of a liberal FDA Monograph that has rained upon them undeniable marketing bounties: legal license to utilize FDA-sanctioned SPF numbers and claims relating to prevention of skin cancer and premature aging from sun damage," he explained. Also helping those marketers were repeated stories in the media about the ozone layer, statistics on the rise in skin cancer cases; and when medical professionals, of all kinds, were interviewed by the media on the topic of sun exposure, they added to the growing public awareness and even alarm about the dangers of unprotected sun exposure. "In all the history of cosmetics or of OTC drugs I doubt any single product category was so blessed by circumstance and serendipity," enthused Davis. "In fact, ten or 15 years ago, any sunscreen marketing executive assembling a wish list of the most wildly unlikely happenings that might affect the market in the mid–1990s would fall far short of conjuring up so many favourable events." Davis said the Estee Lauder annual sun care product sales of $36 million wholesale translated to $100 million at retail.[36]

On August 1, 1993, New York City Bureau of Consumer Affairs acting director Richard Schrader went before television news cameras to complain that high SPF sunscreens were: a) illegal according to FDA ceilings on SPF numbers, and b) a rip-off since they forced consumers to pay exorbitant prices for SPF protection they did not really need. He argued that scare stories about the ozone layer and the hazards of sun exposure manipulated the public into buying something they could have got at a much lower price. Davis wasn't sure a rip-off was involved, but he admitted Schrader had made an important point when he declared that some high SPF sunscreens were indeed too high for the normal consumer. The price issue was one gray cloud on the industry's horizon, he added. The most outrageously priced article Davis knew about was Chanel's Haute Protection Naturelle Natureblock Cream, which cost $27.50 for 3.5 ounces.[37]

Holland Sweet wrote a hopeful article for *Harper's Bazaar* in 1993 in which it was postulated that "safe tanning" was perhaps not an oxymoron. Basis for that hope, said Sweet, lay in the fact that after nearly two decades of preaching the virtues of pale and sunless skin, cosmetics firms and dermatologists were starting to claim there was a way to get a relatively safe tan. Daniel Maes, vice president of research and development at Estee Lauder explained, "Antioxidants in combination with UV filters are making it possible for us to perfect damage-free-tanning formulas." According to Maes, antioxidants were free radical scavengers that acted to combat the changes that occurred in the skin when UV light hit it. Scientists such as Maes were contending that gradual tanning without burning, in conjunction with sun protection that contained UV filters and free-radical scavengers, was the way to a safe tan. Those antioxidants took several forms; Lauder favored vitamins C and E, which it had added to all its sun creams in varying degrees while removing all chemical sunscreens. Lancome's laboratories had synthesized a substance similar to natural melanin and added it to their sunscreen line. Nicholas Lowe, M.D., and clinical professor of dermatology at the UCLA School of Medicine, worried that any seemingly positive evidence on sunning (such as the antioxidant story) could be the excuse those people teetering on the tanning issue needed to go out and lie in the sun. As a dermatologist, Lowe saw his job as one of dissuading the public from suntanning, "because research on the sun's dangers just continue to mount." Much of the article's hope fizzled out near the end when Sweet allowed that many dermatologists were not convinced there was enough evidence to make any claims about antioxidants. "Marketing people are getting too carried away, making claims that are difficult to substantiate."[38]

As 1995 began Schering-Plough (still number one with a 33.1 percent market share) wanted to make the Ultraviolet (UV) Index as ubiquitous as the daily weather report. Plough began testing the National UV Index the previous summer and rolled it out nationally in 200 cities in 1995, calling it simply the Ultraviolet Index, or UV Index, as it quickly became known. A joint effort with the National Weather Service, the U.S.

Environmental Protection Agency, the Centers for Disease Control, and various health groups, the UV Index offered a report on the UV risk level as part of the local weather forecast, including how quickly people would burn if unprotected. The Coppertone brand alone had a 27.1 percent share of the $500 million per year sun care industry and supported the index rollout with National Sun Protection Awareness Week, May 21 to 28, as well as ongoing public service announcements on television and UV Index Centers in retail outlets. Schering-Plough spent $30 million that year on sun care product marketing, including $2 million on the UV Index. Other marketing efforts included Little Miss Coppertone, covered up to promote sun protection. In its spring 1995 catalog a company called After the Stork was selling Sunskins, clothing for children that, according to the ad copy, blocked "50% more of the sun's harmful UV rays than regular clothing."[39]

Mary Tannen reported in the spring of 1997 that there was still no rating system for UVA protection in sunscreens, that SPF numbers referred only to the product's ability to block UVB rays. She felt that most of those products did block some UVA rays as well but conceded, "For now, we will have to rely on those sunblocks whose packaging promises 'broad spectrum' or UVA protections."[40]

That same year business reporter Pat Sloan observed that, after years of touting protection against the sun, some marketers were "once again glamorizing the tan — and promoting products that offer little or no sunburn defense." The two market leaders, Schering-Plough (29.6 percent) and Playtex Family Products (15.1 percent) had introduced lines aimed at teens and sun worshippers who were after a tan. Plough launched Coppertone Gold while Playtex's Tan Express was a sub-brand under the Banana Boat umbrella. Although their most heavily advertised and best-selling products were protective, the two firms were thought to be hedging their bets with the new lines; they were offered largely unadvertised. The move to introduce what were openly tanning products drew criticism from the American Academy of Dermatology and even from some quarters of the industry itself. "We find this confuses the public and is counter to our messages to stay out of the sun and protect yourself from the sun," said a spokesman for the dermatologists. "It's a great concern to us." In 1996, tanning products grew at a faster rate than did products with SPFs of 15 and higher, 15 percent and 12 percent, respectively. Still, zero protection products accounted for only 4 percent of the total industry. A *Seventeen* magazine telephone survey of 500 teen respondents found that 71 percent said they used a sunscreen with an SPF of 15 or higher. Pfizer Skincare Category Director Doug Sweetbaum (it had acquired the brand Bain de Soleil from Procter & Gamble the previous year) remarked that less protective products were not a "long-term sustainable trend and not responsible to society." Ken Meeker, vice president of marketing of sun care for Playtex, defended products such as Tan Express and their low or non-existent SPF for use by teens who might otherwise use nothing, and for the consumer who went on a three-day winter weekend in the sun for color, comparing that person to a binge drinker. "This is the [consumer] who gets drunk once a year. Is it smart? No.... But as a major marketer, we have to offer a broad spectrum of product for different types of consumers," he said.[41]

When *Consumer Reports* did another evaluation article on sunscreens in 1998, CU started by observing that medical science had not proved that sunscreens prevented melanoma. Saving your skin from cancer, the publication urged, involved avoiding the sun at midday, shading your skin with clothing and hats, and covering exposed skin with sunscreen. More than one million new cases of skin cancer were expected in America that year, nearly 50,000 of them would be melanomas. Blacks had a skin cancer risk that was about one-twentieth that of whites. "The details of the sunlight-cancer connection are unclear," admitted CU. "In melanoma, for instance, research appears to show the sun has less influence than does a person's genetic makeup." Moreover, the piece allowed that it was not clear that sunscreen was enough to halt skin cancer. "For one thing, it turns out to be hard to show that people who wear a lot of sunscreen have a lower cancer rate than other people with similar sun exposure. For another, it's not even clear that preventing sunburn has any effect on skin cancer." Nevertheless, no one was urging people to stop using sunscreens, and marketers were "trying their best to promote it."[42]

In separate tests CU tested how much UVA light the sunscreens blocked. The best blockers of UVA, they found, were virtually all those with an SPF of 30 or more and the most waterproof of those labeled with an SPF of 15; they all stopped at least 90 percent of the UVA rays (there was still no existing standard to measure UVA blocking and the SPF numbers still referred only to UVB). But *Consumer Reports* found that some of the products that claimed UVA protection performed poorly in their tests. Prices of sunscreens tested ranged from 34 cents per ounce to $2.02. Special clothing was being sold as a complement to sunscreen. Two prominent, and pricey, fabrics were Solumbra, used in a line of clothing by that name, and Solarweave, made in several different forms by Solar Protective Factory and found in about a dozen brands of clothing. CU tested two shirts that each claimed an SPF of at least 30. Reportedly these fabrics were woven very tightly with Solarweave fabric, said to have a special coating. Tested with those two (the Solumbra cost $75; Solarweave, $55) were five regular shirts: a $9 polo shirt; an Appalachia shirt, $39; a Super-Tee from Land's End, $18.50; a Fruit of the Loom T-shirt (three for $8); and a Hanes Beefy-T, $4.69. Both special shirts were confirmed by CU to yield an SPF exceeding 30, but so did Land's End Super-Tee and Hanes' Beefy-T. The polo and Appalachia shirts had SPFs between 15 and 20, said to be sufficient protection, while Fruit of the Loom's SPF 12 was "a little on the low side." With respect to special clothing for sun protection, CU concluded, "So if you're looking for clothing to shield yourself from the sun, you probably already have what you need in your dresser."[43]

After 20-some years of considering the issue, after its 1978 Monograph, the FDA announced, in 1999, new rules for how sunscreen products, including cosmetics that made sun protection claims, could be labeled. When the rules took effect in May 2001, consumers would no longer see the world "sunblock" because, the FDA noted, nothing completely blocked the sun. All the various rating categories and SPF numbers were to be reduced to just three: SPF 2 to 11 for "minimum" protection, SPF 12 to 29 for "moderate" protection, and SPF 30 or higher for "high" protection. New labels could list "30+" but could not carry a higher specific number because, said the agency, there were no good measures for testing the effectiveness of SPFs higher than 30. The American Academy of Dermatology had urged the FDA to mandate an SPF of 15 as the minimum standard before a product could claim to be a sunscreen at all. Those ratings still applied only to UVB rays, and the government did not change labeling rules for claims of protection from UVA rays. That meant sunscreens that claimed to offer protection from both types of radiation could still call themselves "broad spectrum" products.

After reporting the FDA news, journalist Susan Brink observed that half of all Americans do not use sunscreen while the other half skimp on the amount as they "throw themselves in the path of cancer-causing rays." Added Brink, "The price for this tawdry love affair with the sun: one million Americans diagnosed with skin cancer last year, nearly 42,000 of them with the most lethal form, malignant melanoma." Unmentioned by Brink was that no evidence at all existed to suggest sunscreens prevented melanoma or that exposure in fact caused the disease. Dr. Darrell Rigel, president of the American Academy of Dermatology said, with respect to sunscreens, "People apply 20 to 50 percent of the amount they should." To which Brink added the thought that a day at the beach for a family of four should pretty well finish off a bottle of sunscreen.[44]

A year later, in 2000, the FDA announced that the implementation of the new sunscreen rules had been delayed indefinitely as the FDA, the makers, and the dermatologists struggled over the numbering system, measurement of UVA radiation, and other details. According to the American Cancer Society, melanoma represented only about 47,000 of the nearly 1.8 million cases of skin cancer diagnosed each year, but it caused 79 percent of skin cancer deaths. Researchers at the Queensland Institute for Medical Research, in Brisbane, Australia, reported in September 1999 that sunscreen use reduced the risk of developing squamous-cell carcinoma by 40 percent. But using sunscreen did not reduce the risk of developing melanoma or basal-cell carcinoma. Said to be the first study to test the protective effect of sunscreen on people, it followed 1,383 adults for five years. Writing in the *FDA Consumer* Larry Thompson said, according to a 1998 review article, that most sunscreens did not protect the skin from UVA rays. Although the FDA rules had been delayed, one requirement went into effect on May 22, 2000, as originally scheduled. Under that new regulation, all tanning products that did not contain sunscreen were required to carry the following warning statement on the label: "Warning: This product does not contain a sunscreen and does not protect against sunburn. Repeated exposure of unprotected skin while tanning may increase the risk of skin aging, skin cancer, and other harmful effects to the skin even if you do not burn." Tanning products that did not contain sunscreens and did not protect against the harmful effects of UV light continued to be regulated as cosmetics.[45]

In a June 2001 evaluation, *Consumer Reports* began by declaring the phrase "with sunscreen" seemed as ubiquitous at the drugstore as did "low fat" at the supermarket. Sunscreen could then be found in moisturizers, lip balms, shampoos, hair-styling products, insect repellents, and makeup, among other products. Rit, the fabric dye brand, had created a colorless sunscreen you washed into your clothes. In Europe, Procter & Gamble was planning to sell sunscreen-soaked Pampers Sunnies UV wipes, apparently for places on a baby where the sun did shine. Reportedly, more than one million new cases of skin cancer would be diagnosed in America that year; some 54,000 of those would be malignant melanomas. About 9,800 people were expected to die from some form of skin cancer that year. "The prevalence of skin cancer is attributable in part to a history of unprotected — or underprotected — sun exposure," declared CU. It also argued that sunscreen had been shown to prevent squamous-cell cancer. With respect to melanoma, the organization's stand was more equivocal and confusing. "Although research has yet to prove that sunscreen helps prevent the disease, the evidence is compelling." However, CU undid its own conclusion by its failure to introduce so much as one piece of that "compelling" evidence. According to a 1997 survey, one-half of white women and one-third of white men in the U.S. used sunscreen regularly when sunbathing. Even CU, in this piece, allowed for some benefit from sun exposure, and some need for it, remarking that the sun was important in stimulating the skin to make vitamin D, which helped to maintain bone strength. For most people under 50, said CU, 5 to 10 minutes of sun exposure, two to three times a week in summer, allowed the body to store enough vitamin D for the year. Older people perhaps needed more exposure.[46]

Reporter Helen Fields produced a scare story on UVA rays for a July 2003 issue of *U.S. News & World Report* in which she warned consumers abut sunscreens, even those with a number as high as SPF 30, because the sun protection factor did not rate a type of sunlight that may have played a role in triggering cancer. The danger, she explained, was in UVA radiation, which seemed to suppress a person's immune system and allowed cancer cells to flourish. SPF numbers rated only protection from sunburn caused by UVB rays, Fields emphasized. Yet one hundred times as much UVA radiation reached the earth's surface as did UVB. "Because there's so much more UVA, we find that the UVA wave band in sunlight is more important to immune-system damage," said biologist Gary Halliday of the University of Sydney in Australia. Fields said there were compounds that blocked a lot of UVA but you had to squint at the label to learn if your sunscreen had them. Also, consumers could not rely on the large-lettered claims on the front of the bottle and rarely noticed, emphasized the reporter, "Scientists have recognized UVA's cancer-causing potential in the past decade." While sunscreens often claimed they blocked UVA, their protection from that energy was not as strong as their protection from UVB, noted Vincent DeLeo, chairman of dermatology at St. Luke's-Roosevelt Hospital Center and Beth Israel Medical Center in New York. Bottles that said "broad spectrum" or "UVA" on the front did block some UVA, but how well those products actually protected people depended on the whole formula, said biologist Patricia Agin. Indirectly, one conclusion from the Fields piece was that the consumer was on her own when it came to picking a sunscreen that protected from UVA, a type of solar radiation whose reputation continued to sink. There was no industry standard for measuring UVA protection, and still no federal government involvement (except for occasional warnings to firms making excessive claims). In fact the consumer was alone, and likely confused.[47]

For many decades many Americans had been faithfully obeying the drumbeat of the time — use sunscreen. Throughout that period, skin cancer rates had continued to rise dramatically with seemingly no end in sight. In fact, the increase in skin cancer rates began not long after the arrival of lotions as a popular item. That should have given pause for thought. When two variables moved in tandem that way, causality may not have been involved; it's possible that a third factor could have caused the other two to move together. Still, such a movement in two variables was at least circumstantial evidence. At the very least it should have triggered an investigation. Yet it was a heresy to suggest some type of link between sunscreen use and an increasing skin cancer rate. If those who suggested such disturbing ideas were not heretics to begin with, they were soon branded as such by conventional medicine and science, and banished to the margins of science.

9

Sunscreens, a Discouraging Word: 1990–2004

"...as experts persuaded more and more Americans to use sunscreens, melanoma became an epidemic, with new diagnoses roughly paralleling sunscreen sales."
                                        Michael Castleman, 1993

"To some extent, when you protect only for UVB, it would seem to run a risk for potential skin cancer. UVA is a more damaging ray..."
                                        Jack Surrette, Tropic Tan, 1993

"It's not safe to rely on sunscreens.
                                        Dr. Marianne Berwick, 1998

The idea that common sunscreens might increase the risk of developing skin cancer first surfaced in the mass media with a report in the *New York Times* in 1990 from Natalie Angier. She related that two researchers from the University of California at San Diego suggested that UVA radiation could damage melanocytes, the pigment-making cells that gave rise to melanomas. One of the researchers, Dr. Frank C. Garland (the other was his brother, Dr. Cedric F. Garland) said, "When you block out ultraviolet-b light, you stop the skin from burning, which means that you can stay out in the sun for many hours or many days. So what happens is you end up getting an unnaturally high dose of ultraviolet-a. Sunscreens give you a false sense of security." He added that sunscreens prevented the skin from producing vitamin D, which in laboratory tests had been shown to help prevent damaged melanocytes from turning cancerous. Ordinarily, he explained, the skin used sunlight to synthesize vitamin D. The Garlands based their theory largely on an analysis of general epidemiological data on melanoma and on recent experiments examining the role of vitamin D in cancer prevention. Angier noted that other skin experts, of course, disagreed with that theory, "However, experts concede that many questions remain about the genesis and progression of melanoma."[1]

Almost three years passed before anything more was heard about this theory in the general media, at which point David Bjerklie wrote a piece for *Time* magazine. Death rates for melanoma in the U.S., according to the American Cancer Society, were as follows: 1973 (3,430), 1978 (4,452), 1983 (5,216), 1988 (5,800), 1993 (6,800, estimate). Bjerklie remarked that since 1990 the Garlands (and their research associate Edward Gorham, all San Diego–based epidemiologists) had spread a highly unsettling message; that liberal use of sunscreens might actually increase the risk of melanoma, and then summarized their theory. The Garlands did admit that sunscreens filtered out the most damaging solar rays and prevented sunburn. But, said Cedric, "It's time to step back and to consider whether what we have been doing, specifically the strong use of sunscreens, is working." Having denounced their work in the past, the American Academy of Dermatology continued to blast their conclusions as unfounded, saying they could undermine efforts to educate the sunbathing public about skin cancer. On the sidelines was the FDA, which had not weighed in on the issue but, at this time, asked sunscreen makers to put warnings on their lotions about the harmful effects of overexposure to the sun. Bjerklie said that some 700,000 new cases of skin cancer would be diagnosed in the U.S. that year; 80 percent of them basal cell and 130,000 of them squamous-cell carcinomas.[2]

Then Bjerklie summarized the evidence with respect to the Garland theory. All the evidence gathered from animal experiments and epidemiological surveys, he argued, pointed to UVB as the main culprit in causing basal- and squamous-cell cancer and to the fact that sunburns were caused by UVB while wrinkles were generated by UVA. Malignant melanoma researchers still did not know what caused the disease. Most dermatologists had long assumed UVB had to be a greater threat than UVA and, as a result, he argued, sunscreen manufacturers originally concentrated on blocking UVB. The most powerful formulas developed in the past decade "have provided some protection from UV-A." However, he did admit that none provided *much* UVA protection, if any. On the other hand, the Garlands pointed to one study that suggested that animals exposed to both UVA and UVB developed more cancers than those receiving UVB alone. "Sunburn has been with people ever since there have been people outdoors," said Cedric. "But it can't account for the melanoma epidemic."

That was a reference to an often advanced theory that the number of sunburns a person received, and/or at what time of life they were received, played a role in increasing the risk of melanoma. Garland critics disagreed. "We know that the more sunburns you have, the greater your risk of melanoma," said Dr. Darrell Rigel, a New York University dermatologist. "And we do know that sunscreens stop you from getting sunburn." Rigel did not explain how we knew the first part. However, Bjerklie stepped in to say, "Particularly bad burns suffered in childhood or adolescence appear to increase the risks of melanoma, and a genetic predisposition to skin cancer also plays a role."[3]

Another article published at the same time as Bjerklie's was the one that stirred up the most controversy, and brought the theory prominently to the attention of the general public. Michael Castleman's lengthy piece in the May/June issue of *Mother Jones* magazine was clearly sympathetic to the Garland theory, and very critical of the sunscreen industry. He began by saying that, unfortunately, public health authorities that urged the routine, liberal use of sunscreen "fail to mention that sunscreens have never been shown to prevent melanoma. The medical research community knows this. The Food and Drug Administration knows it. And sunscreen makers know it. Yet, as a result of scientific myopia, bureaucratic inertia, and the almighty bottom line, they've essentially told us to use sunscreen and not to worry." But the Garlands, best known for their work linking sunshine with the prevention of breast and colon cancer, were worried, Castleman continued, and had compiled a body of evidence suggesting sunscreens duped the public into believing they were covered with state-of-the-art melanoma protection, when, in fact, they may be highly vulnerable to the disease. "Even worse, the Garlands' research suggests that sunscreen use might just promote melanoma." Unfortunately for the public health, he worried, the Garlands refused then to discuss their theory for fear of professional ostracism. After they presented their case against sunscreens at a 1990 epidemiological meeting in Los Angeles, both the *New York Times* and *Washington Post* ran articles discussing the Garlands' theory. Other epidemiologists accused the Garlands of grandstanding by speaking to the media before publishing their analysis in a scientific journal. Fearful as a result of that criticism — it had the potential to threaten funding of their other work — the brothers avoided journalists after that. As for the sunscreen industry, it had an obvious interest in keeping the Garlands' theory away from the public eye. At the time of his account, observed Castleman, no one was doing any research on the presence or absence of a link between the sun and melanoma.[4]

Then Castleman turned his attention to the conventional explanations of melanoma. From 1975 to 1992, the number of melanoma cases reported annually in the U.S. tripled, increasing more than any other form of cancer. Since the 1950s, melanoma rates had also risen dramatically among fair-skinned Australians, Canadians, Scandinavians, and the British — it remained extremely unusual for dark-skinned people to get skin cancer. Melanoma then struck 32,000 Americans each year and killed 6,800. "But before 1950 it was quite rare." Dermatologists' major concerns then were basal- and squamous-cell cancers, slow-spreading cancers that usually occurred in white men over the age of 45 who worked outdoors or lived near the equator. Around the beginning of the 20th century, continued Castleman, doctors linked risk of basal- and squamous-cell carcinomas with lifetime sun exposure; the more sun, the more risk. They also discovered a far rarer — and mostly fatal — skin cancer, which came to be called malignant melanoma. At that point doctors believed melanoma had nothing to do with sunlight because it usually appeared in people who spent little time in the sun. Victims of melanoma seemed to have only two things in common; most had fair skin along with red or blonde hair. Physicians concluded nothing more than that melanoma was a consequence of being fair-haired and light-skinned.[5]

However, by the late 1960s, numerous studies revealed a connection between melanoma and the ultraviolet radiation in sunlight, concluding, for one thing, that whites who lived near the equator had higher melanoma rates than whites in temperate climates. Castleman argued that the fact that outdoor workers rarely developed melanoma was apparently explained when researchers shifted their attention from sunlight to sunburn, theorizing that deeply tanned skin protected against melanoma, even though it increased the risk of basal- and squamous-cell cancers. Indoor office workers had brief, intense exposures to the sun, the kind that caused sunburn, which in turn could lead to melanoma. During the 1970s, he continued, scientists used the sunburn theory to explain the dramatic rise in the melanoma rate in the second half of the 1900s. After World War II, they argued, large numbers of Americans became white-collar workers, which limited their sun exposure and, as a result, increased their risk of weekend sunburns. Because melanoma had been associated with teenage sunburns, (the median age for diagnosis was in the 40s), researchers concluded that melanoma, like many cancers, took decades to develop. Thus, with an estimated 25- to 30-year time delay, proponents of the sunburn theory argued that post-war sunbathing resulted in the melanoma epidemic of the 1980s.[6]

However, for Castleman, that theory failed to explain a number of things. For instance, sunburn was a common medical problem long before people started wearing bikinis. Turn-of-the-20th-century medical texts dealt with it, as did folk medicine remedies of the time. Yet melanoma was extremely rare before 1950. Many of the social changes that sunburn-theory adherents attributed to the 1950s—the advent of sunbathing, for example—actually began earlier. Sunbathing first became popular in the 1920s, declared Castleman, "thanks to fashion designer Coco Chanel, who launched a tanning chic after returning from a yachting vacation with a golden tan." If there was a time lag of 25 or so years, then the melanoma epidemic should have started in the 1940s, but it did not. [Actually, of course, the fashion of sunbathing had nothing to do with Chanel and started much earlier than Castleman argued, which only furthered strengthened his point.] Also, some studies indicated melanoma may have had only a short time lag. If that was true, then the factor responsible for the epidemic must have appeared in the middle or late 1950s, at the earliest. Other studies were said to have consistently shown seasonal patterns in melanoma diagnoses, another marker of biological events that had short time lags. The Garlands worried that factor could be sunscreen usage.[7]

When the Garlands took aim at sunscreens that protected only from UVB, many sunscreen makers referred media calls they received to the American Academy of Dermatology, which issued a rebuttal stating, "No studies have suggested direct relationships between melanoma and ultraviolet A." Yet, less than three years later, the Academy was recommending UVA protection and it was then a major focus of sunscreen marketing strategy. Castleman also mentioned the Garlands' idea that by impairing the body's production of vitamin D, a defense against cancer might be removed. According to studies, vitamin D had a hormone-like effect that interfered with the growth of several tumors, including those associated with melanoma and colon and breast cancers. Although people got small amounts of vitamin D from fortified milk and cold-water fish, most of a person's supply was produced when skin was exposed to UVB. By blocking UVB, sunscreens interfered with vitamin D synthesis. One study showed that habitual sunscreen users had unusually low vitamin D levels—sometimes low enough that researchers called them deficient. Another link unexplained by the sunburn theory was that melanoma was correlated with income; that is, the melanoma risk rose with income. Although both professional and clerical workers worked indoors, the former had a significantly higher melanoma rate. One speculation, said Castleman, was that because health consciousness was generally an upper-income phenomenon, sunscreens may have been used more by the affluent. Historically, whites would have been dangerously sunburned long before they received the levels of UVA radiation that they now got in one sunscreen-wearing day at the beach. As Castleman noted, sales of sunscreens were $380 million in 1991, "more than twice as much as a decade earlier. But as experts persuaded more and more Americans to use sunscreens, melanoma became an epidemic, with new diagnoses roughly paralleling sunscreen sales."[8]

According to Castleman, the melanoma epidemic became a major news story six years earlier when the ozone hole opened over Antarctica. However, that thinning of the ozone layer had nothing to do with the melanoma rate in America. In a 1991 report, the Environmental Protection Agency estimated a five percent ozone loss over the U.S. during the previous decade. But the amount of UV radiation striking the country actually decreased a bit, according to the National Cancer Institute, because of another UV filter — that of air pollution. To that date, melanoma epidemiologists were said to be in agreement that the Antarctica ozone loss had played no role in the melanoma epidemic. However, further ozone losses could well lead to soaring melanoma rates in the future.[9]

Sunscreen makers admitted, argued Castleman, that their product had never been shown to prevent human skin cancers. Studies showed that sunscreens prevented squamous-cell cancers in animals, said Patricia Agin, sunscreen product manager for Schering-Plough. "I think they do the same in humans. But ... we don't know for certain. Because there's no animal model for [melanoma], we don't know if sunscreens prevent it. I see no reason to think that they wouldn't, but we have no proof that they do." Jack Surrette, marketing vice president of Tanning Research Laboratories remarked, "To some extent, when you protect only for UVB, it would seem to run a risk for potential skin cancer. UVA is a more damaging ray. We may be hurting ourselves by protecting ourselves too well on the UVB side." Labels sometimes said something like, "Regular use may prevent skin cancer," observed Castleman. With respect to those product labels the sunscreen makers insisted it meant nonfatal squamous-cell cancers, but if the label did not distinguish between melanoma and other skin cancers, then how did the consumer? Also confusing buyers was the fact that most sunscreens carried a seal of approval from the non-profit Skin Cancer Foundation, which claimed to alert people to safe products. More than 130 different sun care products had earned the right to display that seal — for a price. Corporations submitted their products for testing and review, along with $10,000 to display the seal. John Epstein, who sat on the Skin Cancer Foundation's four-member seal review committee, said he could not recall anyone ever being denied the seal, but added that companies that filed inadequate paperwork had to resubmit their requests. The foundation, which boasted celebrity backers such as Tom Selleck,

Lauren Bacall, Dick Cavett, Paul Newman, and Joanne Woodward, earned about 25 percent of its $1.7 million annual budget from corporate donations. Recently the foundation sent 60,000 posters to elementary schools that urged students: "Always use a sunscreen when you go outdoors, no matter the season or the color of your skin."[10]

In conclusion, Castleman conceded that the Garlands openly admitted their case against sunscreens was not airtight; the contention that melanoma had a brief lag time needed corroboration, and a recent study showed no correlation between vitamin D and melanoma risk, for example. Still, he argued that the best theory was the one that answered the most questions and on that basis he felt the sunburn/long time lag theory was shaky because it ignored the studies showing a brief lag time and it did not address why sunburn rarely caused melanoma before the 1950s. Also, it did not address why the melanoma risk was linked to income, and it failed to explain why increases in the melanoma rate had so closely paralleled the rise in sunscreen use.[11]

When industry executive Donald Davis celebrated the growth of the sunscreen industry in the pages of *Drug & Cosmetic Industry* in 1993, he saw a few clouds on the horizon — one was the high price of sunscreens. Another he mentioned was the work of the Garlands. "Even on the basis of preliminary information, it seems premature to arbitrarily dismiss what the Garlands say," he allowed. Davis worried sunbathers had indeed been encouraged that it was safe to stay in the sun longer, made confident that their sunscreen would protect them. Yet if they put too little of the sunscreen on (perhaps in response to its high price) or if it was sweated off or washed off by the ocean, "their confidence may be misplaced."[12]

Writing in *Science News* in 1994, T. Adler reported that new cases of melanoma had doubled since 1980, with about one American in every 105 destined to contract it. Adler observed that Margaret L. Kripke and her colleagues at the University of Texas M. D. Anderson Cancer Center in Houston felt that while sunscreens helped prevent mild skin cancers and sunburn, the exposure to UV rays may have had another, less visible effect that sunscreens failed to stop — impairing the ability of the body's immune cells to fight melanoma. "Protection against sunburn does not necessarily imply protection against other possible UV radiation effects, such as enhanced melanoma growth," said Kripke and her co-workers. In fact, by preventing the pain and redness of sunburn, sunscreen may enable people to stay longer in the hot sun, putting them at higher risk for developing melanoma, Kripke added.[13]

In their study Kripke and the other researchers applied either a sunscreen or an oil-water mixture to the ears and tails of mice. After 20 minutes the team exposed some mice for 20 to 27 minutes to UVB rays, the rays most sunscreens tried to block. They repeated the exposure twice a week for three weeks so the mice received about three times the UVB needed to give them sunburn. After the final session, the researchers injected all of the mice's ears with melanoma cells from genetically identical mice to see how well their immune systems fought off the cancer cells. The group of mice put under the sunlamp had a higher incidence of melanoma tumors than the unexposed mice, stated Kripke. However, the lotion did protect them from sunburn.

Finding that protection against sunburn did not necessarily imply protection against melanoma "is really kind of surprising," ventured Kripke. In an editorial accompanying Kripke's article in the *Journal* of the National Cancer Institute, Howard K. Koh and Robert A. Lew of the Boston University Schools of Medicine and Public Health, commented that the study "reminds us that the pathophysiology of melanoma appears to differ markedly from that of non-melanoma skin cancer." Adler added that other animal studies had found that light not screened out of most sunscreen lotions, such as UVA, "may cause the cell changes that lead to melanoma."[14]

Donald Davis returned to the pages of *Drug & Cosmetic Industry* in 1994 with an editorial on the Kripke experiment wherein he said, "the study should cause red flags to be run up in the offices of sunscreen marketers because it calls into question the possible hazard of prolonged sun exposure...." With respect to the FDA allowing certain label wording— whenever the Monograph was finalized and implemented—Davis felt the study had likely put to rest permanently "the notion that a comprehensive cancer prevention claim has either scientific validity or merit in a marketing sense." In conclusion, Davis argued the Kripke study, together with the work of the Garlands, meant "the honeymoon for sunscreens is about to experience some serious scientific introspection."[15]

Another person skeptical of sunscreen was Dr. Adriane Fugh-Berman, whose article in *Ms* magazine in 1994 discussed whether or not to use it. She argued that whether sunscreens were good or bad for people was a complicated issue and while they clearly prevented sunburn, their effect on skin cancer risk was much murkier. If sunscreens perhaps protected against basal- and squamous-cell carcinomas, there was no clear evidence they protected against melanoma. Until recently, she declared, melanoma was thought to be caused exclusively by exposure to UVB with the tan-producing UVA rays having little to do with burning, and long considered to be harmless. But in the 1980s UVA was identified as harmful. Since 1989 "broad spectrum" sunscreens meant to protect against both UVA and UVB had been available in addition to the older blockers. But, remarked Fugh-Berman, the sunscreens that supposedly blocked UVA only protected against half of the UVA spectrum, and SPF numbers were no indication of UVA protection.[16]

Despite what the sunscreen industry was telling people, continued Fugh-Berman, sunscreens may have provided no protection from melanoma (citing the work of Kripke). Not only did epidemiological studies fail to show a decreased risk of melanoma in sunscreen users, in fact, there was some controversial evidence that the incidence of melanoma was higher among sunscreen users. The most popular explanation was that, in preventing burning, sunscreen allowed sunbathers to stay out longer in the sun that they would have otherwise, thus absorbing massive amounts of the eventually carcinogenic UVA. In addition, studies indicated that alternating exposure to both UVB and UVA with exposure to UVA alone could increase carcinogenicity. Many people failed to reapply sunscreen or used it irregularly, thus establishing that particular pattern of UV exposure.[17]

Fugh-Berman then mentioned the Garlands' theory (blocking of vitamin D synthesis) and that people in the U.S. received 75 percent of their vitamin D from the sunshine, with few getting the recommended daily allowance in their diets—vitamin D was still found mainly in fortified milk and fish such as herring, mackerel, and salmon. The lifetime risk of melanoma for European Americans in the U.S. she put at 10 times higher than for African Americans. Data from Israel showed that Jews of different ethnic origins had different rates, with lower rates of melanoma found among those of darker complexions. Other risk factors (besides pigmentation) included having a lot of moles and a family history of melanoma. In conclusion she declared that even people who were dark-skinned or tanned easily might want to avoid the midday sun but those people could skip sunscreen the rest of the time and get their vitamin D from the sun with little risk. Ultimately, she argued, the best sunscreen was a roof; that is, hats, sunglasses and clothes that covered limbs when a person went outside.[18]

Journalist Michael Castleman, who created such a stir with his 1993 piece in *Mother Jones,* returned exactly five years later, with another piece, this one titled "Sunscam." Curiously, his article made no mention of the Garlands. Instead he mentioned a study that received a lot of press just a few months earlier. According to a survey of new research by epidemiologist Marianne Berwick of the Memorial Sloan-Kettering Cancer Center in New York, there was no evidence that sunscreens offered any real protection against malignant melanoma. "It's not safe to rely on sunscreen," Berwick told the press. The Skin Cancer Foundation (SCF) refuted this at a press conference and continued to tell consumers that "sunscreen should continue to be an integral part of a comprehensive program" to prevent melanoma. People would also mostly hear that advice from dermatologists, felt Castleman, but what they would not learn was that dermatologists got much of their information from the SCF, and the SCF, in turn, was heavily supported financially by the sunscreen industry. He agreed that basal- and squamous-cell cancers were caused primarily by UVB and there was credible evidence that sunscreen helped prevent those two types of cancer, as well as providing protection against the premature aging of the skin. But, he argued, sunscreens did not offer protection against UVA and did not protect against melanoma and consumers did not differentiate between basal- and squamous-cell and melanoma and thus there was a basic marketing dishonesty.[19]

One theme Castleman returned to in this article was the idea that melanoma might develop after a short time lag, instead of after a long time lag, as most conventional researchers believed. Until 1950 melanoma was rare. Then its incidence increased slowly until the mid–1960s, after which its incidence accelerated into its "current epidemic." Arguing against a long time lag was that crowded beaches in the 1920s, and even earlier, seemingly produced no melanomas. Sun care product sales rose from $18 million in 1972 to $500 million in 1996. If melanoma had a 20-year time lag and sunscreen was protective against the disease, then melanoma rates would have leveled off long before 1998. But they had not, and were still climbing. If melanoma developed after a short time lag, say two to five years, then something must have changed a few years before melanoma rates began to inch up in the 1950s, he thought. And that could have been the use of sunscreens, which of course did not offer much protection against UVA, even though many makers touted their products as offering broad-spectrum protection. "I guess there's an inconsistency," said FDA spokeswoman Ivy Kupec. She added that makers "could still say [their product] protects against UV-A because they can do it until we tell them not to." Castleman argued that for sunscreen to live up to its hype, a person had to slop it on thickly and reapply it every few hours, something few people did.[20]

After epidemiologist Marianne Berwick presented her data on sunscreen use and skin cancer at the annual meeting of the American Association for the Advancement of Science (AAAS) in February, 1998, in Philadelphia, the American Academy of Dermatology promptly denounced Berwick's conclusions. In a March press release it called her message "misleading and confusing." Frank Gasparro, of Thomas Jefferson University in Philadelphia, said the academy had a knee-jerk reaction to Berwick's talk. Gasparro, who organized the AAAS session, said Berwick accurately portrayed the data on sunscreen and skin cancer. "Put her conclusions together with basic research on sunscreen chemistry," he contended, "and there is good reason for concern about these products."[21]

In her review Berwick looked at four studies of squamous-cell cancer. Two concluded that sunscreen protected against a skin condition thought to lead to the disease; two reported sunscreens did not protect people from that type of skin cancer. Berwick also reviewed two studies of basal-cell carcinomas—both found that people who used sunscreen were more likely to develop basal-cell cancer than people who did not. She reviewed 10 studies on melanoma. In five of those studies people who used sunscreen were more likely to develop melanoma than were non-users; in three studies no relationship was found; in the other two people who used sunscreen seemed to be protected.[22]

After Berwick released her data, said reporter W. T. Loesch, "media attention reached a state of panic." In interviews with the CBS Evening News and on the ABC website she further stated that "blanket advise to the public to wear sunscreen as protection against ... skin cancer is unwarranted." She explained that the only reason to wear sunscreen was to prevent a sunburn, implying that skin cancer was not somehow related to sun exposure. Later Berwick contacted the American Academy of Dermatology claiming her statements had been misrepresented by the media. Dermatologists remained united against her, and continued to attack her position. Berwick was quoted as stating "I now realize why no one wants to touch this subject.... Although my study found no relationship between the use of sunscreen and melanoma, it doesn't suggest that people should stop using sunscreens, as some people in the press have suggested."[23]

A brief article in 2004 observed that some studies had suggested sunscreens might have increased the risks of melanoma. Then it noted that a recent review of 18 studies by University of Iowa researchers found no link between sunscreen use and melanoma risk. However, those researchers admitted their review also did not prove that sunscreen usage reduced melanoma risk.[24]

To defend itself against critics, the tanning salon industry seized upon the work of Dr. Michael F. Holick, a professor of medicine, physiology, and biophysics at the Boston University School of Medicine. Two years earlier, in 2002, Holick — then also a professor of dermatology — had begun to promote research that avoiding sunlight was itself a health risk, due to the possibility of developing a vitamin D insufficiency. Holick made clear in a 2004 interview that he did not promote tanning, advising people to take only a minimum amount of sun exposure. But he had been a regular speaker at Indoor Tanning Association conventions and the group had used his web site as a public relations tool (it promoted his book). The trade group also awarded Holick a grant of $50,000 a year for three years to study the effects of sunlight on human health.[25]

Although Holick contended that he promoted "sensible sunlight exposure," his colleagues in the dermatology department at the Boston University School of Medicine apparently did not find his approach sensible. Dr. Barbara Gilchrest, chair of dermatology at the medical school and chief of dermatology at the Boston Medical Center, said Holick's activities forced her to reconsider his status as a professor. Said Gilchrest, "Over the years, and in a much more accelerated way in the last six months to a year, Dr. Holick has become the very public poster child for the tanning industry. I talked to him about the fact that he has a serious conflict of interest with the Indoor Tanning Association that could affect his research. He said he did not believe that." Holick argued there was no conflict because the grant was unrestricted, but he did resign as a dermatology professor. "I think people have for far too long been forced to agree with the message that is out there, that is both simple-minded and draconian and putting people at risk, which is, 'Never be exposed to direct sunlight.'" At the tanning conventions, past attendees said that Holick had shown a slide of Gollem, the pale *Lord of the Rings* character, saying, "This is how your dermatologist wants you to look." When a slide of Darth Vader appeared, his comment reportedly was, "And this is your dermatologist."[26]

Writing in *Postgraduate Medicine* in 2004 to the question as to whether sunscreens prevented skin cancer, Ken Landow contended sunscreen use "unequivocally" reduced — but did not eliminate — development of squamous-cell carcinomas. But the nature of basal-cell cancer was such that optimal protection required lifelong control of sun exposure, while the impact of sunscreen usage on the incidence of malignant melanoma remained controversial. He argued that no available commercial products adequately shielded skin from damaging UVA rays, some 95 percent of the ultraviolet light that reached the skin. And current thought, he added, suggested a major role for UVA in inducing genetic changes that ultimately led to melanoma. Noting that the SPF referred to sunscreen's ability to block UVB energy but did not imply an equivalent ability to block UVA rays, he added, "but not even UV-A sunscreens approved by the U.S. Food and Drug Administration adequately perform this function.... UV-A rays still penetrate relatively deeply into the skin and result in generation of free radicals, which in turn leads to relative immunosuppression and a heightened risk of melanoma." Landow concluded, "Sunscreens definitely have a role in this process [protection against sun damage], but overreliance on them as the sole means of risk reduction is inadvisable."[27]

Dr. Bernard Ackerman, 67, was described in 2004 as a "renowned expert" in the field of dermatology and emeritus director of the Ackerman Academy of Dermatopathology in New York where he spent much of his time diagnosing melanoma and other skin diseases. When he returned home from a recent trip to Israel, he was deeply tanned. On that trip he did not use sunscreen, did not give a thought to the hundreds of moles on his body, and did not wear a hat on his bald head. Having found the evidence wanting, he contended that the link between sun exposure and melanoma was "not proven." Studies were contradictory, inconsistent, and failed to make the case. "The field is just replete with nonsense," he added. No evidence existed to show that sunscreen protected against melanoma. Ackerman advised people to stay out of the sun, but to do it to avoid premature aging of the skin. Those who were very fair would be wise to avoid sunlight, which would also help to prevent squamous-cell cancer. It would be a mistake, he reiterated, to assume that avoiding sunlight or using sunscreen would offer protection from melanoma.[28]

Ackerman, who has spent most of his career in academia, published 625 research papers. His list of honors and awards included the 2004 Master Award given to one person a year by the American Academy of Dermatology. Questioning even the existence of the "epidemic" of melanoma proclaimed by many dermatologists—and found in many media accounts— Ackerman remarked that the definition of the cancer had changed over time, leading doctors to diagnose, remove and cure growths that once would not have been called melanoma. Anyone who argued that sun exposure caused melanoma, declared Ackerman, needed to explain why blacks and Asians got melanoma almost exclusively on skin that was not exposed to sunlight; the palms, soles, and mucous membranes. Even in whites, the most common melanoma sites—the leg in women, the trunk in men — were not the most sun-exposed body parts. Taking exception was New York dermatologist Dr. Darrell S. Rigel, who argued melanoma could occur "where the sun doesn't shine." But that was because sunlight suppressed immune cells in the skin's surface that ordinarily held cancer at bay. Ackerman did not believe the immune system argument and responded, "It is a hypothesis to support the hypothesis that sun exposure causes melanoma. But it is not evidence."[29]

With the sun being repositioned after World War II as killer, public participation in sunbathing and tanning, and their attitudes to those practices did change. However, it took time. In the immediate post-war period, sunbathing was a well-established and entrenched fashion. The tan was much sought after with the sun still regarded as healer, at least to some extent.

10

A Fashion Remains: 1946–1979

"This ritual of tanning one's hide is indulged in by young and old, rich and poor, male and female, smart and stupid, fashionable and frumpy."
Bernadine Bailey, 1950

"I always look busy, and I always have a tan."
Aristotle Onasis, circa 1960s

"I can't live without the sun. I like to lie in it all day and soak it up. I like to tan my whole body."
Mrs. Henry Ford II, 1971

So popular was suntanning in the wake of World War II, as it maintained the popularity it had enjoyed for some 25 or more years, that *Fortune* magazine alerted its business readers in 1947 to the estimate that American industry annually suffered the loss of 7.5 million workdays as a result of severe sunburn, and that at least another 7.5 million workers each year struggled through a day's work under the strain of a burn bad enough to impair their efficiency. The magazine worried that this was a relatively high incidence of illness and impairment to result "from a deliberate attempt to draw health and beauty from the radiation of the sun." After explaining the tanning and burning process, the article grumbled that it did not think anything it said "will in any degree diminish the passion of Americans for toasting themselves brown," noting there were "hundreds" of commercial preparations for the prevention of sunburn and the promotion of the painless tan.[1]

Writing about the passion for tanning in 1948 in the *Saturday Evening Post*, journalist J. C. Furnas felt that the modern zeal for sunbathing was something less than an unmixed blessing, although overall the results may have been mildly beneficial. Furnas devoted a brief section to the benefits, such as vitamin D production stimulation, and then a much larger section on the bad effects of tanning. Specifically mentioned were the sun's ability to cause premature aging of the skin and that most doctors were convinced solar exposure caused skin cancer, although Furnas admitted some doctors felt the causal connection was not then well enough established. Despite all that, Furnas admitted, such scientific skepticism about sun exposure had little to do with styles in complexions, and tanning remained a hot fad. In fact, many took it up over the previous years "until there almost seemed something immoral about the occasional heretic" who did not want to sunbathe. With the memory still fresh Furnas recalled the "conscientious industrialists" who went to the expense of installing quartz glass (to let in UV rays) in their offices and plants. The social smartness of tan continued to dominate; sunlamps had sold as many as they had, not as much because they were thought to be health improvers as because they made the user look as if they had just returned from a vacation in the Caribbean. Cosmetics manufacturers began touting products to make women look suntanned whether they sunbathed or not.[2]

When the *New York Times* ran a 1949 editorial on the tanning fashion, it observed, "A quaint custom of the times dictates that a man while on his annual vacation must acquire a deep tan." According to the editor the fad seemed to have started in the 1920s [no mention was made of Coco Chanel as did no article before around 1971. Prior to that time Chanel was completely absent from speculations on the origins of the fad] and soon attracted hordes of followers. In any case, whatever the origins of the cult, argued the editor, "it is clear that the grip it holds on its followers has remained firm.... The truth of the matter is that the average vacationist is lacking in courage. He is afraid to return to his office pasty-faced, for if he does so he will be the object of solicitous inquiry. What was the matter with your vacation?" In conclusion the editor mused, "Some day heroes and heroines again will be fair, pale as the lily.... But that day is not yet. Definitely not."[3]

A year later reporter Ruth Adler took up much the same theme when she remarked "The modern sun cultist turns to heaven's fire out of sheer vanity, to color the skin, to meet the style. The townie dare not return from summer vacation without a bronze facial badge to prove he had a wonderful time." She added, "There still exists a curious belief among sun fanatics that a tan is always lovely, always a sign of health." After the fashion started decades earlier and was taken up by much of the elite class, society doctors began advising their fashionable patients to get outside and to sunbathe, for general health benefits, said Adler. Tanned skin quickly became a fashionable must. Clothing designers got involved by producing skimpier clothing, allowing more skin to be exposed to the sun for tanning purposes. Sales of sunlamps and cosmetics, designed to produce something that looked like a tan, rose dramatically. "The tan vogue spread until it seemed almost immoral not to be sunburned," declared Adler. She did point out the bad effects of the sun, such as the skin cancer link and its ability to prematurely age the skin, as did many other articles of this period, but such warnings had little effect on public behavior. People continued to tan because it was a socially conditioned expectation, because fashion decreed that they should, because everybody else did. People no longer tanned because the sun was a healer; they sunbathed because the suntan symbolized beauty, sexuality, and desirability. It was harder to change that behavior than if people tanned solely because the sun was viewed as healer.[4]

Around the same time another reporter, Bernadine Bailey in *Today's Health,* observed, "Shadings from blush pink to statue bronze offer vivid testimony to America's favorite summer pastime: sunbathing. This ritual of tanning one's hide is indulged in by young and old, rich and poor, male and female, smart and stupid, fashionable and frumpy." A tan was popularly synonymous with exuberant health, she believed, a concept that had a foundation in fact, because the dilation of the capillaries (a result from exposure to sunlight) increased the supply of oxygen to the skin and therefore enriched it. "In other words, a reddish brown skin is healthy as well as fashionable," explained Bailey. Despite that fact, she gave a warning earlier in her article about not overdoing sunbathing due to a possible cancer link. Bailey offered the following concluding advice, "It is advisable to continue sunbathing all summer, even after you have acquired an attractive tan, for the beneficial effects of the ultraviolet rays will continue in spite of your deepened color."[5]

When *Business Week* advised its readers in 1957 on suntanning, one tip offered, for those who wanted to tan, was before they stepped outside into weeks of hot summer sunlight, they first condition themselves with a sunlamp. Readers were advised to buy a sunlamp (about $10) and expose each side of their body to it for five minutes a day, per side, for two or three weeks.[6]

Physician Leo Orris wrote a question-and-answer article in 1961 in the women's magazine *Mademoiselle.* As to the question of whether or not sunbathing had any health value, Orris explained that there did not seem to be more than one scientifically proven benefit from the sun — it promoted the formation in the skin of vitamin D.[7]

Life magazine published an 11-page article in 1961 (mostly photos) on the pleasures and perils of the sun. Actor Cedric Hardwicke recalled that in his childhood the sun was regarded as something to be avoided under parasol or Panama hat. But things had changed dramatically, said reporter Allan Grant, with the sun then being an object of veneration. "Self-broiling on beach and in backyard has become virtually a cultural hallmark of Western society," he added. "In times past a dark tan was the stigma of the working classes. This attitude still prevails in many parts of the world. But in the U.S. the tan has emerged as a status symbol sought after even by ardent white supremacists. Even a scabbed and blistered burn may suffice as an earnest, that the social proprieties are being pursued." According to Grant, 100 million Americans lay in the summer sun and some two to five million of them each year acquired second-degree burns. "Yet, even in their suffering they luxuriate in the notion that their ordeal has made them healthier, younger looking and more attractive to the opposite sex." Grant also argued that only if a sunbather had a vitamin D deficiency would the activity bestow a health benefit; otherwise, there was no scientific evidence to show that sunbathing did any real good. By his count there were at least 100 suntan lotions, creams, jellies, and oils on the market.[8]

Mademoiselle published an article in 1964 telling its readers how to get a "perfect tan." Something of a throwback article, the piece contained not so much as a single word that there may have been negative aspects or consequences from sunbathing. All the article addressed was how to tan extremely, and intensively. Advice given was that the only way to tan, to establish an even base, was to use what was called the rotisserie method. There were a number of rules associated with the rotisserie system, including an urging to do it in private because "the best sunning positions are seldom the most graceful." It was also advised that one never "do anything except lie in position — except while you're doing your back; then you can read" and "Use a cooking timer for each interval" and "Remember to point yourself in the same direction as the sun." Readers were told to rotisserie for the first three days or so, and then spend one full day in the sun. By following that advice, a person had "made their tan" and then could do pretty much as she pleased since, "All the rest is upkeep."[9]

The rotisserie method had four positions that the sunbather had to go through. First position: "Lie on your stomach, palms down; second — or frog — position: "Lie on your back, knees V'd outward." Third and fourth positions: "Lie on your sides, legs scissored apart, one arm over the head, the other out to the side, insides up." Then there were variations to get to the trouble spots. For example, vary the second position to color the neck and under the chin. For successful sunning by using this method, the bather was advised that she needed four preparations: 1) a preventive blocker, 2) a semi-preventive, 3) a lubricant, and 4) a special lotion for later. Said the article, "Each of the above has its own time, place and purpose. You may, while using the rotisserie method, want a blocker on your face and chest, but only a lubricant on your legs." Among other bits of advice was the admonition to take off your sunglasses now and then as one engaged in the rotisserie method, unless one wanted white rings around the eyes.[10]

Then fairly detailed instructions were given for the woman who had only a couple of days to spend in the sun to get a good tan —called "The Crash Tan" plan. It was considered better to have less of a tan, and to deepen it with makeup, than to get overcooked. Next came a section on the use of reflectors in tanning. "A face reflector works best in the middle of the day. A face reflector gives you an hour's worth of sun in 15 minutes— so watch it!" Also, a body reflector had to be rotated to follow the sun, and all its sections tilted to best advantage. "You should emerge for checkups." On cloudy days, *Mademoiselle* advised, "Double your rotisserie time. Use a body reflector. Get out in the noonday sun — even if there doesn't seem to be any." For the sports tan, women were advised to vary their sleeve and neck lines to avoid "definite lines" when on the golf course, for example. Admitting that a tan would eventually fade, this publication still had some advice on how to postpone that eventuality. "Always walk on the sunny side of the street" and "Find a sunny outdoor spot and use a face reflector during your lunch hour — every minute counts!" Also, "Get under a sunlamp." With respect to the best times of the day for tanning *Mademoiselle* advised that in the summer, "Best hours: 10 A.M. to 2 P.M."[11]

Humorist Russell Baker lampooned the tanning fashion in 1965 when he wrote, "Upon returning home from the [sunbathing] ritual, well-tanned celebrants are praised for their duskiness and hungered after by the opposite sex as though a mahogany hide were the badge of great wealth." Added Baker, "It is idle to point out that all this is senseless in a country noted for refusing hamburger service to people who are born tan...."[12]

When *Newsweek* profiled tanning in 1966, it declared "The word this summer is tan, baby, tan," asserting that tanning was a big fashion that summer. And it was a big fashion all the way from teens in Houston, Texas to Paris, France, where office workers prepared for a weekend in the sun by taking vitamin pills and adhering to a pre-tanning diet (no wine or spicy foods) in the belief it would guarantee "the coppery, glowing nectarine shade dictated by editors of the fashion magazine *Aux Ecoutes*." To speed up the process, a few of the sunbathers took bootleg meloxine pills that helped the body manufacture skin pigment when followed by exposure to the sun. Really dedicated sun worshippers arranged themselves into full-length aluminum sun trays (the polished sides reflected the solar rays) or used a face-baking sun reflector that fit around the neck like a huge collar. Only the results counted. "It's so beautiful," said one 44-year-old New York actor as he stared at his own deep tan "and it makes me look young, young, young." In the opinion of the *Newsweek* article, "Youth, a sense of vitality and a strong narcissistic streak are some of the reasons people run for the sun. And a glowing copper tan in the jet age has also become a well-established status symbol that can be worn like Brooks Brothers clothes as a sure sign of affluence."[13]

Less than a year later *Time* magazine looked at the fashion, but emphasized the bad aspects. "I'm an evangelist against this foolish suntanning habit," said UCLA dermatologist Dr. J. Walter Wilson. "But trying to persuade people to stop lying in the sun for hours is as difficult as getting them to give up smoking. *Time* argued that while suntans may have looked good, they were "very bad medicine." After pointing out the standard bad effects of sunbathing, the piece recalled the problem was a relatively modern one, explaining that whites, up through the 19th century (whether out of innate good sense or colonial snobbery), shunned the tropical sun, carried parasols, wore big-brimmed hats and left exposure to non-whites, protected more by their higher level of pigmentation. "But such tanning was not thought of in the U.S. as a sign of health until the 1920s, after sunlight had been publicized as a treatment for tuberculosis." Sitting in the sunlight, said Wilson, was good only for plants. Direct sunlight could do nothing but harm, he warned. "Human beings would be healthy if they lived inside a building or cave all the time and never went out in the sun."[14]

Mademoiselle ran another article on tanning in 1971 that, like its piece a decade earlier, made no mention at all about negative aspects of sun exposure. However, this article was a lot briefer. It also advised the fair-skinned Celtic-type women they might as well forget tanning because, "Try as you may, you'll never organize those freckles into an overall tan." Those women were advised to stick to sun blocks on the beach and to try the tanning preparations that worked, supposedly, without the sun.[15]

As the 1970s began, the tan remained fashionable and desirable, at least if the opinion of influential women carried much weight. Eugenia Sheppard collected quotes from rich and famous women on their attitude to the sun and tanning for a piece in *Harper's Bazaar*. Mrs. Henry Ford II commented, "I can't live without the sun. I like to lie in it all day and soak it up. I like to tan my whole body." Impervious to all the warnings from medical professionals about the aging effect of too much sun on the skin,

Ford said it had not got to her yet. In the winter, and at Grosse Pointe, Michigan, she used a sun reflector to keep her glowing tan. Model and actor Marisa Berenson was said to throw caution to the wind and take the sun for hours. "I love to get roasted. I turn almost black. It makes me feel healthy," she explained. Betsy Theodoracopulos (a member of a Greek shipping family) loved the sun but she was so fair-skinned that she could only take it in small doses. "I feel it's necessary to be tanned, but I get my tan in short takes when I'm winter skiing," she said. In the opinion of Mrs. Charles Revson, "A good tan makes any woman look at least ten years younger. I used to sit in the sun from nine to six. Now Charles has persuaded me that I can get the same effect in an hour or two. If I use the right lotion, I tan instead of burning and it lasts longer." Actor Merle Oberon said she never sat directly in the sun. Although her skin always looked slightly tanned, she explained it was just from being outdoors, in and out of the sun, and from swimming almost every day of her life. Mrs. Oscar de la Renta (wife of the designer) observed, "A light tan is easy, but turning parchment black is definitely unsexy, to say nothing of passé." De la Renta added, "The body can take any amount of sun, but I try to give my face only about two hours a day, and only fifteen minutes at a time, even when I cover it with oil or lotion."[16]

Sheppard argued that whether women wanted to tan to look sexier, younger, healthier, or wealthier — since originally a tan was synonymous with more leisure in the right places— their love for the sun, itself, "is something different and apart. It has a man-woman connotation." Men, she thought, cared less for the sun than for the results and that more of them used the sunless bronzers than did women. As a result, they could come home from work, gray with fatigue, but look like lifeguards an hour later. As New York society woman Anita Tiburzi put it, "I love a man with a tan."[17]

About the same time Sheppard was collecting her data, reporter Lee Edson wrote a long piece on the dangers of exposure to the sun and the hazards of tanning. She had nothing good to say about the sun. Noting that more and more doctors were then engaged in warning Americans about the sun's dangers, Edson conceded, "Yet despite the medical guidance available — and a burst of warnings from the American Cancer Society— the fact is that the myth of the sun culture remains as pervasive in the United States as the cult of youth." Doctor Frederick Urbach, chairman of the Department of Dermatology at Temple University's Skin and Cancer Hospital in Philadelphia, said, "It is a myth to believe that exposing the body to the sun is automatically good for you." Then he added, "Of course my 17-year-old suntanned son isn't going to listen to such warnings. At his age he can't look ahead to trouble at 40."[18]

Industry executive L. Stambovsky returned to the pages of *Drug &* *Cosmetic Industry* in 1972 to come to the defense of tanning and the sun products industry. Just a few years earlier in that same trade publication he had attacked the suntan lotion industry. He then felt the $100 million per year suntan industry continued to sustain "severe and relentless attack from those who see suntanning as a major health threat." He pointed out that those attackers would have sun worshippers believe their enjoyment "of the cosmetic and other benefits of solar radiation" also subjected them to premature aging, skin cancer and a handful of other maladies. Many of those warnings, he declared, "are without basis in fact, are downright erroneous, or are based on half-truths." Stambovsky then went on to outline much of the evidence against sun exposure, as put forward by the medical community, but did little to attempt to refute it, except to note that solar radiation did possess a dual character — benign and malignant — although the same could be said for "water, exercise, food, heat, cold, and sex."[19]

With respect to exposure to sunlight Stambovsky concluded that while "intemperate exposure is definitely injurious, controlled exposures to within dermatologic tolerance are healthful and beautifying." In a throwback to articles of an earlier time, he contended that the sun provided humans with psychological benefits as well as clear medical benefits, such as lower blood sugar, increased body calcium, slightly lower blood pressure, growth, and more supple skin that manifested improved tone. Then he listed in a chart the all-cause mortality statistics (for 1968 from Metropolitan Life): January, 192,000; December, 185,000; March, 163,000; February, 162,000; August 158,000; July, 156,000; November, 156,000; April 153,000; October, 153,000; May 152,000; June 149,000; September, 144,000. Death rates peaked in the winter, then lessened as the days (and the solar radiation) grew longer. He remarked that he was not saying the differing death rates were due solely to solar radiation and that there were other factors, but nevertheless, "the most persuasive and unarguable distinction between winter and summer is the difference in solar radiation." Next he cited a 1939 study that showed that the rate of skin and lip cancer among Navy personnel was several times higher than that of the general population, while their cancer mortality rate (all types of cancer) was 50 percent lower than that normally expected for such a group. He argued that a systematic exposure to the sun might function as a protective device against cancer in general. Such studies, said Stambovsky, if sufficiently proved, "could give the marketers of suntan lotions, creams, and similar products enough ammunition to considerably expand their market."[20]

Writing in the *New York Times Magazine* in 1974, James Conniff said that, to hear some dermatologists talk, any unnecessary exposure to the sun was a mistake and the "adoption of suntanned skin as an essential element of a glamorous appearance is dangerous and foolhardy. The power of fashion is such, however, that few expect Americans to give up on the sun any time soon — some of the dermatologists sport rich tans themselves even as they discuss the subject in alarming terms." Still, Conniff conceded there were some benefits to sun exposure, in addition to the psychological benefits acknowledged even by the American Medical Association. Some doctors spoke of certain skin conditions being improved, that tanning could reduce blood pressure and serum cholesterol levels for days and even weeks.[21]

With tanning being as fashionable as it was, and as pervasive and popular as it was from, roughly, the 1920s through to the 1980s, some inventions were dreamed up over the years, to assist in the tanning process. One of the first such devices was unveiled in 1928 at a meeting of the American Physical Society in Pasadena, California. Dr. Robert C. Burt told of a new instrument he had invented and named the "Erythemameter." It purportedly measured sensitivity of a person to erythema, the medical term for sunburn. Burt's instrument was a light-tight box (containing a quartz lamp) from which the UV rays could escape through a hole about two inches square. That opening was placed directly against the base skin of the person being tested. A set of filters in back of that hole cut off more and more of the rays so that the skin at one edge got the full impact of the rays from the lamp, while the skin at the opposite side received none. After being exposed to this device for 10 minutes, the skin became burned at the side receiving the most rays. The distance that the burned area spread measured the person's sensitivity; it showed how long of an exposure a person could stand to ultraviolet rays of any intensity.[22]

Burt announced he had another invention — one that measured the intensity of UV light either from the sun or an artificial source. So portable and easy to use was the instrument, predicted Burt, "that the day may come when up-to-date bathing beaches will have an observatory giving out the intensity of the sunburn light in the sun, so that each person may stay out just long enough to become a delicate brown, without becoming severely burned." [Obviously, he was anticipating today's ubiquitous UV index, a part of all summer weather forecasts.][23]

At the annual meeting of the American Institute of Electrical Engineers held at Swampscott, Massachusetts in 1949, Hoyt Scott, an engineer with the General Electric Company, introduced a sunburn meter that told sunbathers when to get into the shade. Scott explained the meter consisted of filters and light-sensitive cells that recorded on a dial the number of minutes of sunlight necessary to produce a pink glow or a bad burn.[24]

A rotary apparatus patented in 1954 by one Nicholas M. Kambourakis of New York City offered the sunbather the assurance of an even, all-around tan. The user strapped himself in and, as he revolved, he was uniformly exposed to the sun's rays. Coming with a wide canvas strap across the middle, and a footrest, the machine had a U-shaped frame along with a pillow. The bather stretched out in the apparatus face up. When he wanted to revolve he fastened a strap across his forehead, another across his middle, and attached a number of "fine, soft threads" at various other points; then he touched a switch. In motorless versions of the machine, the user turned himself by grasping a ring or using a pedal. Referring to the discomforts of conventional methods of sunbathing the inventor explained, "To secure an even tan over the entire body it is necessary for a person frequently to assume various awkward and tiresome positions."[25]

Peter M. Winter of Chevy Chase, Maryland, was awarded patent 3,597,054 in 1971 for spectacles that gave the wearer warning of UV radiation, so that he could determine how long he should lie on the beach. Set in the eyeglasses frame, outside the normal field of view but within peripheral range, were chips of a material that changed color under UV light. Noting flashes of these colors out of the corner of his eye, the wearer of the glasses could decide when the radiation had reached his discomfort point.[26]

In 1975 the American Cyanamid Company of Stamford, Connecticut, received a patent for a sunburn "Dosimeter," designed to let people estimate the effects of the sun's rays on their skin in time to avoid overexposure. It was a disposable device in which a test zone of plastic contained chemicals that showed irreversible color changes when irradiated in the sunburn-causing range. Near it on the device was a color standard in the shade to which the same chemicals changed after a predetermined exposure. The user compared the test zone with the standard to judge whether to protect his skin from further rays.[27]

A sunburn alert system came on the market in 1988. Called the "UV Sun Sensor," it was also a disposable adhesive patch to be worn on the skin; it featured a white dial that turned red to indicate the onset of sunburn.[28]

A few years later, in 1991, an inventor in Southern California came up with a device that measured a person's exposure to UV light and sounded an alarm when it was too great. Invented by Nahum Gat, an aerospace engineer in Manhattan Beach, the device combined UV sensors with an electronic processor that compared the dose of radiation with data on danger levels for people with different skin pigments. Users were able to program the device to identify which of six basic skin types they were, as well as the level of protection in any suntan lotion they may have been wearing. When solar exposure passed a designated level, the device literally sounded an alarm.[29]

Yet another new product that warned sunbathers when it was time to seek shade came on the market in 1992. Worn on the skin or clothing, the Sun Alert Ultraviolet Warning Badge contained, in the center, a picture of the sun that had been treated with photochemicals. With exposure to UV rays the little sun changed color from blue to green to yellow to orange, matching colored rings around the sun on the patch that said, respectively, no exposure, alert, caution, and burn. Manufactured by Xytronyx, Inc., a San Diego bio-tech firm, the badge came in versions for unprotected tanning, for children, and for adults wearing sunblock with SPF 15 or higher. A package of five badges retailed for $3.99.[30]

At the same time, Sun Sports International, based in Newark, Delaware, was marketing a credit-card size tanning gauge that measured the strength of the sun's UVB rays and that recommended the type of sunscreen to be used.[31]

By the end of the 1970s, the increasing number of warnings about sun exposure was starting to have an effect. Anti-sun articles increased as did the reported consequences of exposure, presented in an escalating and exaggerated way. Starting to crack was the pervasive idea held by the general public that a bronze skin signaled health and success. That was an idea epitomized in the words of Artistotle Onasis, who used to say, "I always look busy, and I always have a tan."[32]

11

A Fashion Fades:
1980–2004

"The glowing tan, once a symbol of abundant health and leisure, now hovers between tobacco breath and needle tracks as grounds for social shunning."

Stephen Rae, 1985

"The suntan is absolutely out unless, of course, you're George Hamilton."

Jackie Collins, 1988

"The sun is to Bob Dole what Big Macs are to [President Bill] Clinton."

New Yorker, 1995

Typifying changes in the tanning fashion was the 1983 report that Nancy Reagan was one of 400,000 Americans treated for basal-cell cancer in 1982. In the following year she had several spots of keratosis removed from her face to prevent a recurrence. President Ronald Reagan also had a skin cancer spot removed from his nose during the time he was in office. On New Year's Day 1983, Nancy Reagan resolved to stay out of the sun.[1]

Still, old attitudes were resistant to change. In 1984 a group of dermatologists found that most Americans loved their suntans so much they refused to use a sunscreen even after being told by medical experts that tanning was unhealthy and damaged the skin. Researchers at Pennsylvania State University's College of Medicine in Hershey, using 350 subjects, found that only 5 percent of the group used a sunscreen while sunbathing, even after they had been warned by medical experts that sunning was a major cause of skin cancer, prematurely aged skin, and wrinkling. According to the study, 78 percent of respondents believed that a tan looked healthy, and 72 percent thought it made them look more attractive.[2]

In a 1985 op ed satirical piece in the *New York Times* on the changing attitude toward this fashion, Stephen Rae wrote that his summers began to unravel after he learned the suntan was déclassé. "The glowing tan, once a symbol of abundant health and leisure, now hovers between tobacco breath and needle tracks as grounds for social shunning," he said. A passion for being pale, he continued, seemed to have begun in the early years of the Reagan Administration after "a scare campaign mounted by the sun tan lotion companies to promote their new graded sun-screen formulas worked all too well."[3]

A national survey of 1,013 adults and 126 teenagers (12 to 17 years old), conducted in October 1986 for the American Academy of Dermatology, revealed that 66 percent of adults and 70 percent of teens said a tan made them look healthier. Thirty percent of adults and 50 percent of teens admitted they intentionally worked on a tan; 23 percent of adults and 33 percent of teens took no precautions while tanning. Approximately 54 percent of the adults and 37 percent of the teens declared they knew that sun exposure could cause skin cancer.[4]

Another survey, conducted around the same time for the American Academy of Dermatology and the Avon Foundation, canvassed 50 fashion leaders who were said to be "virtually unanimous" in their opinion that the dark tan, once considered fashionable, was no longer in vogue. The main reasons for caution under the sun were fears of premature aging and skin cancer. Those polled included such fashion leaders as Helen Gurley Brown, the editor of *Cosmopolitan* magazine, and Eileen Ford, head of the famous New York City modeling agency, Ford Models. Said Brown, "There are still addicted-to-tan people who will never conquer the addiction. The reason the rest of us are more careful is because of all the information being disseminated. You just could not avoid knowing, at this point, if you can read, that heavy suntanning does cause skin cancer." Ford told the researchers, "Today's style is a healthy glow, not sun-baked skin."

Nevertheless, there were some dissenters as to the supposed decline of the fashion. Bo Wunsch, a spokesman for Silver Solarium, a tanning equipment importer in San Francisco, explained that there were then more than 275,000 commercial tanning beds in America and "It is not only the fashion in this country it is the fashion throughout Western Europe." Tom Neighbors, manager of Eurotan Halsted, a Chicago tanning parlor that had about 100 customers a day, said "I really don't see tanning ever going out of style to be honest with you. It's been around forever."[5]

According to reporter Mary McIver, in 1988, many modeling agency spokesmen insisted they had always discouraged their models from tanning; and with tans then growing more unfashionable, more agencies were said to be insisting their models stay out of the sun. Said Sharon Dorais, the director of Sharon Dorais Modeling and Talent International in Vancouver, "The first thing I say to the girls is, 'No suntanning.'" She added, "Today's look is pale on pale, with very, very fair skin. This year, we are looking for people who have hardly ever exposed their skin to the sun. As a model, the more alabaster you look, the more work you will get." Noted author Jackie Collins observed that "Hollywood wives have finally realized that their perfect skins are going to crack if they go out into the sun. The suntan is absolutely out unless, of course, you're George Hamilton." The latter, at age 48, was an actor almost as well known for his tanning regimen as for his screen roles. Hamilton followed the sun with a legendary dedication. According to his publicist, Jeffrey Lane, the actor "suns every day." Added Lane, "It is something he has done for years." All of Hamilton's movie contracts reportedly said that while he was filming on location, he had to be flown to a sunny climate once a month. His friend, movie star Elizabeth Taylor, was also described as a dedicated tanner. Screenwriter William Stadiem recalled that when he met the 56-year-old actor beside the pool of her Bel Air home, she conducted the entire meeting holding a sun reflector.[6]

Still, tanning remained important to many Americans, despite the fact that in 1987 skin cancer struck 500,000 Americans and killed 8,000. For thousands of people nationwide, tanning remained a ritual as routine as going to the movies. Tanning centers continued to spread rapidly with the number of salons increasing some 55 percent, from 11,202 to 17,405, in the course of one year. Steve Goodhue, the owner of Sundays, a tanning salon franchise with outlets in Denver, Los Angeles, Dallas, Washington, D.C., and San Francisco, remarked "Every summer the press comes out with anti-tanning articles that say pale is in. Irrespective of what you might hear through the grapevine, 99 percent of the American population still thinks they look better tan." In a Gallup poll taken in August 1987, of 1,147 people aged 13 and over, 60 percent said that a tan made them feel healthier and 30 percent said they then tanned more than ever. Said Steve Bobowski, vice president of marketing for the Schering-Plough (Coppertone) firm, "What we're seeing now is a shifting away from the deep, dark tan to a more golden glow." Yet when a *New York Times* reporter made a trip to several Long Island New York beaches, he found that parasols, visors, and sunblock lotions hardly outnumbered the bodies greased with tanning oils or left unprotected. "I hear a lot of people talking about the dangers of the sun," said Peter Erwig, a lifeguard for the previous five years at Navajo Beach in Amagansett, Long Island. "But they still come out here and bake. I guess they're sort of addicted to it, like coffee."[7]

Hard-core tanners, those least concerned about caveats in the late 1980s, were teenagers, according to dermatologists and beauty experts. People most likely to heed warnings from groups such as the American Academy of Dermatology were said to be women in their 40s and 50s who were just discovering "the sun's toll on their skin." Said Diane Young, owner of a skin-care center in Manhattan, "Many of my clients still want to look tan, but they realize the long-term effects are not worth dealing with, so they use bronzers. And as the population grows older and as cosmetic surgery becomes more popular, many women know that the effects of their surgery will not hold up as well as in the sun." Yet the reporter argued, "But for many of these women, pale will never be attractive." Dr. G. Thomas Jansen, president of the American Academy of Dermatology, observed that the idea put out by the tanning salons—that they are safer than the sun itself—was simply not true. Nevertheless, many conceded that vanity overrode health considerations for many tanning buffs. Typifying that attitude were the comments of Risa Hope, a 33-year-old toy designer in Manhattan. "I get very used to looking tan and I feel sickly when it fades." For Arthur Appleman (a 40-year-old Manhattan lawyer who went to a tanning salon at least twice a week throughout the year) a tan was a sign of success. "When I'm tan, I work better and my business is better, because my clients think I must be a fine attorney who can afford to travel to expensive, hot places in the winter. Publicist Jeffrey Lane explained that his client George Hamilton was "as brown as he's ever been." Hamilton was unavailable for comment for that article because, explained Lane, "George is on a boat in the south of France, doing lots of you know what."[8]

A survey conducted in 1987 for the American Academy of Dermatology revealed that 96 percent of all adult respondents could name at least one negative effect of the sun. And 54 percent of those singled out skin cancer.[9]

An editorial in the *New Republic* magazine in 1988 declared that since the link between sunlight and skin cancer was well known, the position of all right-thinking people was that the deliberate exposure of skin to sunlight for the purpose of acquiring a tan "is almost criminally foolhardy—like smoking." He cited the president of the American Academy of Dermatology, who said, "You cannot get a tan without damaging your skin"; the Skin Cancer Foundation saying, "The term 'healthy tan' is a contradiction in terms"; and an expert featured in *Conde Nast Traveler* magazine who recommended a sunscreen that was the equivalent of "standing in a dark basement at midnight." According to the editor, "This consensus about tanning is rapidly becoming part of the new Puritanism — an issue, like drugs, about which your piety is measured by how extreme a position you're willing to take." Acknowledging that the risk of developing fatal cancer from heavy sunning was much smaller than the risk of getting it from heavy smoking, the editor went on to state that there was no such all-or-nothing-at-all dilemma regarding suntans, as there was with smoking. "Yet the rhetoric of the new heliophobia rarely allows for any middle ground." Skeptically he added that, although dermatologists struggled to prove otherwise, there was no proof that UV rays, at times other than around midday, were cancerous at all. Overwhelmingly he felt the greatest danger came from sunburn and not mere tanning, accepting the idea that the risk of getting skin cancer, and even prematurely aged skin, was determined primarily by a person's experience as a child, not on a person's tanning behavior as an adult. "We certainly don't have to do as some dermatologists suggest and drench ourselves in maximum-protection sun blocks everyday as routinely as brushing our teeth," the editor concluded.[10]

Several researchers, led by Arthur G. Miller, conducted experiments in 1990 on attitude toward a tan. In one experiment, with 205 student respondents, a vignette procedure was used in which subjects were asked to record their impressions of a target person (no tan, tan, intentional tan). No photos were used, just text. In the tan condition, the target was described as having a dark suntan due to participation in outdoor activities; while in the intentional tan condition, the target was described as having a dark suntan due to sunbathing frequently. Subjects perceived the target in the tan condition as more attractive than in the no-tan condition. Ratings for the intentional tan target were less positive than for the tan condition though still more attractive than in the no-tan condition. For the trait of vanity, ratings were highest for targets in the intentional tan condition. No effects were obtained from the sex of the target or the sex of the respondent. Researchers concluded that information regarding the presence of a suntan generally increased the perceived social attractiveness of the target. Persons with a tan were judged to be more attractive, popular, sexy, and so forth. Miller presumed that social image accounted, at least in part, for the considerable effort, expense, and risk millions of people underwent in their quest for a tan. It was an image consistent with what the researchers found from a sample of college students, returning from spring break, who told them, when asked about their major goals for a successful vacation, that a well-developed tan was very high on the list. However, despite the overall importance of a tan, the researchers argued that the vanity rating indicated a kind of stigmatizing impression attached to those who intentionally engaged in efforts to manipulate their attractiveness. "The impact of a suntan thus is not a simple halo. Subjects acknowledged the predominately positive attributes of a suntan while simultaneously indicating the impression of a specifically negative facet to this image," said the researchers.[11]

A second experiment by Miller and the others consisted of three parts. In the first part, the 227 respondents were divided into three groups based on a questionnaire of their own tanning behavior (low, medium, high). Part two measured their attitude toward the risks of tanning and the issues pertaining to skin damage and cancer in another questionnaire. Part three was the screening of a 30-minute videotape originally aired on PBS that included a thorough survey of the risks involved in tanning and the case history of one woman in her late 20s with skin cancer, purportedly from a history of intense tanning and occasional sunburning.[12]

In that experiment subjects with higher reported tan levels were more likely to endorse a belief in the association between tanning and physical attractiveness. Respondents making their judgments after seeing the videotape were less likely to endorse the tan/attractive linkage than were subjects responding to those items before seeing the tape. Relative to those in the medium and low categories, respondents in the high tan category were more likely to indicate that the pleasures of a tan were worth the risks. Researchers concluded that a major pattern was the systematic linkage between the subjects' tan-level category and his or her endorsement of what could be termed the "tan stereotype." That is, people with high tan levels were more likely to acknowledge the positive attributes of a dark tan — attractiveness, confidence, healthy appearance, and so forth. Those in the high-tan group were less convinced about the perils of tanning than were subjects in the low and medium groups, suggesting to the researchers that a degree of resistance or denial may have been at work. High-tan subjects reported a lower usage of sunblocks, compared to the other two groups. Female subjects found the videotape to be more convincing than did male respondents, leading the researchers to conclude, "We would suggest that women in this study generally displayed a more realistic, self-protective orientation toward the risks inherent in suntanning."[13]

Two studies conducted by the American Academy of Dermatology in 1987 and one in 1989 by Opinion Research showed everyone was still not convinced about the dangers of tanning. In the first survey, half of the teens and 45 percent of adults under 35 reported they intentionally worked on a tan. The follow-up survey showed those figures remained basically unchanged, although people acknowledged that sun exposure was bad for their skin. But among adults, sunscreen use was up from 35 percent to 41 percent.[14]

Marita Broadstock led a team of researchers in 1991 that conducted an experiment on Australian teens with respect to their attitudes about tanning. Australia had the highest rate of skin cancer in the world, with two out of every three Australians said to be likely to develop some form of skin cancer during their lifetime. A survey there in 1989 of adolescent students indicated that 70 percent were using inadequate protection from the sun, yet 97 percent of those respondents knew skin cancer was a dangerous disease, and 56 percent viewed themselves as vulnerable. In a different survey (1990) it was found that more than half of the respondents said they felt healthier with a suntan, and 66 percent thought they looked healthier although only 18 percent believed that a suntanned person was healthier. Yet another study (1984) also found a positive stereotype associated with tanning; 72 percent believed that tanned skin looked more attractive than untanned skin and 78 percent believed that having a suntan made a person look more healthy than not having one.[15]

Broadstock's experiment involved 191 adolescents with a mean age of 14, drawn from schools in the State of Victoria. Stimuli were 32 different color slides featuring a model photographed from hip-level up. Male and female models were used with the attire varied (casual attire versus swimwear) and the tan level varied (no tan, light tan, medium tan, dark tan). Results confirmed that a tan was judged healthier than having no tan. Perception of healthiness increased with tan level from no tan to a peak at medium tan, and decreased for a dark tan. The dark tan was judged as less healthy than the light or medium tans. For the trait of attractiveness, the same patterns of judgments were recorded. Overall, researchers concluded that there was a preference for a medium tan over a light tan, with a dark tan and no tan being clearly less preferred. It was confirmed that there was a strong preference for tans over no tans for those adolescents. "The results of the present study confirm that suntan is an important physical feature affecting adolescent perceptions of healthiness and attractiveness," concluded the researchers. "These findings confirm that perception of both healthiness and attractiveness are affected by level of suntan."[16]

Similar behavior took place in other parts of the world. Eduardo Betancourt had worked for 13 years as a lifeguard on the beaches of Punta del Este, Uruguay, as of 1992. Seven hours a day he watched his Uruguayan compatriots and vacationers from Argentina lie out in the sun and develop dark tans. [Many articles at that time dealt with the hole in the ozone layer in that part of the world.] Betancourt said he had not seen much change in the people over those 13 years, "Before they didn't use creams. Now they say they're a little worried about the ozone, so they put a lot of cream on. They think cream will protect them totally. They still come at 10:00 in the morning and lie baking in the sun until 5:00 in the afternoon," he said. Both the Argentine and Uruguayan governments had mounted what were described by reporter Nathaniel Nash as "tiny" public health campaigns warning about the summer sun. But results were spotty. Said sunbather Manuel David, "You don't want to be told not to go into the sun. The people still want to be burned. They want to go back to Buenos Aires dark, dark, dark."

At a local shop, Hawaiian Tropic 30 Ozone Sunblock, imported from the U.S., was said to be selling well, even though it was very expensive at $21 for four ounces. Dr. Anna-Maria Salazar, a dermatologist at the Mautone Clinic in Punta del Este, said she had seen dramatic changes in patients in recent years. Five years earlier she had seen one case of melanoma every 18 months, but by 1992 she was seeing 10 cases a year. Basal- and squamous-cell skin cancers used to be confined only to patients more than 60 years of age, she added. But such cancers were then appearing in 25–35 year olds. Salazar said other physician colleagues confirmed those trends. Unexplained was why this dramatic increase had happened only in the last five years. The previous December, the Health Ministry in Chile had begun a serious public awareness campaign to persuade Chileans to "enjoy the sun in a healthy way."[17]

Researchers Simon Chapman, Robin Marks and Madeleine King did a study that rated 3,971 photos of models from the midsummer editions of six Australian fashion magazines (*Cosmopolitan, Cleo, Dolly, Vogue, Mode*, and *Woman's Day*) for the period 1982 to 1991. Photos were rated for tan on a nine-point scale, for the presence of hats, for sun-protective clothing, and for being set in the shade. It was remarked that while fashion norms had prescribed suntans in that period, public health organizations in Australia had been attempting to counter that fashion through campaigns about the risks of exposure to UV rays and through efforts to promote the wearing of protective yet fashionable clothing and hats.

Results of the study revealed that, with the exception of the 1990–1991 period, there were an increasing proportion of light tans on models over the years. Male models were more likely to be deeply tanned than were female models. Also, the proportion of models wearing hats followed an increasing linear trend across the decade. However, 75 percent of the photos set outside were taken in unshaded settings. In those unshaded settings, 17 percent of the women and 5 percent of the men wore hats. Of the models overall, 86.6 percent were female; 96.8 percent were Caucasian. Over the decade there was an increasing proportion of light tans (ratings one and two) and a decreasing proportion of dark tans (7, 8, 9), except in 1990–1991. Men had a mean tan rating of 5.10 and women had a mean tan rating of 3.98. Models in swimwear had a mean tan rating of 5.47, compared with a 3.89 rating for models in other types of clothing. In a different study of attitudes toward suntans in the Australian state of Victoria, 51 percent of the 3,100 people surveyed said they felt healthier with a suntan and 20 percent said they believed that "a suntan protects against skin cancer." With respect to his own study, Chapman concluded, "The changing trend in the depth of tans in fashion magazine models in Australia over the last decade is an indication that suntans are now perceived as being less fashionable."[18]

Back in America *Glamour* magazine reported in 1993 the results of its first-ever tanning survey, of some 6,000 of its readers. Those results, thought the magazine, proved "we have begun to mend our ways." The survey revealed that 58 percent of the respondents tanned in the summer of 1992, 42 percent did not. Nearly nine out of 10 readers reported using sunscreen and they had been using it for an average of 3.6 years. Thirty-six percent said they used sunscreens with an SPF of 15 or more and 15 percent used products with SPF 25 or higher. Sixty-seven percent declared they spent less time trying to get a tan than they had five years earlier; 33 percent reported they felt guilty about tanning. Fear of skin cancer was cited by 69 percent as the reason for doing less tanning, while 57 percent said it was a fear of wrinkles. Fully 17 percent of the respondents had become year-round sunscreen users, wearing cosmetics—from foundation to hand cream — with screening agents. Sixty percent had tried self-tanning products and 59 percent of those who did liked the results. Of those who liked the results, 64 percent approved of self-tanning products because they gave a tan without skin damage; 53 percent, because they could be used all year; and 36 percent, because it helped maintain a summer tan. Of the 42 percent of the respondents who reported they had not gotten a tan the previous summer, 60 percent said it was because they feared skin cancer. That fear increased with age, climbing to 82 percent in respondents over the age of 35.[19]

Despite its survey indications that the tan was falling out of favor, *Glamour* went ahead, in the article that reported its survey results, to discuss at length the tanning methods, the types of sunscreens available, and provided self-tanning tips. *Glamour* listed the pros and cons of six different tanning methods: self-tanning creams, tanning with sunscreen, tan-accelerating lotions, natural tanning with sunscreen, tanning salons, and tanning pills. All six methods reportedly had "cons" and the last four methods had no "pros." That is, it was clear that none of the last four methods was recommended. Also discussed were the newest sun protectors, broken down into four categories: extended-wear sunscreens, broad-spectrum sunscreens, chemical-free sunscreens, and moisturizers with sunscreen.[20]

According to the Roper Organization of New York City, between 1987 and 1992 the share of adults who actively sought a suntan dropped two percentage points, while the share that avoided tans increased by two percentage points. A larger share of Americans, as of 1992, shunned tans, compared to those who sought them (29 percent versus 22 percent), but 48 percent did not care one way or the other about getting a tan. About 80 percent of those polled by Roper used one or more forms of protection when they went out in the sun; 55 percent wore sunglasses, 34 percent wore a hat, 31 percent used a sunscreen, 13 percent used special protective creams for the nose and the face, and 9 percent used beach umbrellas. Young adults were the most likely to seek a tan, with 38 percent of adults under 30 wanting a tan, 23 percent in the 30 to 44 age bracket, 15 percent of the 45 to 59 year olds, and 8 percent of those aged 60 and older. More than one-third of people aged 45 and older described themselves as positively sun-shy. Affluent Americans were most likely to both seek a tan and avoid one. Twenty-five percent of adults in households with incomes of $50,000 and up wanted a tan; 19 percent, in households with incomes less than $15,000. On the other hand, 33 percent of the high-income households avoided the sun, compared to 30 percent in the low-income category. Women were found to be slightly more likely to want a tan than men (by 23 percent to 20 percent) but also much more likely to avoid the sun (35 percent to 22 percent). Most men, however, 56 percent, didn't think about the sun one way or the other.

Hats were mostly worn by people age 45 and older, with men 38 percent more likely than women to wear a hat — perhaps due to their bald heads or thinning hair. In the South, 40 percent of adults wore a hat; 33 percent in the West and the Midwest; 25 percent in the Northeast. While 37 percent of women reported that they used a sunscreen, only 25 percent of men did so. Usage of sunscreens peaked among adults in the 30 to 59 age range. Sunscreen users were more likely than non-users to have incomes of $30,000 or more and to be well-educated. Sunscreen use in the South and the Midwest stood at 28 percent, 34 percent in the Northeast, and 37 percent in the West.[21]

Journalist Peter Marks reported in 1995 that although the culture of tanning had changed dramatically, there were still many who followed the fashion. He found 20-year-old college student Kelly Mercein tanning at Jones Beach, Long Island, New York. "I am fully aware of what the sun can do to me," she told him. "My mother yells at me every day. But I guess I am 20 and I feel invincible." Marks added, "Yet like cigarette smoking and alcohol consumption before it, tanning is now an activity with a warning label that many are choosing to ignore." Dr. Mark Leary, a professor of psychology at Wake Forest University, felt that for some people the cosmetic benefits simply outweighed the health risks. Four years earlier he surveyed 300 Wake Forest students and found that more than 90 percent went into the sun at least occasionally to "enhance their tan." In a follow-up survey, his researchers questioned 200 sunbathers in central North Carolina and found that about 12 percent were so obsessed with being tan that they felt they could never get tan enough, a group Leary called the "tan insatiables."

As a researcher, Leary was interested in what it was that prompted people to go out and pursue a tan, even though negative messages about sun exposure abounded. "I've found it has to do with people's concerns about the impressions that other people form of them, and that people who are more concerned about others' impressions of them are more likely to work on their tans," he declared. Marks said he thought "dangerous" sunbathing might also have persisted because, unlike with smoking and alcohol abuse, tanning was "a vice seemingly without a secondary victim." Nowhere did people find buttons or labels expressing sentiments such as "Thank you for not tanning" or "We mind very much if you tan." However, Marks admitted that, in ads, Little Miss Coppertone then wore a T-shirt, a hat, and sunglasses. "It is no longer chic to have a dark tan," Russ Elliott, vice president of advertising for Schering-Plough Health Care Products (Coppertone) told Marks. He said views on sun worship had changed so radically in the previous decade that the sun lotion market had shifted from an almost total emphasis on perfecting the tan to one of protecting the skin from the sun's harmful effects. "It's no longer the tanning market," he added. "It's the health-care market." For the most part, thought Marks, tanning remained an activity for young, white people who believed pale was unacceptable. The people at Coppertone reportedly said the average black person had in his or her skin a natural Sun Protection Factor of 8, while white people had a natural SPF of 0.[22]

During afternoons at the Capitol building in Washington, D.C., in the mid 1990s, Senator Bob Dole often sat on the terrace of his Capitol office, his head angled directly into the sun's rays. "Dole Beach" was what his staff had dubbed their boss's favorite hideaway. Everyone who had worked for him knew that sneaking out to catch some sun was a regular part of his daily schedule. "The sun is to Bob Dole what Big Macs are to [President Bill] Clinton," a press secretary explained. Dole spent nearly an hour on the terrace in the sun three or four times a week and sported what was described as a "deep, luxurious George Hamilton–style tan." Monthly trips to his Florida condo maintained the tan over the winter. One of his staff described Dole's color as "vigorous bronze." Called a sun worshipper of the old school, the Senator exposed himself to the sun's rays without protection; no lotions, no sunscreens, and so on. Self-tanning preparations were out of the question because, said an associate, "He would never fake a tan."[23]

Australian authorities had engaged in vigorous and continuous public education campaigns about the dangers of sun exposure since the early 1980s. Yet as recently as 1988, according to reporter Patrick Perry, 69 percent of Australians believed that suntans were desirable. By 1992, though, that figure had dropped to 48 percent.[24]

Writing in *Harper's Bazaar* in 1996, Emily Prager produced almost a nostalgia piece, sort of mourning the total loss of the deep tan and perhaps, soon, the light tan. Hollywood's young actresses—Winona Ryder, Bridget Fonda, Gwyneth Paltrow, Mira Sorvino, and Nicole Kidman — said Prager, were all untanned, "ghost-white" compared with the likes of those who went before them, such as Jane Fonda, Farrah Fawcett, and Ali McGraw. On the other hand, Jennifer Ramey, an agent at Women Model Management, observed that her very young models liked to tan. "Young people think that the more tan you are, the more affluent you look."

In 1990 George Hamilton launched the George Hamilton Sun Care System — a line of tanning products that told the user how to become a "tanmaster." Roundly denounced by dermatologists, the Hamilton line was defunct by 1996. Agreeing that there had been a huge attitude change in the previous 10 years in the general perception of the dark tan, Prager added, "We have yet to reach the point where we see even the lightest tan for what it truly is: pigmentation as the result of skin damage. Why, after all the information we've been given about the danger, do we persist in seeing a tan as attractive?" In answer to that question Dianne Osborne, a spokeswoman for the Estee Lauder firm said, "We just believe that white fat looks a lot worse than tanned fat. And of course, for years wellness was associated with a tan. If you were pale or palish, you seemed more fragile, not as robust or as full of life." Karen Flinn, spokeswoman for Lancôme's, observed, "The sun makes you feel energized and healthy. People don't want to give that up."[25]

When the American Academy of Dermatology had a survey conducted for them in 1995, it was revealed that nearly 60 percent of adults under the age of 25 admitted to working on a tan; one to two million had a serious tanning habit, going to tanning salons on an ongoing basis. Also disclosed by the survey was that only one sunbather in three bothered to use sun-screen.[26]

From July through September of 1991, researchers led by Howard K. Koh conducted a nationwide telephone survey of 2,459 whites about their sunbathing habits and their sunscreen use. Respondents were classified into three groups: non-sunbathers, infrequent sunbathers (engaged in the habit one to 10 days in the previous year), and frequent sunbathers (11 or more days). Respondents were also classified into "routine" users of sun-screen (if they used it always or often) or as "sporadic" users if they used it sometimes, rarely or never. Percentage breakdown for non-sunbathers (1,019) was as follows: women, 40 percent; men, 43 percent; Both men and women, aged 16–25, 25 percent; 26–40, 34 percent; 41–60, 43 percent; over 60, 69 percent. Those with lower education (high school or less), 48 per-cent; middle education (two years of university), 41 percent; higher edu-cation (four years university), 37 percent. For infrequent sunbathers (818) the numbers were: women, 33 percent; men, 34 percent; 16–25, 41 per-cent; 26–40, 32 percent; 41–60, 36 percent; over 60, 22 percent; lower edu-cation, 30 percent; middle education, 32 percent; higher education, 38 percent. For the frequent sunbathers (622): women, 27 percent; men, 23 percent; 16–25, 34 percent; 26–40, 34 percent, 41–60, 20 percent; over 60, 9 percent. Those with lower education, 22 percent; middle education, 27 percent; higher education, 25 percent. Mean age of the respondents was 42 years; 55 percent were women, and 28 percent were college graduates.[27]

In that Koh survey, 59 percent of the subjects reported sunbathing at least once during the previous year. Women, those in the youngest age group and those in the highest education group, were most likely to sun-bathe at least once. Twenty-five percent were frequent sunbathers; women, younger respondents and those at middle and higher education levels were most likely to sunbathe frequently. Among the 530 subjects who had sun-bathed on one or more days in the month prior to the interview, 248 (47 percent) reported using sunscreens routinely; only 36 percent of the men used sunscreen routinely, as compared to 53 percent of the women. Edu-cation level appeared to be related to sunscreen use. Respondents in the lowest education group used sunscreens least frequently (38 percent ver-sus 53 percent and 55 percent). Routine users were more likely than spo-radic users to use sunscreen with an SPF of 15 or higher; of routine users, 45 percent did not use an SPF 15 or higher; while among the sporadic users, 60 percent did not use sunscreen with the recommended SPF of 15 or higher. Those in the youngest age group were less likely than those in other age groups to use sunscreen with an SPF of 15 or higher.

In summary, only 47 percent of the 530 subjects reported routine sunscreen use, and of those people, only 55 percent used sunscreen with an SPF of 15 or higher. Overall, then, said Koh, only 25 percent of sunbathers routinely used a sunscreen with a recommended SPF 15 or higher. Koh also found that men, those in the lowest education group and those in the youngest age group, were less frequent users of sunscreen. Figures for sunscreen use among sporadic users (282 of 530) were as follows: women, 47 percent; men 64 percent. Both men and women 16–25, 62 percent; 26–40, 48 percent; 41–60, 53 percent; over 60, 57 percent. Those with lower education: 62 percent; middle education, 47 percent; higher education, 45 percent. Numbers for sunscreen use among routine users (248 of 530) were: women, 53 percent; men, 36 percent; 16–25, 38 percent; 26–40, 52 percent; 41–60, 47 percent; over 60, 43 percent. Those with lower education, 38 percent; middle education, 53 percent; higher education, 55 percent.[28]

According to figures from the American Academy of Dermatology, the number of people using sunscreen jumped from 35 percent in 1986 to 53 percent in 1996. However, the number of people who suffered sunburn had also increased, from 30 percent in 1986 to 39 percent in 1996.[29]

Other figures from the Academy indicated 20 percent of adults (18 and older) used a sunscreen with an SPF of 15 or greater in 1996, up from 6 percent in 1991, with usage rates by women growing a little faster than rates for men. Use of a product with SPF 15 or higher was 7 percent among women in 1991, 22 percent in 1996; numbers for men were, respectively, 4 percent and 17 percent. Women's use of any sun care product was stable at 35 percent in both years, with men's share increasing to 28 percent in 1996, from 24 percent in 1991. SPF 15 or greater products comprised 15 percent of all sun care products in 1991; 62 percent in 1996. According to American Academy of Dermatology research, the percentage of adults who thought a tan looked healthy declined 10 percentage points between 1986 and 1996. But even with the drop, 56 percent of adults said a tan suggested good health. And adults were only slightly more likely in 1996 than 10 years earlier to say they minimized their sun exposure, at 23 percent, compared to 19 percent in 1986. More than 75 percent of teens (aged 12 to 19) said they knew sun exposure damaged skin. And 72 percent reported using sunscreen at least sometimes. As with adults, teenage girls were more likely than their male counterparts to use sunscreen always or often, at 46 percent compared to 30 percent. Yet adult-like perceptions of the positive attributes of tanned skin persisted with young people. Two-thirds of teens said they looked better, healthier, more sophisticated, older, and thinner with a tan.[30]

In 1997 officials of England's National Ballet ordered 60 dancers, scheduled to perform in an upcoming production of "Swan Lake," to stop sunbathing because they were no longer considered pale enough to play their roles. Said National Ballet spokesman Jim Fletcher, "Some of the dancers have been away on holiday and look more like lobsters than swans."[31]

Then there was a report on a reversal in the fashion of tanning. According to surveys by the American Academy of Dermatology, 84.5 percent of people under age 25, polled at the start of the 2002 tanning season, said they looked better with a tan, up from 61 percent in 1996. "Oh yeah, teenage tanning is back," said Atoosa Rubenstein, editor in chief of *Cosmo Girl* magazine. "We're seeing the beginning of the trend now, and it's only going to get bigger." Her explanation for the trend, echoed by dermatologists with adolescent patients, was the influence of bronzed pop stars like Britney Spears and Christina Aguilera, combined with "a current wave of nut-brown fashion models who have supplanted pallid beauties of the 90s...." Dr. Darrell Rigel, professor of dermatology at New York University. said. "I'm definitely seeing more teenagers interested in tan and being tan than I used to. If you look at fashion magazines, from the mid–80s to the mid–90s, less tan people were fashionable. In the last few years, you see the tan look coming back. That's what made the difference."[32]

Journalist Deborah Netburn, reporting on that supposed trend toward more tanning, said a decade earlier warnings from dermatologist on the perils of sun exposure seemed to have an effect, dampening the interest in tanning among girls and young women, "But now the old obsession is back with a vengeance." Molly Nover, beauty director of *Cosmo Girl*, aimed at teens, traced the new obsession to a shift in fashion a few seasons earlier. According to Nover it all started in 2000, when the models in the Chanel and Valentino and Guess ads that year were all well tanned. At the spring fashion shows in 2002, designers were putting a combination of baby oil and bronzers on the models, to create a tanned look. Rubenstein, in explaining this supposed new trend, emphasized the influence of pop stars as role models, "Britney and Christina are 90 percent responsible for this trend. Britney is really tan and she dresses to accentuate that tan. She is No. 1 on every guy's list, and even if girls can't dance like her or don't have a body like hers, at least they can be as tan as she is." When Aguilera was being photographed for the cover of *Cosmo Girl*, said Rubenstein, her first request to the makeup artist was "Make me four shades darker." Debbie Then, a psychologist who worked with teens in Los Angeles remarked, "We can never underestimate the importance that girls and women place on their looks and their appearance, especially with regard to the opposite sex." She added, "It is not that they are vain or conceited; they are realistic in the way they are reacting to societal pressures." Dr. Mark Taylor, associate professor of dermatology at the University of Oklahoma Health Sciences Center, observed, "This is a battle of attitudes. Pick up any fashion magazine and you'll see beautiful people with dark tans. Young girls look at them and try to emulate them because this is what is attractive to the opposite sex."[33]

The idea that tanning was making a comeback, at least among young females, provoked an editorial from the *New York Times*, which first pointed to a study in the journal *Pediatrics*, which found that most teens did not use sunscreens and that girls were more likely than boys to sunburn. With respect to a celebrity-fueled tanning trend the editor advised, "But celebrities rarely disclose the gap between illusion and reality by telling readers that their picture-perfect tans come from cosmetics." A change in attitude was necessary, starting with public education, asserted the editor, "As role models, singers and actresses are in a position to urge young women to use sunscreen and enjoy the sun in moderation without risking their health." The idea that tanning was making a comeback did not reappear in the media after Netburn's piece, which perhaps indicated this had been about a reporter searching for a unique slant to a story rather than pointing to a real trend.[34]

A little more evidence that tans might be making a fashion comeback (albeit mostly of the sunless variety) surfaced at the time of the motion picture Academy Awards in 2004. Best-actress winner Charlize Theron was said to have got most of her tan the old-fashioned way, during a 10-day trip to Brazil. But she still opted for a color boost in the hours before the Awards ceremony from makeup artist Shane Paish, who used a tanning cream to make her face match her body, he explained. Then, he dusted her body with Terra Bella Bronzing Powder by Christian Dior ($33). "I wanted to give her a '30s-esque look," said Paish. Actor Naomi Watts also received a pre-show dusting with Dior powder, according to the Dior people. Reportedly that was also how Jennifer Garner, Lucy Ciu, Kirsten Dunst and Hilary Swank maintained their glow. Jennifer Lopez had a supply of Dior Bronze Instant Glow Self Tanner ($26) to keep her tan deep.[35]

As the tan held sway as desirable in the post-war period, at least from the mid–1940s through the 1970s or so, it was accompanied by two parallel developments, each of which was designed to remove the sun itself from the suntan process. Of course, it was all perfectly sensible since the sun was unreliable and capricious; sometimes it was there, sometimes it was not. Sometimes it was too ferocious for anyone to be basking in its rays. Sometimes it rained all weekend. In much of America the sun was gone all winter, at least in the sense of being an effective tanning agent. And tanning took time, lots of time. A person had to lie in the sun for hours, and hours. Wasn't there a better way? There was, actually there were two of them. The sunlamp limped along and seemed likely to disappear but then returned with a vengeance around 1978, reinvented as the tanning salon, or tanning parlor. Method two was the cream you rubbed on, the pill you swallowed, or the stuff you sprayed on that produced a tan without the sun.

12

The No-Sun Suntan:
1946–2004

"[In] six minutes a week you can look as if you just stepped off the beach at Acapulco."
                                    Alice Sutherland, 1979

"Young, carefree and hooked on sunlamps."
                                    Deborah Netburn, 2002

"Science is on the threshold of introducing packaged suntan — a tiny pill you'll pop into your mouth..."
                                    Harry Kursh, 1956

"You take a pill. You get a tan. Welcome to the 1980s."
                                    Louise Fenner, 1982

When Westinghouse Electric Corporation moved its 350 employees into its new Chicago offices in the spring of 1951, one "first" that it claimed for the new office was for the artificial sunlight that the workers basked in each day. A total of 220 fluorescent sun lamps had been installed to cover all work areas. During an eight-hour day, an employee reportedly got the equivalent of 15 minutes of sunshine. Sunlamps in private offices could produce a tan in less time, if the executive chose to adjust them.

"After the first few weeks under the sun lamps, most employees had good tans, and one or two looked as if they got too much sun at one time," commented reporter Don Baker. Two or three employees preferred to have the lamps above their desks turned off, and one bald worker wore a skullcap. Westinghouse said the cost of operating one 40-watt sun lamp for a year was little more than a dollar, which it regarded as "cheap insurance against winter absenteeism caused by the common cold." Baker thought Westinghouse was the first sizable office to offer suntans to its employees on a year-round basis, but other large firms— U.S. Gypsum among them — were reported to be planning similar facilities. However, the fad for UV lighting in plants and offices had actually peaked back in the 1920s and 1930s and had largely disappeared from the scene by 1950. Westinghouse was simply very late in following that trend, and no other firms followed its lead. That fad disappeared because, of course, it did nothing to increase worker productivity—from reduced absenteeism or from some general energizing effect—and that is why the few companies that utilized UV light in their facilities had turned to it.[1]

Home sunlamps continued on at a steady, if unspectacular pace. Little attention was paid to them until 1977, when the U.S. Food and Drug Administration (FDA) proposed safety standards for the estimated one million sunlamps sold annually in the U.S. Proposed standards for the machines, then slated to go into effect in 1978, included that sunlamps be sold with protective eyewear and that timers be incorporated into the lamps to turn them off after 10 minutes. According to FDA Commissioner Donald Kennedy, about 10,000 sunlamp injuries requiring emergency room treatment were reported in 1974; that figure increased to 12,000 in 1975. Kennedy explained that many of the injuries occurred because people fell asleep under sunlamps that did not shut off automatically, resulting in sunburn and eye injuries. "If the [proposed] standard does not significantly reduce injuries, we will seek other means to protect the public, including the possibility of restricting sales of these products to prescription use only," warned Kennedy. As well, the new rules would modify sunlamp bulbs so they fit only into sockets with timers, preventing use in conventional sockets. Sunlamps would additionally be required to include a warning "clearly visible during use," saying ultraviolet radiation could lead to premature aging of the skin and skin cancer. Lastly, the agency wanted to ban the sale of sunlamps emitting certain short waves of ultraviolet radiation [UVB] that are "particularly dangerous and not necessary for tanning."[2]

Before the FDA got very far, a new fad had struck in 1978. Late in that year, reporter Diane Weathers in *Newsweek* related that the latest rage was tanning salons, like the Plan-A-Tan Salon in Orange, California, which had three-foot cubicles rigged with ultraviolet lamps and reflective wallpaper. One of its customers, Alice Sutherland (who set her timer for 90 seconds), said, "If you don't have the time to get a natural tan, this is the next best thing. For six minutes a week you can look as if you just stepped off the beach at Acapulco." Enthused Weathers, "It's the newest way to fool Mother Nature — the indoor tanning spa that provides a quick, convenient way to keep a tan all year round." Reportedly, it all started when Tantriffic opened in 1978 in Searcy, Arkansas, and signed up 500 customers in the first four months. By December 1979 there were Tantriffic franchises in 81 locations with 3,000 more outlets projected. Its major rival was Plan-A-Tan with nine outlets in the U.S. and Canada. Plan-A-Tan founder Jim Crabtree predicted that in five years every shopping center would have a tanning salon. With names like the Sun Spot, the Solarium, and the Endless Summer Tanning Salon, many operations were outfitted with beach chairs and thatched-hut motifs. Customers paid from $35 to $50 for 15 visits, each of them lasting from one to 15 minutes.[3]

Salons arrived around the same time as the concept of "sun as killer" was peaking, at a time when the perils of sun exposure were taking center stage. Thus, medical experts warned that the quickie tanning treatments were rife with hidden costs. Excessive exposure to UV light, said the doctors, encouraged premature aging, stimulated hereditary skin diseases, damaged unprotected eyes and was the major cause of skin cancer. "With what medical science already knows about the skin's reaction to ultraviolet rays, walking into one of those tanning booths once a week is a dumb thing to do," said Dr. John Epstein of the University of California at San Francisco Medical Center. Most salon devotees, said Weathers, "Come out of sheer vanity. They insist that a coppery hue makes them healthy looking and that a tan out of season is a mark of affluence."

Barbara Cohen, a customer of the Caribbean Sun Indoor Family Tanning Centers in Atlanta, remarked, "It's only $2 a visit. That's a whole lot cheaper than Florida." Salon owners maintained that tanning parlors were safe because they set time limits on sessions and screened out easy burners with medical questionnaires. However, health and government officials were not convinced. Already the FDA had received complaints from patrons who had been overexposed at salons. The agency was then pressing tanning centers to adopt stricter controls and to warn customers of the potential hazards. At the time, the California Board of Cosmetology was investigating its state's tanning businesses. Tanning salon customer Robert Duncan, manager of a fast-food restaurant in Costa Mesa, California, rationalized his visits by declaring, "Something is going to get all of us one day, so why worry about it? If tanning is going to kill me at least I'll be a good-looking corpse."[4]

Six weeks later *Time* magazine reported on the hot new fad and that at least a dozen outfits with names such as Tantalize, Tantrific Sun, and Tan Four Seasons had opened scores of the "indoor bronzeries" in the previous 12 months. According to this account the idea was born in August 1978 in Searcy (population 11,000) when three entrepreneurs converted half of an old house into the first tanning clinic. After word got around, other entrepreneurs picked up on the idea and investor money began to flow. Despite their 300 days of sunshine a year, Californians were particularly taken by the fad; one Plan-A-Tan salon in Orange enrolled 2,100 members in its first six months of operation. Franchises for Plan-A-Tan then cost up to $35,000 with the franchisor providing the equipment and the décor, which *Time* described as "often early Gilligan's Island: rattan and white wicker furniture, palm trees, sometimes thatched roofs on the tanning 'huts.'" Operators were said to charge customers $35 and up for a series of 20 visits, and $125 or more for a year's unlimited tanning. A few offered life memberships for $500. Tanning salon profit potential was said to be high because the overhead was low and there was no product cost.[5]

Time went on to describe a typical stand-up booth in a salon as being about three feet square and lined with reflectors and Westinghouse UV lamps of varying lengths that looked like fluorescent lights but emitted an average total of 580 watts of long- and medium-frequency UV rays. Doctors had long used such lamps to treat serious skin conditions, said the account; tanning spa operators had merely put them in tanning booths. One minute under the lamps was said to equal an hour in the summer sun. Salon operators reportedly provided eye goggles and took some precautions to see that patrons did not get burned. Customers filled out cards describing their sensitivity to the sun; people with obvious skin problems, such as psoriasis, were supposedly turned away. Booths had timers that turned off the lamps after a set period, usually one to five minutes. As of May 1980, the FDA was to require tanning clinics to post warnings of the hazards of UV exposure.[6]

That FDA standard was first proposed prior to the existence of any tanning salons. Regulations adopted finally by the FDA applied to both sunlamps bought for home use and the devices used in tanning spas. Standards adopted included that each lamp had to have a timer that automatically turned the lamp off after 10 minutes of operation; each lamp had to also have a manual switch so the user could turn the lamp off at will; sunlamp bulbs had to have a special base so they could not be used in an ordinary light socket. Additionally, there had to be a warning label on the sunlamp fixture that said "Danger — Ultraviolet radiation" with directions to follow instructions and a caution that overexposure could cause eye injury and sunburn, with the possibility that repeated exposure could cause premature aging of the skin and, ultimately, skin cancer. That label also had to state the minimum safe distance between lamp and user, the maximum safe exposure time, and a warning about the necessity of wearing protective goggles. It was estimated that the special requirements established by the FDA applying to sunlamps manufactured after May 6, 1980, would add $14 to the cost of each sunlamp. The FDA pointed out that tanning booths were potentially more hazardous than were home-use sunlamps because of the greater intensity of UV radiation in the booths. As of April 1980, it was estimated that there were about 1,000 tanning salons around America.[7]

A little later, in 1980, *Consumer Reports* said that the 1,000 or so existing salons that had sprung up charged $2 to $5 per visit, and patrons typically took a "course" of 10 to 20 progressively longer exposures from 30 seconds to 15 minutes. "Daily visits are encouraged in the beginning, followed by weekly maintenance visits to help you keep 'that healthy, sexy glow all year round,'" explained the story. Most tanning booths were said to use standard fluorescent ultraviolet bulbs that emitted burning UV rays, but increasing numbers of booths were beginning to use bulbs that emitted mainly the longer-wave UVA or tanning rays. UVA rays, said *Consumer Reports*, did not burn as much as UVB, and much longer tanning times were required — from 15 minutes to two hours or more.[8]

New York State Attorney General Robert Abrams announced in August 1980 that he had reached an agreement with several tanning parlors in New York City, requiring them to post warnings of possible health hazards on their premises. Patrons of the parlors were to be made aware that hazards accompanied the use of sunlamps, explained Abrams. Since there was no statute regulating tanning spas on the books, those parlors had probably agreed after some "moral suasion," since they could envision harsher measures coming in legislation if they had declined to be persuaded by Abrams.[9]

More bad publicity was directed at the salons at the start of 1981. Scientists from the National Aeronautics and Space Administration conducted a study and concluded that people in indoor tanning booths might be exposed to two times more "cancer-inducing ultraviolet radiation" than was found in natural sunlight. From the study it was determined that inexpensive radiation meters used in such booths could seriously underestimate exposure, resulting in more severe burns and greater long-term radiation hazards than operators and users might expect. According to the findings, the amount of UV radiation was 30 percent greater when the bulb was first turned on than after it had been burning for 10 hours. Researchers also concluded that radiation exposure in tanning booths could be highly uneven, with the user getting "fried" on one side while other parts of the body might be only minimally affected. According to the American Medical Association, tanning salons were then opening at a rate of 10 a week.[10]

By the spring of 1981, the glow had faded from the industry. "It was too much blue sky," said Fred Tippen, president of Wonder Tan, an Atlanta-based company, when asked what happened to all those tanning parlors. "Everybody thought it was easy money." In the very beginning, a franchise fee of from $7,000 to $30,000 seemed to be about the only cost to enter the initially booming industry, with profits quickly piling up. But, said the *New York Times*, by the spring of 1981, there had been an abrupt and sustained shakeout in the industry. "There's a sense that we had our fun and now we're through," worried Cindy Street, president of the National Association of Sun Tanning. While Street and others in the industry were still convinced there "are good monetary reasons to be in the tanning business," she also admitted, "we are not the next Colonel Sanders."[11]

Commenting on the factors leading to the decline, William Richey, president of both Sun Tan, and the International Tanning Manufacturers Association, said, "people got the impression that you could make" tanning booths "out of anything; all fluorescent fixtures were safe; anything you built would work; people were putting them together in their garage." When dermatologists began to urge the FDA to take notice of the problem, the industry, collectively, did not take much notice. "Today we are cooperating 100 percent" with the government, said Ritchie, which had since ruled that tanning equipment was covered by its "medical devices" regulations and had to carry appropriate warning labels. Also, explained Ritchie, there was the problem of summer. That is, the business proved to be seasonal. Thus, most operations were incapable of sustaining themselves unless they were run "parasitically" as part of a racquet club, beauty shop, and so on. Tanning parlors did not do very well as stand-alone businesses.[12]

Grady Mason, the former president of Tantriffic, the Arkansas company that was the first to franchise tanning parlors, remembered the dream of big money in the beginning. When he and his associates decided to begin franchising, they didn't even have a sales force, recalling, "All we did was get a couple of suites in the Holiday Inn in Memphis." He said, "In three days we sold a quarter of a million in franchises; people were waiting in the hall for a chance to talk to us. As of spring 1981, Mason sold real estate for a living. Tantriffic, which once had 100 operating franchises, and commitments for 100 more, was then bankrupt. Fourteen of the 15 other companies that had at one time been franchising tanning salons also reportedly shut down. Only Richey's Sum Tan still sold complete turnkey outlets, and most of them were then purchased by beauty parlors, health clubs, and so on, as add-ons to existing businesses. Nobody in the industry was sure how many tanning parlors still existed in the U.S., including Street, whose organization sold the only newsletter that dealt with the industry. Street added that she was confident the industry would soon be thriving again. "It's settling down now," she said. "The tanning idea is still a good concept." Richey agreed, saying he felt tanning devices "fit in with the American way of doing things." When asked why he explained, "Face it, this is a vain society. People want to tan. The public will always want a tan."[13]

Not long after the ink dried on the reports of their decline or even demise, reports surfaced that they had returned, as hot as ever, as strong as ever. They were a fad and a craze once more, according to reporter Richard Zoglin, writing in *Time* magazine in 1985. First, though, he mentioned the character Zonker Harris, tanner extraordinaire in the popular comic strip "Doonesbury." To prepare for big tanning competitions like the George Hamilton Cocoa Butter Open, Zonker spent hours under the sun with an old-fashioned reflector. Martin Rothschild, president of Rothschild Sunsystems in Albany, New York, remarked that the ordinary person who could not afford a vacation could get a lasting tan for a fraction of the money. "It used to be just movie stars and captains of industry who looked good. Now a lot of ordinary people are beautiful too." According to Zoglin, while no precise figures were available, tanning centers were sprouting up all over and taking in an estimated $300 million a year. At one of the trendiest of the outlets, Hollywood's Uvasun, such celebrities as Liza Minelli, Rod Stewart, Mariel Hemingway and even George Hamilton, spent upwards of $30 an hour to maintain their tanned looks. Less exclusive outlets charged between $3 and $15 for 30 minutes in the artificial sunlight.[14]

Zoglin reported that indoor tanning was becoming a year-round activity. "I used to call in to work sick so that I could lie out in the sun," said Lola Lanza of Houston, Texas. "Now I can just come here on my lunch hour." Jeannie Frazier, who spent $60 a month at tanning spas to cultivate her tan, felt a salon tan "is better than the sun. You don't get hot, and you don't get sand all over." As to why the centers had become a hot craze again — although Zoglin did not mention the initial craze from around 1978 to 1981 — he felt it was due to an advance in technology. New tanning machines at the outlets reportedly blocked out most of the sunburn-linked UVB rays in favor of UVA, which promoted a more gradual tan. The most popular commercial tanning device then was a clamshell-like tanning bed. A customer lay down on a plexiglass surface, closed the lid and relaxed as lights from above and below "baked him to a golden brown." However, Zoglin then pointed out that while UVA was less likely to cause an immediate sunburn, doctors warned it could produce the same bad effects, such as aging of the skin and the risk of skin cancer. "There is no such thing as a safe tan," declared Darrell Rigel, a dermatologist who taught at New York University's School of Medicine. Rob Bernstein, who spent 30 minutes each workday at a tanning salon in Dallas, enthused, "I think a year-round tan is a good, successful, power look. It's just a part of good grooming." And, in the dead of winter a tan implied that the wearer had the money and leisure to travel. Explained Jeff Russell, of Evanston, Illinois, "It's a conversation piece. People are always asking, 'Where have you been?'"[15]

A few months later journalist William Schmidt also wrote about the new fad. But, like Zoglin, Schmidt was also short of numbers. According to him the trend had even spread to rural areas and to areas in the South, where the mostly plentiful, year-round sunshine and warmth might have been expected to blunt any growth in the tanning industry. Greater Tusca-loosa, Alabama, reportedly had eight tanning centers; one charged $10 for a 15-minute session; another advertised eight visits for $25. One of the eight centers, Cherry Miller's Tanning Salon, had three tanning beds and was open six days a week from 7:30 A.M. to 9 P.M. Even though it was the end of May, most of Miller's time slots were said to be booked.[16]

By later in the 1980s, a growing number of problems were reported with tanning centers, including eye injuries, as some of the outlets ignored FDA standards. Two 16 year olds tanned for 45 minutes straight without supervision and without goggles at the Jack LaLanne Health Spa in New York. A spokesman for the club said patrons who used the tanning booths were not given goggles and that the lamps stayed on constantly. Said a reporter, "Tanning salons are unregulated and unlicensed in most states, including New York, and they do not always warn patrons of the health risks involved in artificial tanning. Nor do they always follow safety pro-cedures recommended by the Food and Drug Administration." Under a 1980 regulation, the FDA required sunlamp manufacturers to provide con-sumers with timing devices, warning labels, safe exposure schedules and goggles. But, once the lamps were bought by salon operators, the agency had no authority over their use under current law unless they were tam-pered with or falsely advertised, according to Robert T. Handren, Jr., deputy director of the FDA Center for Devices and Radiological Control, which oversaw tanning regulation.[17]

Another problem, explained Handren, was that the FDA lacked the manpower to police the growing number of tanning centers in the U.S. Instead it was encouraging local governments to pass regulations. That lack of government control, added Handren, had tempted some salon own-ers to remove warning labels and circumvent automatic timers so that people could tan for longer periods than recommended by the agency. In some cases it came to the attention of the FDA that people had been allowed to tan without goggles or had been told the goggles were unnecessary — "a dangerous falsehood since ultraviolet radiation passes through closed eyelids," said Handren. According to an agency spokesman in Washington D.C., 350 warnings were issued nationwide in 1986 to tanning salons not complying with regulations. There were then an estimated 15,000 centers in America. New York City health officials had responded to an increasing number of complaints about skin and eye injuries from tanning machines by announcing they were in the process of drafting an ordinance that would license and regulate such places.[18]

In 1986 the FDA went so far as to close one of the centers that had received warnings. At Midnight Sun, a Manhattan salon, the agency confiscated lamps in January because an undercover investigator discovered that operators were telling patrons that goggles were unnecessary, which was considered to be false advertising of the machine. Several lamps there were also found to have been rewired to bypass automatic timers so that salon operators could control them from a front desk. Midnight Sun corrected the problems and was back in business later in 1986.[19]

One 1988 estimate put the number of tanning centers in America at 18,000 salons, many of them parts of existing businesses such as health clubs. Dr. Stephen Katz, chief of dermatology at the National Cancer Institute, declared, "These things are hazardous." Based on a survey of 62 hospitals, the Consumer Product Safety Commission estimated that there were 1,781 hospital emergency room visits nationwide in 1987 for injuries related to tanning booths. Despite such dangers, Ohio was the only state that then regulated the tanning industry — although several other jurisdictions were considering legislation. Most tanning center patrons were said, by reporter David Brand, to assume they were protected because the type of radiation produced in most tanning machines was largely UVA. Brand also pointed out that many medical researchers believed UVA exposure might promote skin cancer. "The presumption, based on animal studies, is that if you go into an indoor tanning salon, then go out into the sun, you increase the risk of skin cancer," explained Dr. Nicholas Lowe of UCLA.[20]

After conducting a survey of 100 tanning salons in eight states and the District of Columbia, the organization, the U.S. Public Interest Research Group, said nearly half the 183 machines in the salons they studied did not bear a federally required warning label; 45 percent of the machines did not bear the warning label the FDA had mandated that the manufacturers affix to the machines from 1980.[21]

A team of researchers, led by Jennifer Oliphant, conducted a 1994 study in the form of a self-administered questionnaire given to all students in grades 9–12 from a suburban high school in the St. Paul, Minnesota, metro area. There were 1,008 respondents— 88 percent white, 51 percent female, ages ranging from 13 to 19. It was a study designed to measure the use of commercial tanning facilities by adolescents. Overall, 34 percent of the students reported using a tanning facility; that is, 51 percent of the 511 females and 15 percent of the 469 male respondents. Most of those tanners (72 percent) reported indoor tanning infrequently (less than once a month or on special occasions). However, 28 percent of all tanners tanned at least once a month at a salon with 15 percent reporting they tanned once a week or more. Usual length of a tanning session ranged from five minutes to more than 60 minutes; the majority of tanners reported sessions lasting from 21 to 30 minutes. More than 40 percent of the tanners reported not always wearing goggles and 17 percent reported never wearing them. Approximately 16 percent of the tanners had experienced one or more eye problems, including pinkeye, eye burns, or sandy or gritty eyes. Fifty-nine percent of the tanners reported some skin injury, including burned, blistered or peeled skin and/or rashes.[22]

In Oliphant's study, tanners were asked to report the instructions and warnings they received from operators at the outlet where they tanned most frequently. More than half related they were not always told to wear goggles; more than 25 percent said they were never told to limit their time per session; half reported that they had never received a warning about the health risks of indoor tanning, and less than 50 percent had ever noticed a sign on the premises warning of the health risks of tanning. Of 314 respondent tanners, 42 percent were always told to wear goggles; 16 percent were usually told; 14 percent were told sometimes; 28 percent were never told. Of the 305 respondents who answered the question as to whether they had received warnings about the health risks of indoor tanning, 30 percent received a written warning; nine percent received a verbal warning; 11 percent received both; 50 percent received no warnings.[23]

All respondents were asked to respond to true/false statements regarding the risks of indoor tanning. Sixty-one percent knew that closing their eyes or covering them with cotton balls while tanning was not enough protection; 71 percent knew that indoor tanning was not safer than tanning in natural sunlight; 79 percent knew that indoor tanning could cause skin cancer; 77 percent were aware that damage could occur from tanning even without a sunburn. The tanners were found to be as knowledgeable as those who had never tanned indoors. In Minnesota, commercial tanning facilities were said to be readily available. For example, 33 tanning salons with a total of 150 tanning beds were located in the suburban area where students included in Oliphant's survey lived, or one tanning bed for every 1,200 students. Oliphant concluded that, of the 22 states that then regulated commercial tanning facilities, only about half required parental consent for use of commercial tanning facilities by minors, and none prohibited their use by minors. That was despite recommendations made by the American Academy of Dermatology, the American Medical Association, the Skin Cancer Foundation, the American Cancer Society, and the United States Public Interest Research Group for prohibition or severe limitations of use by minors, and adults.[24]

At Beach Bum Tanning in Manhattan in 1995, business was said to be booming. Nationally, the industry was said to generate more than $1 billion in sales annually. Rob Stein, general manager at Beach Bum, said 100 people came in to his facility on an average day for a 25-minute dose of artificial sunlight.[25]

One study published in April 2002 in the *Journal* of the National Cancer Institute suggested that users of tanning lamps were 2.5 times more likely to develop squamous-cell cancer and 1.5 times more likely to develop basal-cell cancer than people who did not use the devices. By this time, 27 states had regulations limiting teen access to tanning centers, including Ohio, Louisiana, and California. Texas passed a law in 2001 requiring adolescents aged 13 to 15 to be escorted to a salon by a parent, and those aged 16 to 17 to have a parent's written permission before attending. Typically the tanning industry — then said to be a $5 billion annual business — opposed regulations. In April 2002 Missouri legislators rejected a bill that would have required teens to have written parental consent before using tanning beds. Joe Levy, spokesman for the Indoor Tanning Association (a trade lobby group that represented 11 percent of the nation's 45,000 salons) said that about 30 percent of salon customers were women aged 20 to 30, and five percent were females aged 16 to 20, based on a 1997 survey by his group. He dismissed any link between skin cancer and tanning salon lamps by saying that many of the alleged victims were people who were tanning before 1975, "back when they were using home units which were dangerously high in UVB radiation."[26]

When Richard Palmer studied the indoor tanning facility density in 80 U.S. cities in 2002, he said the industry did $4 billion in sales annually, from approximately 50,000 tanning salons and 28 million customers. A marketing study conducted by a tanning bed manufacturer suggested that more than 70 percent of clients of commercial tanning facilities were Caucasian females between 16 and 49 years of age. Palmer argued there was a positive association between tanning bed use and cutaneous malignant melanoma (from a survey of studies). For his survey he collected data from late 1997 through early 1998 for the 80 cities. Municipalities with the greatest density of tanning facilities were as follows: Dayton, Ohio, 182,044 population (102 tanning facilities, 56.03 facility density per 100,000 population); Syracuse, New York, 163,860 (67, 40.89); Grand Rapids, Michigan, 189,126 (76, 40.18); Minneapolis, Minnesota, 368,383 (134, 36.38); Pittsburgh, 369,879 (133, 35.96); Providence, Rhode Island, 160,728 (54, 33.60); New Haven, Connecticut, 130,474 (34, 26.06); Rochester, New York, 231,636 (57, 24.61). Municipalities with the least density of tanning facilities were: Detroit, Michigan, 1,027,974 (13, 1.26); El Paso, Texas, 515,342 (6, 1.16); Los Angeles, California, 3,485,398 (39, 1.12); Honolulu, Hawaii, 365,272 (4, 1.10); New York, New York, 7,322,564 (57, 0.78).[27]

For the 80 cities in the sample, the mean number of tanning facilities was 50.33 with a range of from four (Honolulu) to 134 (Minneapolis). Palmer found that with the exception of tanning facility legislation, each predictor variable had a statistically significant association with facility density. That is, cities with a relatively high percentage of whites, a low percentage of daily sunshine, and a lower normal daily temperature had greater facility density. Cities with relatively low January temperatures, higher annual precipitation, and a low to medium household income had greater facility density. Finally, cities at higher latitudes had greater facility density.[28]

Lauren Lyster wrote a 2003 article that gave a brief history of the highlights on indoor tanning in Los Angeles. In 1981, two years after tanning centers began to open in New York, they began to appear all over Los Angeles; most of those tanning beds emitted UVB radiation. One year later Uvasun opened its first outlet, in West Hollywood, said to be one of the first salons in America to use beds that emitted mostly UVA rays. By 1989 more than 100 tanning salons were in operation in Los Angeles. Mystic Tan arrived in the city in 2001, at Uvasun. For $32 patrons stepped into a booth to be sprayed with magnetically charged tanning solution and emerged 60 seconds later with a color coating said to last from four to seven days. Another advance occurred, in June 2002, when Fred Segal Beauty in Santa Monica introduced the airbrush tan: customers were exfoliated, then sprayed with tanning solution. It was a process that took an hour, but the color was supposed to last up to two weeks.[29]

A study published in the *Journal* of the National Cancer Institute found that 51 percent of high school girls visited tanning salons at least four times in 2002. Journalist Jaime deBlanc-Knowles pointed out the dangers involved and argued that cases of basal- and squamous-cell cancers increased for people exposed at a young age to UV radiation. Tanning beds posed a particular risk, said Margaret Kargas, associate director of the Center for Environmental Health Sciences at Dartmouth Medical School "because [they] mimic sunlight and provide such an intense, concentrated dose of ultraviolet rays." States were still imposing legislation to curtail access to tanning facilities, especially because young women were a fast-growing segment of users of such facilities. In January 2003, the Ohio state legislature passed a law requiring salons to obtain written permission from the parents of tanners under 18. New Hampshire and Connecticut had proposed similar laws but faced strong opposition from the Indoor Tanning Association. Salons commonly claimed tanning beds were a safe alternative to baking outdoors and argued that the UV rays emitted by sunlamps seldom produced a reddish sunburn. Yet, said the American Academy of Dermatology, tanning devices emitted almost three times the intensity of natural sunlight. Tanners, said deBlanc-Knowles, seemed convinced that establishing a "base tan" would protect them from sunburn, an idea dismissed as myth by dermatologists. A study published in the *American Journal of Epidemiology* found that young women who tanned in salons at least 10 times a year had seven times the melanoma rate as did non-users of the centers. Such findings outraged the American Medical Association, which favored a complete ban on commercial tanning. One young woman who used tanning salons said, with a typical lack of concern, "Everything is bad for you these days, so why not?"[30]

Barry Zale, whose name adorned a jewelry store in many of the nation's malls (he was heir to his family's billion-dollar retailing empire, which included jewelry stores in Europe and Australia), turned his attention to tanning parlors in 2004. He and his wife Cindy owned the Southern Nevada franchise for Dallas-based Palm Beach Tan. Said Zale, "We're going to take tanning salons from a mom-and-pop business to the superstore concept." There were then nearly 40 company-owned Palm Beach Tan stores in Dallas and six franchises in America. Zale's superstores were envisioned to contain 20–25 tanning beds whereas most strip mall tanning salons at the time typically had only five or six beds. His company also owned the rights to Mystic Tan, an ultraviolet-free system that provided a spray-on tan. It was Zale's hope to open some 20 stores in the Las Vegas area over the coming three years. He estimated that 75 percent of his customers were women between the ages of 18 and 45. Palm Beach Tan stores were open 24 hours a day, seven days a week and, explained an account, "The company's employees are skin-care certified and members of the International Tanning Association. They've mastered the art of moisturization, understand the effects of UV light and have comprehensive knowledge of all skin types, the company says."[31]

Another relative newcomer to the industry was Planet Beach, described as one of the fastest growing tanning salon franchises in the country. CEO

Stephen Smith opened the first one in New Orleans in 1995 and awarded the first franchise in 1996. By early in 2004 there were about 203 Planet Beach outlets in the U.S., Canada, and Australia, with another 275 locations in various stages of development. Company spokeswoman Toni Marie Vinterella said the main change in the indoor tanning industry had been employee and consumer education. "Back in the old days, they'd stick you in a bed, turn on the timer for 30 minutes and not care whether you burned or not," she explained. "Now all our employees have to complete course work so they can inform the customer what lotions to use, how long to stay in the bed based on skin lightness and the positives and negatives of UV light. We never say it's safe." Dermatologists continued to lobby hard against them. Eric Finley, section head of dermatological surgery at the Ochsner Clinic Foundation in New Orleans, called tanning salons "absolutely terrible" and said there was no such thing as a healthy tan. According to the Centers for Disease Control and Prevention, an estimated 700 hospital emergency department visits per year were related to tanning salon exposure."[32]

Popularity of the tanning salons showed a strong increase in the years around the Millennium. According to the American Academy of Dermatology, whose position was that children should not be allowed to use indoor tanning facilities, the use of tanning salons by people under 25 more than tripled between 1996 and 2003. Reporter Jane Schwanke observed that people using tanning devices had 2.5 times the risk of developing squamous-cell cancer than those who did not use the salons, and 1.5 times the risk of developing basal-cell cancer. A 2003 survey of 6,903 non–Hispanic white adolescents, aged 13 to 19, revealed that 36.8 percent of the females had used the parlors at least once, as had 11.2 percent of the males. Also discovered was that 47 percent of the 18 to 19 year olds had been to an indoor parlor at least three times. Another study, of college students, determined that half the respondents were indoor tanners and 98 percent of the tanners were aware of the inherent dangers. By 2004 the indoor tanning industry was estimated to be generating revenues of around $5 billion annually.[33]

California was one of 27 states that had passed legislation requiring minors to have permission from a parent or guardian to use tanning beds or booths (as of mid–2004). Customers under the age of 18 were said to make up about 12 percent of tanning spa clients. Jeff Nedelman, spokesman for the Indoor Tanning Association, said there had been a renewed assault on the industry by legislators in 2004. The spray-on tan, introduced in popular form in 2000, had lured in customers once wary of tanning salons, parlor owners declared. The spray-on method was generally endorsed by dermatologists, who had been putting increasing pressure on the ultraviolet tanning industry as the salons attracted more and more teenage clients. Nedelman predicted that Americans would make 28 million visits to tanning spas in 2004. According to the trade publication *Looking Fit*, more than 2,500 stand-up spray-on units would be in place by the end of 2004, a growth of 200 percent over the previous four years. By contrast, there were about 25,000 salons in the U.S. that offered UV tanning, some with just one bed or booth but others with as many as 30 or more devices. Tony Passarello, chief marketing officer for Palm Beach Tan (then with 67 locations) said the spray-on tan was growing faster than anyone had expected. Palm Beach Tan outlets averaged 20–25 ultraviolet beds, and then included up to four spray-on booths.[34]

The U.S. Federal Department of Health and Human Services added, in 2002, ultraviolet light to its list of human carcinogens. UV tanning took place in tanning beds or booths (the client lay down or stood up) sandwiched by UV light (behind plexiglass). A base tan required four to six sessions with the cost in New York City varying from $10 to $60 a session. The spray-on tan was a liquid solution that typically combined aloe vera, a bronzer, and dihydroxyacetone, or DHA, a chemical that interacted with the skin to produce a brown color over several hours. Treatment costs ranged from $30 for spraying in a stand-up booth, to $150 for a professionally hand-applied tan.[35]

Wondering why people did not listen to the warnings about the risks of sunlight, a group of researchers, writing in the *Journal of the American Academy of Dermatology*, reported they sought out volunteers who regularly went to tanning salons and invited them to use tanning beds at no charge over a period of six weeks. Fourteen volunteers — 13 women and one man — came in twice a week and were directed to one of two seemingly identical tanning beds. But one of the beds was equipped with a UV filter and the other wasn't. When the volunteers were given mood assessments after the experiment, those who had not been shielded from the UV light consistently seemed to be more content and more relaxed. And when the group was given the opportunity to come in on a post-experiment day and select one bed or the other, 11 of the 12 who showed up headed straight for the bed that provided UV light. Researcher Dr. Steven R. Feldman, professor of dermatology at Wake Forest University Baptist Medical Center in Winston-Salem, North Carolina, commented, "They're lying out on their backs and they're saying, 'Ah, this feels good.' These people are getting their little hit of UV."[36]

Legislative efforts to strengthen regulation of the tanning industry continued and in January 2005 at least 29 states had some form of regulation, and more were in the works. A major aim of the newer laws was to limit the use of indoor tanning facilities by young teens, or even to ban them from the spas altogether. Reportedly the industry was adding some 1,000 new customers every month and was projected to grow to the point where it produced $7.5 billion in revenue annually, over the coming three to five years. A tougher law went into effect on January 1, 2005, in California that prohibited minors under the age of 14 from using tanning salons and required written parental permission for anyone aged 14 to 17. A recent North Carolina statute prohibited people 13 and younger from using tanning facilities without a prescription from a doctor specifying a medical condition, such as psoriasis, which required treatment with UV exposure. New Hampshire required tanners under 18 to have parental consent and those under 14 to have a written order from a physician.[37]

Going one step further were the preparations that claimed to produce a tan on the user without benefit of sunlight, either natural or artificial. Such concoctions reached their peak in the post World War II years, but they were not entirely absent before that time. A 1912 account in the *Los Angeles Times* related, "Of recent years more than one patent wash, guaranteed to produce a permanent tan, has been put on the market." Cheapest of the lot was said to be a chemical, permanganate of potash, which was used simply by diluting it and applying it to the skin. Some two years earlier, in 1910 at a chemists' convention, a Los Angeles chemist declared that judging from the way his sales of permanganatic went up in the summer, a considerable portion of the August tan in his district "came out of the bottles."[38]

In 1923 the same newspaper reported that enterprising beauty parlors were showing every shade of tan in face powder with the result that it was no longer necessary to lie on the beach in the sun for hours to get a tan. "Some there are who contend that a woman with creamy skin, untouched by the sun, protected by harem veil or sunshade when she stirs abroad, is all the more alluring," went the account. "But the younger generation disputes this edict."[39]

When reporter J. C. Furnas wrote about suntanning fashion in the *Saturday Evening Post* in 1948, he mentioned that bathing beaches, suntan preparations and dark glasses were all commercial propositions that owed their success to the sun cult. But one "crying need" was still to be satisfied. And a fortune awaited the person who invented a harmless substance to dye people the color of cigarette tobacco all over. "Diluted walnut juice and potassium permanganate, sometimes satisfactory, wears away in a week or ten days," grumbled Furnas. Yet he was convinced that somewhere in nature the answer probably existed, and the market was ready because, "It takes time and bother to acquire a real tan. More people than care to admit it consider the sunning process irksome and dull."[40]

Those who tanned poorly, or not at all, had their hopes raised in 1956 by an announcement that there was, perhaps, a pill that could make sensitive skin darken quickly to a "gratifying bronze" under the sun's rays. Developed by Dr. Thomas B. Fitzpatrick, and two other scientists at the University of Oregon Medical School, the pill contained 8-methoxypsoralen (8-mop for short), which stimulated the body's natural production of melanin, the pigment that formed the tan. Note that this pill supposedly worked, in some vague fashion, in conjunction with the sun. When the doctor accidentally stumbled on that effect of the drug, while doing other research with it, he went on to test it for tanning on healthy volunteers, including 41 fair-skinned inmates of Arizona State Prison. More testing was needed but Fitzpatrick hoped that in two to three years (based of his encouraging early results) a pill a day would banish painful sunburns from the beaches.[41]

By the time media reports about 8-mop began to appear in mid–1956 the drug had been used in preliminary testing on about 100 persons over the previous three years. Science reporter Ray Shrick declared, of that testing, "striking results" of tanning had shown up in people who had never tanned. Large-scale tests that were to involve 2,000 volunteers were then said to be in the planning stage, thanks to a $72,000 grant from the U.S. Public Health Service. According to Shrick, 8-mop worked internally to build up a person's natural defenses against sunburn with the drug speeding up the normal process of getting a tan. The skin went through a period of mild reddening, then tanned at a rate several times faster than normal. Some physicians reportedly were already prescribing 8-mop for sun protection; the drug had been on the market for treating other conditions. Said a man closely associated with the tests, "It's phenomenal. You wouldn't believe it to see these people — even redheads— go out of here all white one week and come back the next with a deep rich tan." Those 8-mop pills cost 15 cents each. Convicts involved in the early tests were chosen for their fair skin, and had no sun on their backs in the previous six months. They were paid $5 a day for sunning on the prison baseball diamond.[42]

Another of the many laudatory, uncritically accepting articles about 8-mop at that time was one by Harry Kursh in the *American Mercury*. He enthused, "Science is on the threshold of introducing packaged suntan — a tiny pill you'll pop into your mouth before heading for open sunshine." Kursh went on to conclude, "and that agonizing pre-tan burn, or that laborious process of careful, gradual exposure in the sun, may be eliminated entirely."[43]

Another who sang the praises of 8-mop was science reporter Wesley Griswold who declared, "It appears likely that a fine mahogany hue for all, except a wretched few who are truly allergic to sunshine, may be obtained in as short a time as three days."[44]

At the end of 1956 a warning against the indiscriminate use of the newly developed pills taken to promote quick suntanning was issued at a meeting of the American Academy of Dermatology. Dr. Norman B. Kanof of New York University Post Graduate Medical School said the pills might induce skin cancer in susceptible persons. Kanof reported that some patients were asking for the pills to perpetuate a so-called "banker's tan" acquired during short winter vacations in the South.[45]

When Dr. S. W. Becker of the University of Illinois addressed the American Academy of Dermatology at the end of 1958, he said that the highly publicized suntan pills not only protected against sunburn and increased tanning, but were helpful in fighting eczema, vitiligo (white spots) and psoriasis. According to Becker the chemicals in those pills acted as photosensitizers. When taken by mouth the patient became more sensitive to sunlight for about eight hours. If the skin was exposed to a small amount of sunlight at that time, the horny (top) layer of the skin thickened. After about two weeks of daily exposure, the horny layer became quite thick and provided a filter that protected the skin against sunburn and at the same time produced a good tan. Despite such praise, the 8-mop pills promptly disappeared, at least as tanning agents.[46]

Even more attention was focused on the next development in the no-sun suntan. Advertising claims for what pharmacists across the U.S. termed "the hottest thing in the drug trade" were being investigated in the spring of 1960 by the National Better Business Bureau. But manufacturers of the products in question — alleged to tan the human body without exposure to UV light — were confidently going ahead with major promotional efforts. The original, and most widely advertised of the bottled suntans was Man-Tan, made by Drug Research Corporation of New York. It was introduced in September 1959 as the "after-shave lotion that tans you without the sun." Drug Research also made its sibling, Positan. According to the advertising trade publication *Printers' Ink* the tanning ingredient of Man-Tan and its counterparts was dihydroxyacetone. Reportedly the makers had conducted exhaustive laboratory tests on humans that had shown Man-Tan to be safe on all types of human skin. Reference to the safety tests were featured in the product's advertising, which also guaranteed a "golden tan the very first day you use Man-Tan or pay nothing!" Commercials were before and after dramatizations.

Ad agency account executive George Bailey declared that the first half of a spot was filmed on a Friday before the model had used the product; the second half was shot on a Monday, after the model had used Man-Tan over the weekend. Bailey insisted no type of makeup was used in the shooting of the ads. A color ad in *Look* on March 15, 1960, for Man-Tan contained the following statement, "Sworn affidavits from model and photographer prove these fotos were taken without special lighting, makeup or retouching. The 'after' foto shows the actual result of using Man-Tan." Positan, then being sold in Florida, was essentially the same as Man-Tan except that it contained a sunburn preventative.[47]

A complaint against Man-Tan and Positan, however, was issued by the Post Office on December 29, 1959, stating that a mail-order promotion for the products was fraudulent. According to Bailey, the complaint referred to a mail-order testing the previous spring, and subsequent advertising was amended to suit the Post Office. With respect to the safety of the products, the American Medical Association (AMA) told *Printers' Ink* the maker of Man-Tan had sent the AMA a report of its animal studies, and on the basis of the evidence it had seen thus far, the AMA said the product seemed to be relatively safe for topical use. Man-Tan's first commercial rival appeared in variety store chains and in a few drug stores, around February 1960 — Magic Tan (manufactured by Leonet Corporation, a subsidiary of Welded Plastics, New York). It sold for 98 cents, compared to $3 for Man-Tan. A second competitor, Tano-Rama, had been out only for a couple of weeks but had already been heavily advertised on New York radio and television. It sold for $1.75.[48]

For its first full year on the market, 1960, Man-Tan's ad budget was estimated at around $3 million, 60 percent of that — $1.8 million — earmarked for television. Man-Tan addressed its 60-second filmed messages primarily to men, with special attention devoted to the viewing habits of younger men. Those before and after-themed ads were said to build product appeal by following a model through the transition from "pale and pasty-faced" to "tan and terrific" as the accompanying audio described it — with less than subtle hints as to the favorable effect it would all have on women. Also, those ads emphasized the product was not a paint, stain, or makeup (it was a clear liquid), but rather an item that acted chemically on the skin's top layers to produce a tan with the qualities of a natural suntan. Shots of the model wiping his tanned face with a handkerchief that he afterwards held up to the camera, unsmudged, were designed to indicate Man-Tan's relative permanence. A caption superimposed over the ad on the screen declared, "Safe — Medically Tested."[49]

All the hype over the new suntan-from-a-bottle products caused *Newsweek* to herald, in May 1960, "a new industry: The artificial suntan."

Noted by the account was that bathroom tanning had already made inroads in the market for suntan lotions and that farmers in Kansas, lifeguards in Florida, sallow urbanites, and teen-age girls had all picked up the fad. There were then said to be at least a dozen brands on the market, from Man-Tan and Positan to Tan Tone, Rapid Tan, Magic Tan, Tan-O-Rama, Tansation, and Tanfastic. An ad for Man-Tan proclaimed "From office white to Caribbean tan in about six hours."[50]

Newsweek said the key ingredient in all the brands remained dihydroxyacetone, known for years as an obscure colorless chemical with limited uses (an antidote for cyanide poisoning, for one) and the annoying property of leaving a lasting brown stain. John Andre, president of a small New York mail-order firm, Drug Research, Inc., got the idea in 1959 that what annoyed chemists might be welcomed by the public. He added alcohol and scent to dihydroxyacetone to make an after-shave lotion he called Man-Tan and sent out mail-order feelers. That produced what Andre called a "tremendous" response, which Drug Research fed with a number of full-page magazine ads and television commercials. The company expected to sell about $15 million worth of its tanning products in 1960. Andre toned down his ads, at the request of the U.S. Post Office, eliminating, among other things, implications that Man-Tan supplied any significant amount of vitamin D, that it "tans like the sun" or that a single application was enough for a tan. (At least three applications, 20 minutes or so apart, were necessary to avoid a blotchy job.) Man-Tan was then being tested by the FDA. The company was also hopeful that consumers would learn to read the label as they applied the product, washing their hands after each application (rather than complaining about stained fingers), and applying the lotion down to their collar line. "Sometimes it's easy to tell who is wearing Man-Tan and who has a natural tan," explained Drug Research's marketing vice president Michele Mazzocco, "just by looking at the backs of their necks." All the rivals to Man-Tan then were small companies, although sizable competitors were beginning to show up. Plough's Coppertone division had just launched its own suntan in a bottle product, called Q.T.[51]

Around the same time ad trade journal *Advertising Age* also reported there were a dozen competitors in the tan-in-a-bottle field. Drug Research was then launching two new products, Miss Mantan and Super Man Tan (for a super tan, not super men) in competition with its own Man Tan, Positan and Tan Perfect. Miss Mantan was described as a moisturizing foundation and night cream with tanning properties that would "tan years off your looks in hours." Drug Research was then said to be expected to do at least $12 million in sales in 1960 on its tanning products—about 45

percent of its total business—and would spend $5 million out of a total
ad budget of $6.5 million on those tanning products. An ad for the Rol-
ley company product Tansation declared "All 'no-sun' tanning lotions in
America became obsolete. Tansation is here. Tans you fastest of them all
in or out of the sun!" Positan ads promised a "New type suntan lotion
works with or without sun!" Prices of the tanners ranged from 89 cents
for a two-ounce tube of Tansation to $6 for four ounces of Miss Mantan.
Most averaged around $1.50. Noted by this account was that several of the
products suffered from having too weak a solution of the browning chemical, which produced a blotchy look. And some of the tans produced by
these products had been more yellow or orange than brown.[52]

A list of recommendations for the media to consider as a basis for ad
copy acceptability of tanning preparations was suggested in a 1960 bulletin from the National Better Business Bureau after a study of the field
that year. Recommendations included: 1) no claim should imply that these
preparations tanned the skin in a manner similar to that of the action of
UV rays; 2) no unqualified claim of safety should be made until adequate
research and testing was done; 3) advertising should not claim unquali-
fiedly the color produced looked like a "natural tan" or that users could
obtain the exact shade desired. Another recommendation was that claims
of faster action, more natural-looking color, deeper shades, and so on,
should not be made unless competent clinical data was available to substantiate such claims.[53]

Later in 1960 *Good Housekeeping* magazine conducted its own investigation of tanning products, which it said, "are advertised as being able
to produce natural-looking tans within several hours of application. Thereafter, it is claimed, regular use enables you to maintain a tanned appearance as long as your like." Using 25 female volunteers, this magazine
studied 11 brands and found that more than half the women in their study
reported they were dissatisfied with the results. "Although artificial tans
of various shades were produced, only a few were considered to match the
glowing promises made for the preparations." Observing that almost all
of the self-tanners lacked screening agents and thus offered no protection
from sunburns, the publication added that the results of its tests "seemed
difficult to reconcile with advertising claims which promise 'glorious
golden tans' or 'the most gorgeous tan you ever had.'"[54]

Trained beauticians employed by *Good Housekeeping* checked the volunteers after the first four applications. "On about 90 percent of the skin
test areas there was some form of discoloration such as a streaky, blotchy
appearance, particularly where the skin folds at the knee, knuckle, ankle,
elbow and wrist. The stains were similar to those of iodine residue. The

color of flat skin surfaces ranged from pinky orange to muddy yellow-orange. Few, by any standards, were 'gorgeous tans.'" Subsequent checks were made the next day and then four days later but the unevenness and blotchiness remained. Regardless of the price paid (it varied from 20 cents to 87 cents an ounce), the 11 lotions and creams tested were found to perform in a fairly similar manner. For use on the face, neck, chest, arms and legs, the amount needed averaged about six to eight ounces a week.[55]

In a final check three weeks later the volunteers were asked by *Good Housekeeping* for their own reactions to the self-tanners— specifically what they liked and disliked about the products. Two-thirds said there were some aspects they liked. However, all but one woman reported they disliked the preparations in at least one respect; fewer than 25 percent of the respondents said they would try the products again. Another observation from the study was that in applying the products, palms and fingers could become stained and that those stains were difficult to remove with soap and water.

According to this story many dermatologists had no objections to their patients using these products externally. One physician explained he personally felt it was preferable to get a tan from a bottle than to overexpose oneself to the sun. Because they were cosmetics, the products did not have to be submitted to the FDA for safety tests before they were marketed. But the FDA had done some tests on its own and concluded the products were safe to us as directed on the label.[56]

A report from a group of doctors in the AMA publication *Archives of Dermatology*, still in 1960, after testing the active chemical in self-tanners (DHA for short) on 200 people, declared the products to be safe as the medical researchers found no signs of primary or allergic reaction. *Newsweek* felt the results from that study were a relief to sun worshippers because "To status seekers, a deep, year-round suntan is an impressive symbol of upper-crust leisure. Besides, the tan minimizes wrinkles and makes teeth look whiter."[57]

Journalist William Vath reported on the self-tanners in the AMA publication for lay readers, *Today's Health*, in 1961. He explained that for years John Andre had had the idea for such a product and had struggled to find a formula, corresponding with herb gardens around the world for ideas. Then a few years earlier he came across a 1920s medical journal describing experiments with a chemical called DHA that was used in treating diabetes. That article noted a side effect: patients who swallowed the drug developed stained teeth. In the first six months, Andre's company sold six million bottle of Man-Tan for a retail total of $20 million. The tan or coloring produced by a self-tanner gradually wore off over five to 15 days as a result of the normal shedding of surface skin cells. Vath observed that indications were those products did not provide "an even, natural-looking tan."[58]

According to Vath, the National Better Business Bureau had received complaints from consumers that the products produced yellow and orange colors and other complaints about the color being uneven and/or blotchy, after applications. Those physicians who reported on safety in the *Archives of Dermatology* had also observed, "It is extremely difficult to obtain a uniform tan." Both the *British Medical Journal* and the *British Journal of Dermatology* reported the same complaints with the latter declaring that if the products were inexpertly applied, "the user may induce a streaked and bizarre pattern which may detain him or her in the home for a week until normality had been regained." In his article, Vath declared these products were harmless but did not live up to their claims of natural and even tans.[59]

Writing in *Reader's Digest* later in 1961, Fred Dickenson said that when Man-Tan was first introduced, "the response was a merchandiser's dream. Drugstores were sold out within hours" and the enthusiasm for a tan from a bottle soon swept Great Britain and much of the rest of Western Europe. Dickenson's piece was full of praise and largely uncritical, one of the last such articles as Man-Tan and its counterparts faded away. Many people probably used them once but hardly anybody went back for a second bottle. The color produced was blotchy on most people and not the color of a natural tan, streaky or not. Those effects had been fairly well publicized by the time Dickenson's article came out, but he glossed over them with barely a mention: "Uniformity and evenness of color depend in part on skill in application."[60]

Self-tanners did not disappear, they simply became obscure as the hype faded when reality clashed with the illusion of the self-tanners' ad copy. Business reporter Lorraine Baltera observed in 1975 that instant tanning products fell into two basic types — items that tanned the skin several hours after application, such as Coppertone's QT, or products that tanned instantly upon application, such as the company's one-year-old SuddenTan. Unlike cosmetic bronzers that were water soluble, these instant tanners would not wash off with soap and water, but wore off gradually within a few days. Sea & Ski had recently added Instant Summer Tan, a non-water-soluble product that tanned instantly upon application. The Sea & Ski line already included Indoor/Outdoor, a QT-type tanning product. Coppertone's ad themes included, "Got a minute, get a tan" for SuddenTan, "Tans in three to five hours with or without the sun" for QT, and "Whatever your kind of skin, there's a Coppertone for you" for the regular line. Although the major suntan product makers had never taken cosmetic bronzing entries seriously, said Baltera, such products had remained on the market for several years. Their marketing failure was ascribed, by many sources, to a lack of advertising and promotional support. Helena Rubenstein, Inc., had discontinued its Sun Country Bronzing line as did Lanvin-Charles of the Ritz with its Sun Bronze Collection. Elizabeth Arden, Inc., was marketing Self Tanning lotion, not a cosmetic, but an instant tanning product, which contained no sunscreen agent.[61]

Touting the newest no-sun suntan product to arrive, in 1982, Louise Fenner announced in the pages of the government publication *FDA Consumer*, "You take a pill. You get a tan. Welcome to the 1980s." Those pills contained two food colors, chemical replicas of substances that occurred naturally in some plants. After a week or two the dye accumulated in the skin and produced a tan. But, said Fenner, there was a catch. "For one thing, the tan doesn't look quite right. It has a distinct orange tinge, especially in the palms and soles of the feet." Also, of course, the pills provided no protection against sunburn. "It's merely a dye job, and a costly one at that." The pills ranged from about $20 to $30 for a month's worth. First developed in Europe, these tanning pills surfaced in Canada and, around 1981, in the U.S. They contained synthetic versions of the natural coloring substances beta carotene and canthaxanthin, which belonged to the family of compounds called carotenoids and were responsible for much of the yellow, orange and red coloration in plants. For example, beta carotene gave carrots, apricots, peaches, melons, and so on, their distinctive color.[62]

Labels on those products, related Fenner, recommended taking several tablets a day for two or three weeks, then smaller doses to maintain the color. Dosages were based in part on body weight. Supposedly the effects of the tanning pills started to show up as an "outdoor glow" on the skin about a week after the first pill was swallowed. When the palms became orange-tinged, the user was told to cut down his intake. If the pills were discontinued, the tan faded at about the same rate as it appeared. What these tanning pills did, essentially, was to give the body such an overdose of color that some of it accumulated in the blood, skin and fatty tissue and certain organs such as the liver. Most of the color passed through the system unabsorbed, giving many consumers brick-red stools. Estimates were that an average person's intake of beta carotene (it was added to many processed foods— both substances had been approved by the FDA as color additions in foods and drugs— to enhance their appearance) was about 0.3 milligrams (mg) per day. For tanning pills with a recommended start-up dose of three or four tablets a day, that meant an intake of 12 to 16 mg. of beta carotene a day. Neither product was approved for use in ingested products intended to color the human body. According to the

Food, Drug and Cosmetic Act, manufacturers had to petition the FDA for approval of any new use of a color additive. Therefore, until the agency gave its approval, the use of beta carotene and canthaxanthin in oral tanning products was illegal. The FDA was then investigating tanning tablets and had taken some regulatory steps to keep them off the market. It had refused entry to some 40 shipments of the tablets manufactured outside the U.S. and was then maintaining an import detention alert on further shipments. One petition for the use of canthaxanthin in an oral tanning product had been submitted to the FDA and was then under review.[63]

A warning issued by the Better Business Bureau of Metropolitan New York in 1985 stated, "We warn consumers not to use tanning pills, as the safety and efficacy of tanning pills have yet to be determined," said Barbara Opotowsky, president of the bureau. A warning had been issued after the Bureau investigated two mail-order concerns offering oral tanning products— New York–based Long Life Products and Chicago-based Brothers Pharmaceutical. According to Opotowsky, an advertisement for the tablets from Long Life said, "Now you can have a perfect tan without aging your skin or risking your health," while an ad from Brothers declared, "Beautiful Tan tablets help you tan naturally.... So safe it'S GOOD for you." When the Bureau asked the companies to substantiate their claims, they received no response. Those pills contained canthaxanthin and up to that time the FDA had still not approved its use in ingested products intended to color the human body; it still seized any such items it found trying to enter the U.S.[64]

Several years passed and then, in 1992, reporter Terry Trucco covered the issue again. He began by noting that, for many people, the very notion of self-tanning products produced bad memories of blotchy orange skin. But now there was a new generation of products that could turn the skin brown without the sun and, said Trucco, "properly used, can provide a golden skin tone that is safe, smooth and convincing." Said Dr. Nelson Lee Novick, a Manhattan dermatologist, "You may have to experiment before you find one you want. But you can get a much more natural color now." There were then reported to be 35 such products on the market priced from as little as $5 for 3.75 ounces of Coppertone Sunless Tanning Extra Moisturizing Lotion to $20 for 4.2 ounces of Lancome Personalized Self-Tanning Lotion. Coppertone alone had five different product lines (including a reformulated, updated version of QT). For 1991, sunless tanners accounted for 15 percent of the $530 million market in sun care products, up from 10.5 percent in 1990, according to figures from Solomon Brothers. Though most manufacturers claimed to have a unique formula, the basic component of the sunless tanners remained DHA. It reacted with the amino acids in the skin, turning it darker in about three hours. At the end of his article Trucco admitted that getting the color right could still be a problem, as could getting an even application on the various parts of the body.[65]

A month later Jean Seligman wrote a brief article in *Newsweek* about the new boom in self-tanners. She thought the lure of a fast fake tan that looked almost real, combined with growing fears of skin cancer, had sparked a new interest in the sunless items. Some of the new self-tanners sported glamorous French names like Crème Solaire Anti-Rides (Clarins, $18.50 for 2.7 ounces). According to Seligman, dermatologists welcomed this new development, because any tanning that did not involve the sun reduced a person's risk of premature aging and skin cancer. "It's a sensible alternative to tanning in the sun or going to a salon," said Dr. Nicholas Lowe, clinical professor of dermatology at UCLA. However, Lowe admitted he thought the results from self-tanners "don't look like a natural tan, except perhaps in artificial light, at night."[66]

Increasingly sunless-tanners (non–UV) became available at spas and salons. A 2004 article remarked, indirectly, on how much they had improved in quality over the years when it commented, on those tanners, "All procedures show immediate, natural looking results, and the color is relatively non-transferable." Acknowledging that the more time spent in the sun, the more quickly the skin aged, this account added, showing the tie between tan and health, and tan and beauty lingered on. "Beauty experts say a youthful appearance, healthy glow and radiant skin are always in style. However, achieving this look often requires time in the sun." Profiled briefly were three types of sunless tanners, all of which had to be applied by a person at an outlet (not at home by the self). One was Mystic Tan, a fine mist of aloe vera-enriched solution sprayed on to the skin; a second method was airbrush tanning wherein an aesthetician airbrushed tanning solution onto the skin. Third was the autobronzant application. That was said to be the most hands-on approach, used at spas, wherein an aesthetician manually applied a self-tanner, sometimes called autobronzant tanning cream, to the skin.[67]

Sally Blenkey-Tchassova had a tiny New York City salon, Brazil Bronze, to which her clients came, stripped naked, and stood before her as she misted their bodies with a bronzing solution dispensed through a pressurized air gun (like the one used to spray paint cars, only smaller). Offering shades with names such as "Exotic Dancer" and "WASP Housewife," a 20-minute treatment at Brazil Bronze cost $50. "One minute you're white and the next you look like you've spent the week in St. Tropez," commented Sally.[68]

Consumer Reports evaluated seven sunless tanners in October 2004 and found those products gave most of the 19 staffers who tested them a fairly realistic tan that lasted about three days. These were all self-application products and all used the chemical dihydroxyacetone, which the magazine declared was not harmful. Such products were not replacements for sunscreen, and the chemical tan gave no protection against sunburn. Sunless tanners were said to be expensive, the cost ranging from $2 to $10 per tan. With a liberal application of the products necessary to achieve good results, the publication advised that a consumer could not expect more than two applications from a four-ounce container. Most of the tanners tested were sold in pharmacies for $6 to $15 for a container of from three to six fluid ounces, although Lancôme Soleil Flash Bronzer, a department store item, cost $26 for five ounces. These products had names such as "Tan Overnight" (Sun Laboratories), "Sunless Tanning Crème" (Banana Boat), and "Endless Summer" (Coppertone). Late in June 2004 the Food and Drug Administration ordered seven companies to stop selling pills or capsules containing the chemical canthaxanthin that claimed they tanned the skin and protected against sunburn and cancer, as the agency continued to fight against tanning products that contained that chemical.[69]

13

Conclusion

Suntanning, and the image of those who tanned, went through a huge change in less than a century. At the very beginning of the 20th century in America, white people avoided the sun, at least those who could do so. Getting a tan was the mark of a lower class person who was forced to toil outdoors; the upper classes were not forced outside and typically shielded themselves with parasols during the times they had to be outside. In the colonial empires maintained by white colonizers it was the locals — almost always non-white — who did whatever unpleasant work had to be done outside in the hot sun. Thus, there was also a racist interpretation of tanned skin — white was the preferred color. Tanned skin was associated with the underclass and the "inferior" subjects in the far-flung colonial empires.

However, attitudes were changing due to a variety of factors. One was a shift in working conditions brought about by the industrial revolution that drove the members of the working class off the land and into factories. As the 20th century dawned it became increasingly likely that a worker toiled indoors, rather than outdoors, and maintained a white complexion. At the same time members of the ruling classes began to engage in more outdoor activities, sports and games such as tennis, nature walks, and others. Women were becoming more active outdoors as they were treated more equally. For example, they took to bicycle riding in large numbers.

Still, the single most important reason for the change started around 1890 with the first medical reports that promoted the sun as a healer, with respect to tuberculosis initially, and later rickets and various other ailments. Many medical personnel wrote their own articles on the power of the sun as healer while even more gave interviews to journalists who reported the miracles of the sun in a usually uncritical way. Relentless hype about the powers of the sun came, over time, to overwhelm any class and race issues with regard to a tanned skin color. Articles in the form of beauty tips and columns for female readers featured home remedies on how to get rid of tan (it was lumped in with various skin problems such as acne) as late as the period 1900 to 1905. But interpretations were then being revised. By around 1908 tanning among white people had become established as a fashion and as stylish, at least in certain quarters. It was well entrenched by World War I, although it was not as pervasive as it would become when it really took off after the war. Prior to World War I tans were sought even for children, such was the power of sun worship of the time.

Suntanning as an activity spread rapidly through all parts of society in the 1920s, driven by an enormous number of articles about the sun as healer, articles that continued to be overwhelmingly uncritical of an ever-expanding number of exaggerated claims about the power of the sun. So popular did suntanning become that sun therapy was given its own name — heliotherapy. People in general were urged by almost all members of the medical community to get as much sun as possible; there was a consensus that children should also engage in regular sunbathing, even for infants as young as a month old. A slightly more critical stance toward the sun as healer began to creep into articles in the 1930s but the relentlessly glowing medical reports had succeeded in getting most people involved in tanning whenever possible and in believing such activity was medically helpful and perhaps even medically necessary.

Articles on the fashion of tanning in the 1920s and 1930s began to stress that a tan made a person look better, appear healthier, and become more attractive to the opposite sex. Tan as style began to replace tan as healer or medicine as fashion leaders and trendsetters took the place of doctors and other medical professionals as interpreters of tan. As an example, Hollywood actresses were canvassed in 1930 to find out their position on tanning.

Such was the popularity of suntanning in the period 1920 to roughly 1945 that it spawned several new industries. One involved the birth of the home sunlamp, a device that was very popular in the 1920s and 1930s. People were often urged to turn to home sunlamps, especially in the gloomy winter of the northern part of the U.S., to make sure they got their "medicine." When it was discovered that ordinary window glass blocked the UV tanning rays, it sparked an unsuccessful search for an inexpensive substitute glass. A few companies went so far as to install sunlamps in their plants or offices, convinced that such UV exposure would cut down employee absences and also improve the efficiency of their employees in some vague way, because "Doctor Sun" — as the orb was often called — was believed to provide some general energizing, or tonic effect. Such applications and hype had mostly disappeared by around the time of World War II.

Some medical reports from the time prior to World War II had noted the damaging effects of the sun on people — such as premature aging of the skin, wrinkle production, and cancer of the skin. However, such reports were infrequent and got lost among a torrent of praise. And if they did not get lost, then they were ignored.

As the post–World War II period began, the number of articles critical of the sun increased slowly and then dramatically, from about 1980 onward. Warnings about the sun and its effects became more and more strident as increasingly exaggerated threats were presented; as new and bizarre diseases were laid at the feet of the sun. Skin cancer numbers were trotted out to terrify the public and were sometimes used in a meaningless way, and sometimes used in an inappropriate way. Launched in the period was the sunscreen industry, beginning with a few tanning lotions but soon expanding to present a bewildering array of sun care items to the public. Aided by the government, and the shrill scare stories in the media, the sunscreen industry developed the SPF numbering system and the UV Index (now a ubiquitous part of most media weather reports) and saw the sales of its products grow rapidly.

By limiting UV exposure, sunscreens were supposed to reduce skin cancer rates. Yet to this day the rates have continued to rise, despite the fact that sunscreens have been used for decades. When the industry was challenged in the 1990s with the obvious question of why there was no leveling off, or decrease in skin cancer rates, such challenges were brushed aside. Critics' theories were not refuted; their questions were not answered. Rather, they were simply pounded down as heretics. Branded thusly meant, of course, that any points raised did not have to be addressed, since scientists were not involved, only heretics.

In post–World War II America, tanning did slowly become less fashionable, over time. By the end of the 1990s the tanner was sometimes equated with the cigarette smoker or the alcohol abuser. Still, sunbathing had not entirely disappeared. So equated had a suntan become in earlier periods to health, wealth, leisure, attractiveness, sexuality, and so on, that it was a difficult behavior to eradicate completely. By the 1980s and 1990s, actor George Hamilton — perhaps the world's best known tanner — was mocked more than admired for his hobby.

One development in the post–World War II era was an increased role for the no-sun suntan in the form of tanning parlors and self-tanners. With a first appearance in America in 1978, at a time when the anti-sun hysteria was just getting under way, the success of such places seemed unlikely. But they survived and continued to hold down a spot — albeit minor — in the tanning industry. Self-tanners had, of course, the backing of medical professionals since no UV rays, natural or artificial, were involved. However, they have never been able to produce anything that remotely resembled a natural tan.

Less than 100 years after the suntan's tentative arrival among white people as a medical aid and fashion, it had been driven back, as a killer. However, it remained a fashion and therefore still claimed adherents. After tanning was adopted, the medical grounds for the habit were all later shown to be false. Time would tell, perhaps, what resolutions would result with respect to current claims about the suntan as killer. The medical establishment had found that what it was largely responsible for creating — the desire for a suntan — was something it could not easily reverse.

Notes

Chapter 1

1. "Sun talk." *Mademoiselle* 73 (May, 1971): 210; June Weir. "Summer sense." *New York Times Magazine*, May 9, 1982, p. 77.
2. Alexandra Greeley. "No safe tan." *FDA Consumer* 25 (May, 1991): 16.
3. "Want a shot of sunshine." *Time* 138 (December 2, 1991): 85.
4. Emily Prager. "The timing of the tan." *Harper's Bazaar* 129 (May, 1996): 127; Susan Brink. "Sun struck." *U.S. News & World Report* 120 (June 24, 1996): 62.
5. "Bare heads and sunshine." *New York Times*, July 14, 1905, p. 6.
6. "Sunlight declared the enemy of man." *New York Times Magazine*, April 21, 1907, sec 5, p. 2.
7. *Ibid.*
8. *Ibid.*
9. *Ibid.*
10. "Our energy due to the sun." *New York Times*, May 15, 1911, p. 3.
11. "Made her beautiful." *Los Angeles Times*, January 13, 1901, p. 5.
12. Mrs. Henry Symes. "How to be healthy and beautiful." *Los Angeles Times*, August 3, 1902, p. C7.
13. Mrs. Henry Symes. "Chats with correspondents on health and beauty topics. *Los Angeles Times*, September 20, 1903, p. E10.
14. "Pretty on $1 a week." *Los Angeles Times*, January 27, 1907, sec 7, p. 2.
15. Simon Chapman, Robin Marks and Madeleine King. "Trends in tans and skin protection in Australian fashion magazines, 1982 through 1991." *American Jour-*

nal of Public Health 82 (December, 1992): 1678.
16. Marvin Harris. "The rites of summer." *Natural History* 82 (August, 1973): 20.
17. *Ibid.*
18. *Ibid.*
19. "Newport to war on smoking by women." *New York Times*, May 3, 1908, p. 11.
20. "Bottled sunburn." *Los Angeles Times*, September 21, 1912, sec 2, p. 10.
21. "Advises bathers against sunburn." *Los Angeles Times*, July 31, 1917, sec 1, p. 4.
22. "Sunbaths for chilly babies." *Los Angeles Times*, November 4, 1915, sec 2, p. 3.
23. F. Scott Fitzgerald. *The Beautiful and Damned*. Middlesex, England: Penguin, 1966, p. 26.

Chapter 2

1. R. I. Harris. "Heliotherapy in surgical tuberculosis." *American Journal of Public Health* 16 (July, 1926): 689; Paul E. Bechet. "Common sense under the sun." *Hygeia* 20 (July, 1942): 507.
2. "The sun cure." *Scientific Monthly* 16 (May, 1923); 555.
3. Woods Hutchinson. "Light refreshments." *Saturday Evening Post* 197 (May 2, 1925): 16
4. C. W. Saleeby. "Sunlight and disease." *Nature* 111 (April 28, 1923): 574
5. "The sun as a surgeon." *Literary Digest* 48 (February 28, 1914): 427
6. "Modern sun-worship: II — its history." *New Statesman* 18 (October 8, 1921):

10, 12; Lee Edson. "Warning: prolonged exposure to the sun can be harmful to your health." *New York Times*, August 8, 1971, sec 10, p. 14.

7. C. W. Saleeby, op. cit., p. 575.

8. "The sun as a surgeon," op. cit.

9. *Ibid.*

10. "More solar surgery." *Literary Digest* 48 (June 13, 1914): 1432–1433.

11. William Brady. "The sun cure." *The Independent* 79 (September 21, 1914): 414.

12. "Doctor sun." *Literary Digest* 58 (August 31, 1918): 26.

13. "More sunlight!" *Literary Digest* 66 (September 11, 1920): 128, 130.

14. "Revolving sun baths." *Scientific American* 125 (September 3, 1921): 170.

15. "Modern sun-worship III — its high priest and his temple." *New Statesman* 18 (October 15, 1921): 42–43.

16. "More light." *New Statesman* 18 (November 12, 1921): 163.

17. C. W. Saleeby. "The advance of heliotherapy." *Nature* 109 (May 20, 1922): 663.

18. "The new sun worship." *The Survey* 49 (October 15, 1922): 109–110.

19. "Heliotherapy arrives." *New Statesman* 21 (April 28, 1923): 76.

20. "The sun cure." *Scientific Monthly* 16 (May, 1923): 555, 557.

21. "Sunlight therapy's value certain in tuberculosis." *New York Times*, March 2, 1924, sec 9, p. 18.

22. "Eating sunshine to cure tuberculosis." *Current Opinion* 76 (June, 1924): 831.

23. "Sun's actinic rays are magnets for tourists." *New York Times*, January 18, 1925, sec 8, p. 18.

24. Woods Hutchinson. "Light refreshments." *Saturday Evening Post* 197 (May 2, 1925): 16, 51–52.

25. *Ibid.*, p. 52.

26. James A. Tobey. "Curing disease by sunlight." *Current History Magazine* 22 (June, 1925): 455.

27. Floyd W. Parsons. "What price sunshine?" *Saturday Evening Post* 198 (July 25, 1925): 6, 73.

28. *Ibid.*, pp. 74, 76.

29. J. Clarence Funk. "Sun worshipping in Pennsylvania." *American Journal of Public Health* 15 (September, 1925): 764–765.

30. "Sun ray baths save baby." *New York Times*, October 18, 1925, p. 6.

31. D. T. Harris. "The biological action of light." *Scientific Monthly* 21 (November, 1925): 504–505.

32. Edwin E. Slosson. "The progress of science." *Scientific Monthly* 21 (November, 1925): 551.

33. *Ibid.*, pp. 551, 554.

34. "Questions the need to abolish disease." *New York Times*, May 21, 1926, p. 14.

35. "Use sunlight on rickets." *New York Times*, June 15, 1927, p. 48.

36. John W. M. Bunker. "Light and life." *American Journal of Public Health* 16 (July, 1926): 677.

37. R. I. Harris, op. cit., p. 692.

38. Robert E. Fitzgerald. "Perrysburg — a mecca of heliotherapy." *American Journal of Public Health* 16 (September, 1926): 893, 895.

39. Charles Sheard. "Cheeks of tan." *Hygeia* 5 (May, 1927): 222.

40. Benjamin Harrow. "Meet doctor sunshine." *Hygeia* 5 (November, 1927): 580, 582.

41. Madelein G. Revell. "A place in the sun." *Public Health Nurse* 19 (November, 1927): 538–541.

42. Crag Dale. "Beware of sunburn." *Popular Mechanics* 49 (May, 1928): 754–756.

43. Edgar Mayer. "Sun-bathing and sunlamps." *The American Journal of Nursing* 33 (August, 1933): 740–746.

44. Henry Laurens. "Sunlight and health." *Scientific Monthly* 42 (April, 1936): 323–324.

45. Allen S. Johnson. "Hot weather hazards." *Hygeia* 15 (June, 1937): 508.

Chapter 3

1. "Woman near death from beach sunburn." *New York Times*, June 25, 1921, p. 2.

2. "Topics of the Times." *New York Times*, June 27, 1921, p. 12.

3. "Warns against sunburn." *New York Times*, July 19, 1924, p. 4.

4. "Sunburn leads to death." *New York Times*, July 17, 1925, p. 7.

5. "Perils of the summer sun." *Literary Digest* 86 (August 15, 1925): 20.

6. "Wynne warns of sunburn peril." *New York Times*, July 31, 1930, p. 10.

7. "Are you a heliophobe?" *Literary Digest* 106 (August 2, 1930): 26.

8. "Economic loss from sunburn is put at $1,400,000 a year." *New York Times*, June 8, 1931, p. 1.

9. Jerome W. Ephraim. "The truth about sunburn." *American Mercury* 35 (July, 1935): 365–367.
10. Frederick S. Bigelow. "Colds and where to catch them." *Saturday Evening Post* 208 (November 30, 1935): 34.
11. "Paba for sunburn." *Newsweek* 21 (May 17, 1943): 70.
12. "Sunburn delays draft." *New York Times*, June 22, 1943, p. 21.
13. "The advantage of tan." *Literary Digest* 78 (September 22, 1923): 27–28.
14. D. H. Lawrence. "Sun." in *The Complete Short Stories*, vol II. New York: Penguin, 1976, pp. 530–536.
15. Lulu Hunt Peters. "Diet and health." *Los Angeles Times*, July 6, 1922, sec 2, p. 8.
16. "Not even skin deep is beauty." *Los Angeles Times*, September 2, 1923, sec 3, p. 15.
17. How to Take a Sun Bath (ad). *Los Angeles Times*, July 25, 1926, p. K27.
18. Gulielma F. Alsop. "Health via sunlight." *The Woman Citizen* 11 (July, 1926): 37.
19. "Sunburn beneficial only when gradually acquired." *New York Times*, July 29, 1928, sec 8, p. 2.
20. Simon Chapman, Robin Marks and Madeleine King. "Trends in tans and skin protection in Australian fashion magazines, 1982 through 1991." *American Journal of Public Health* 82 (December, 1992): 1678.
21. "Take your sunshine in small doses." *Literary Digest* 98 (August 4, 1928): 22.
22. "All shades of tan are now seen on New York's streets." *New York Times*, August 19, 1928, sec 7, p. 9.
23. "A sun-tan mode." *New York Times*, June 16, 1929, sec 8, p. 8.
24. "Ways to get a stylish tan." *New York Times Magazine*, June 23, 1929, sec 5, p. 19.
25. Stuart Chase. "Confessions of a sun-worshipper." *The Nation* 128 (June 26, 1929): 762–765.
26. "Sun devotionals." *New York Times*, July 6, 1929, p. 12.
27. Mildred Adams. "Modern worshippers of that old god, the sun." *New York Times Magazine*, July 7, 1929, sec 5, pp. 12–13.
28. James J. Walsh. "Sun tan: the latest fad." *The Commonweal* 10 (August 7, 1929): 358.
29. *Ibid.*, p. 359.
30. E. E. Free. "Tan fad to furnish new facts to science." *New York Times*, August 11, 1929, sec 9, pp. 3, 10.

31. "Sun baths in London planned by Lansbury." *New York Times*, September 19, 1929, p. 34.
32. "Heavy coat of tan is called harmful." *New York Times*, September 28, 1929, p. 20.
33. Floyd W. Parsons. "Sun worship." *Saturday Evening Post* 202 (November 16, 1929): 28, 213.
34. *Ibid.*, pp. 213–214.
35. Gerald J. O'Gara. "Health rays." *Sunset Magazine* 65 (July, 1930): 11–14.
36. "Puts ban on sun bathing." *New York Times*, July 19, 1930, p. 28.
37. Alma Whitaker. "Sun tans win in movieland." *Los Angeles Times*, July 27, 1930, p. B9.
38. *Ibid.*, pp. B9, B17.
39. "Asks solariums in Chicago." *New York Times*, July 20, 1930, sec 2, p. 3.
40. "Athletics rising greatly in Soviet." *New York Times*, August 31, 1930, sec 3, p. 4.
41. Leonard Falkner. "The burning question." *American Magazine* 110 (August, 1930): 100.
42. "Beauty and sunburn." *New York Times*, August 15, 1931, p. 12.
43. "Return of the red skin." *The Commonweal* 16 (June 15, 1932): 173.
44. "Sun-bathers seek Manhattan roofs." *New York Times*, July 10, 1932, sec 10 & 11, p. 1.
45. "The sun: a doubt." *The New Statesman and Nation* 4 (September 10, 1932): 281–282.
46. "Sun bathers warned to beware of liquor." *New York Times*, July 1, 1935, p. 21.
47. John W. Harrington. "Sun-bathers on increase." *New York Times*, July 5, 1936, sec 10, p. 5.
48. "Auto toll laid to sun bathing." *Los Angeles Times*, August 5, 1937, p. 4.
49. "Suntan." *Life* 11 (July 21, 1941): 55–58.
50. Lulu Hunt Peters, op. cit.
51. "Babies and sunshine." *Literary Digest* 79 (December 1, 1923): 27.
52. "Sunny sea beaches good for children." *New York Times*, September 14, 1924, sec 8, p. 11
53. "Old doctor sun." *Literary Digest* 87 (October 17, 1925): 28.
54. Frederick F. Tisdale. "Sunlight and health." *American Journal of Public Health* 16 (July, 1926): 697–698.
55. "Urges sunlight hour for children."

New York Times, October 6, 1929, sec 3, p. 6.

56. Gerald J. O'Gara, op. cit., p. 12.

57. Edgar Mayer. "Sun-bathing and sun-lamps." *The American Journal of Nursing* 33 (August, 1933): 741.

Chapter 4

1. "Credits 60,000 cures to artificial sun." *New York Times*, October 2, 1924, p. 24.

2. "Sun lamps to tan cheeks of members of Congress." *New York Times*, February 13, 1929, p. 1.

3. "Warns as to sun bathing." *New York Times*, February 18, 1929, p. 10.

4. "Upholds ultra-violet ray." *New York Times*, January 29, 1930, p. 2.

5. "Sun's rays the great healer." *The Canadian Magazine* 73 (April, 1930): 43.

6. "Sunlight." *Hygeia* 8 (August, 1930): 704.

7. Leonard Falkner. "The burning question." *American Magazine* 110 (August, 1930): 98.

8. Henry D. Hubbard. "New vistas opened by invisible rays." *New York Times*, October 18, 1931, sec 9, p. 4.

9. "Chicago sun bathers must wear something." *New York Times*, March 22, 1932, p. 4.

10. Edgar Mayer, M. D. "Sun-bathing and sun-lamps." *The American Journal of Nursing* 33 (August, 1933): 745.

11. Waldemar Kaempffert. "Invisible light is put to work for man." *New York Times Magazine*, May 8, 1927, sec 4, p. 4.

12. *Ibid.*, pp. 4–5.

13. "Glass houses for health." *New York Times*, July 1, 1927, p. 20.

14. "Housing heads urge end of smoke evil." *New York Times*, January 31, 1929, p. 15.

15. "Cornell to fight colds." *New York Times*, November 3, 1930, p. 30.

16. "Children at Cornell bask in violet rays." *New York Times*, March 27, 1932, p. 25.

17. "Says we will sleep under violet rays." *New York Times*, February 11, 1931, p. 28.

18. "Ultra-violet rays used in an office." *New York Times*, December 28, 1931, p. 14.

19. "Says cancers yield to electro-surgery." *New York Times*, September 7, 1932, p. 7.

Chapter 5

1. H. H. Hazen and Florence B. Biase. "Sunlight and the skin." *American Journal of Nursing* 33 (August, 1933): 747–748.

2. Martha Parker. "Danger in the sun." *New York Times Magazine*, July 9, 1944, p. 32.

3. "Our energy due to the sun." *New York Times*, May 15, 1911, p. 3.

4. "Medical progress." *New York Times*, January 9, 1929, p. 30; "Doctors urge care in using ray lamps." *New York Times*, January 9, 1929, p. 33.

5. "The good and evil of getting tanned." *Literary Digest* 106 (August 23, 1930): 30.

6. "Paris doctor warns against sun bathing." *New York Times*, June 25, 1933, p. 1.

7. "Linking cancer and sun bathing." *New York Times*, July 30, 1933, sec 4, p. 5.

8. "Sunlight and cancer." *New York Times*, October 30, 1933, p. 16.

9. Paul E. Bechet. "Common sense under the sun." *Hygeia* 20 (July, 1942): 507, 538.

10. "Smoker's cancer laid to sunburn." *New York Times*, April 8, 1941, p. 18.

11. *Ibid.*

12. "Exposure to sun helps prevent cancer deaths." *Science News Letter* 37 (March 30, 1940): 198–199.

Chapter 6

1. Ruth Adler. "Fun to fry." *New York Times Magazine*, July 9, 1950, p. 33.

2. Bernadine Bailey. "Sun tan pro and con." *Today's Health* 28 (July, 1950): 45, 55.

3. Veronica Lucey Conley. "While you tan." *Today's Health* 30 (July, 1952): 35.

4. "Big sky, big burn." *Time* 24 (December 14, 1959): 72

5. "The sun also burns." *Time* 81 (June 21, 1963): 43.

6. Harold F. Blum. "Skin cancer and sunlight." *Science* 145 (September 18, 1964): 1339.

7. "Sunshine: hazardous to your health." *Consumers' Research Magazine* 63 (April, 1980): 32–36.

8. Jane Ogle. "Facing up to sunning." *New York Times Magazine*, June 14, 1981, pp. 108, 120.

9. Matt Clark. "Suntans and skin cancer." *Newsweek* 99 (June 14, 1982): 85.

10. Claudia Wallis. "Bring back the parasol." *Time* 121 (May 30, 1983): 46.

11. Bernice Kanner. "The selling of suntans." *New York* 16 (August 8, 1983): 19.

12. Jane E. Brody. "Protecting skin from sun's rays." *New York Times*, May 22, 1985, pp. C1, C10.

13. Jean Seligman. "Catching dangerous rays." *Newsweek* 105 (June 24, 1985): 69.

14. Mary McIver. "The sun's killing rays." *Maclean's* 101 (June 13, 1988): 36–42.

15. William Bennett. "Sun: the new wisdom." *Vogue* 179 (June, 1989): 204, 206.

16. Cheryl A. Sweet. "Healthy tan — a fast-fading myth." *FDA Consumer* 23 (June, 1989): 11.

17. "A.M.A. describes tanning hazards." *New York Times*, July 25, 1989, p. C7.

18. David Reuben. "Suntans can kill you." *Reader's Digest* 136 (June, 1990): 119–120, 122.

19. Alexandra Greeley. "No safe tan." *FDA Consumer* 25 (May, 1991): 16–21.

20. Naomi Freudlich. "The sun vs. your skin: a survival guide." *Business Week*, July 1, 1991, p. 91.

21. "For people who have fair skins, suntans may raise gallstone risks." *New York Times*, February 5, 1992, p. C12.

22. Katarzyna Wandycz. "Safe sun." *Forbes* 152 (July 19, 1993): 212–213.

23. Susan Brink. "Sun struck." *U.S. News & World Report* 120 (June 24, 1996): 62, 66.

24. Mary Tannen. "Seeing the light." *New York Times Magazine*, May 11, 1997, p. 54.

25. "Beware the unruly sun." *Newsweek* 133 (June 21, 1999): 81–82.

26. Adam Liptak. "Mother is jailed after children are sunburned." *New York Times*, August 21, 2002, p. A10.

27. "Charges eased in sunburns." *New York Times*, August 22, 2002, p. A18.

28. Howard Markel. "So what's a responsible sun worshipper to do?" *New York Times*, August 25, 2002, sec 4, pp. 1, 3.

29. Donna Wilkinson. "Why do men get sunburned?" *New York Times*, June 21, 2004, p. F5.

Chapter 7

1. Bernice Kanner. "The selling of suntans." *New York* 16 (August 8, 1983): 19.

2. "Sunburn jelly." *Newsweek* 27 (January 21, 1946): 89.

3. "Preventing sunburn and promoting tan." *Consumers' Research Bulletin* 23 (June, 1949): 13–15.

4. "Sunburn preventives." *Consumer Reports* 15 (July, 1950): 291–294.

5. "To tan without burning." *Consumers' Research Bulletin* 33 (June, 1954): 31–33.

6. John J. Abele. "Suntan lotions enjoying day in sun." *New York Times*, July 13, 1957, pp. 21, 24.

7. "Suntan — safe or dangerous?" *Consumer Bulletin* 41 (May, 1958): 27–29.

8. "Sun-tan preparations." *Consumer Reports* 26 (July, 1961): 394–397.

9. "Balms away! Sun worshippers face heavy barrage from lotions makers this summer." *Advertising Age* 34 (June 10, 1963): 18–19.

10. "The sun also burns." *Time* 81 (June 21, 1963): 43.

11. L. Stambovsky. "The sunburn business." *Drug & Cosmetic Industry* 102 (May, 1968): 43.

12. *Ibid.*, pp. 43–44.

13. *Ibid.*, pp. 186, 188.

14. "Sun worship." *Today's Health* 48 (June, 1970): 37, 39.

15. James P. Forkan. "Sun shines on marketers of tanning sunburn product." *Advertising Age* 41 (June 22, 1970): 72.

16. "Suntan preparations." *Consumer Reports* 36 (July,. 1971): 408, 411.

17. Lorraine Baltera. "Suntan products leaning to protection themes." *Advertising Age* 46 (May 12, 1975): 10.

18. *Ibid.*

19. "Suntan preparations." *Consumers' Research Magazine* 58 (August, 1975): 20–22.

20. Angela Taylor. "All about the sun: a new turn on tans." *New York Times*, June 1, 1977, p. C9.

21. Pat Sloan. "Here comes the sun care." *Advertising Age* 49 (May 29, 1978): 3.

22. "Woman tells a suntan-oil company how to soothe her." *New York Times*, July 28, 1979, p. 41.

Chapter 8

1. "Sunshine: hazardous to your health." *Consumers' Research Magazine* 63 (April, 1980): 34–35.

2. "How to survive a season in the sun." *Consumer Reports* 45 (June, 1980): 350–351.

3. *Ibid.*, pp. 353–354.

4. *Ibid.*, pp. 354–356.

5. Pat Sloan. "Suncare '82 outlook partly cloudy." *Advertising Age* 53 (February 15, 1982): 45.

6. Barbara Rudolph. "Don't let the sunshine in." *Forbes* 129 (June 21, 1982): 80.

7. *Ibid.*

8. *Ibid.*, p. 81.

9. Bernice Kanner. "The selling of suntans." *New York* 16 (August 8, 1983): 19.

10. *Ibid.*, pp. 19–20.

11. Pat Sloan. "Sunscreens shine in cosmetics." *Advertising Age* 56 (May 6, 1985): 70.

12. Lisa Belkin. "A fierce fight over the sun." *New York Times*, May 31, 1986, p. 35.

13. *Ibid.*, pp. 35, 37.

14. "Sunburn index gauges risk." *Prevention* 38 (August, 1986): 7.

15. *Ibid.*, p. 8.

16. Pat Sloan. "Suncare marketers raise their screens." *Advertising Age* 58 (May 25, 1987): 1, 66.

17. Deborah Blumenthal. "Some doubts about new cosmetics for tanning." *New York Times*, January 16, 1988, p. 33.

18. "SPF: the sun-profit factor." *Newsweek* 111 (June 27, 1988): 44.

19. Robert Brody. "Playing the numbers for a lighter tan." *New York Times*, July 24, 1988, sec 3, p. 17.

20. Robert Brody. "A tanless society by the year 2000?" *New York Times*, July 24, 1988, sec 3, p. 17.

21. Robert Brody. "Fear takes the sting out of high prices." *New York Times*, July 24, 1988, sec 3, p. 17.

22. Pat Sloan. "Coppertone ads tout beauty on the beach." *Advertising Age* 60 (March 6, 1989): 67.

23. Cheryl A. Sweet. "Healthy tan — a fast-fading myth." *FDA Consumer* 23 (June, 1989): 12–13.

24. Dero A. Saunders. "New under the sun." *Forbes* 144 (August 7, 1989): 134.

25. Joan C. Hamilton. "Sun protection? There's a rub." *Business Week*, June 11, 1990, p. 22.

26. *Ibid.*, p. 23.

27. "Sunscreens." *Consumer Reports* 56 (June, 1991): 400–405.

28. "Environment helps accelerate consumer demand for sunscreens." *Drug & Cosmetic Industry* 149 (August, 1991): 30, 32.

29. "The bottom line." *Economist* 320 (September 14, 1991): 33.

30. "Miami's icon of kitsch faces toppling over the bottom line." *New York Times*, August 25, 1991, p. 28.

31. Toddi Gutner. "Protection racket." *Forbes* 150 (August 17, 1992): 90.

32. *Ibid.*

33. Pat Sloan. "Getting a tan, family style." *Advertising Age* 64 (January 25, 1993): 12.

34. Donald A. Davis. "Sunscreen." *Drug & Cosmetic Industry* 153 (August, 1993): 25–26.

35. "Sunscreen lowers risk of melanoma." *New York Times*, October 14, 1993, p. B9.

36. Donald A. Davis. "Defining the sunscreen market." *Drug & Cosmetic Industry* 153 (December, 1993): 28, 32.

37. *Ibid.*, p. 34.

38. Holland Sweet. "Back to the bronze age?" *Harper's Bazaar* 126 (May, 1993): 126, 130+.

39. Pat Sloan. "UV index backs sunscreen surge." *Advertising Age* 66 (January 30, 1995): 11.

40. Mary Tannen. "Seeing the light." *New York Times Magazine*, May 11, 1997, p. 54.

41. Pat Sloan. "Tan is back, and new brands skimp on protection." *Advertising Age* 6 (June 2, 1997): 22.

42. "A spectrum of sun protection." *Consumer Reports* 63 (May, 1998): 20–21.

43. *Ibid.*, pp. 21–22.

44. Susan Brink. "So much for sunblock." *U.S. News & World Report* 126 (June 14, 1999): 65.

45. Larry Thompson. "Trying to look sunsational." *FDA Consumer* 34 (July/August, 2000): 16–19.

46. "Sunscreens." *Consumer Reports* 66 (June, 2001): 27.

47. Helen Fields. "Burned by SPF." *U.S. News & World Report* 135 (July 21, 2003): 51.

Chapter 9

1. Nathalie Angier. "Theory hints sunscreens raise melanoma risks." *New York Times*, August 9, 1990, p. B10.

2. David Bjerklie. "Does sunscreen save your skin?" *Time* 141 (May 24, 1993): 69.

3. *Ibid.*

4. Michael Castleman. "Beach bummer." *Mother Jones* 18 (May/June, 1993): 33–34.

5. *Ibid.*, p. 34.

6. *Ibid.*

7. *Ibid.*, pp. 34–35.

8. *Ibid.*, pp. 35–36.

9. *Ibid.*, p. 36.

10. *Ibid.*

11. *Ibid.*, p. 37.

12. Donald A. Davis. "Defining the sunscreen market." *Drug & Cosmetic Industry* 153 (December, 1993): 34.

13. T. Adler. "Sunscreen can't give blanket protection." *Science News* 145 (January 22, 1994): 54.

14. *Ibid.*, p. 55.

15. Donald A. Davis. "Boggy ground." *Drug & Cosmetic Industry* 154 (March, 1994): 22.

16. Adriane Fugh-Berman. "Sunscreen or smoke screen." *Ms* 5 (July/August, 1994): 19.

17. *Ibid.*, pp. 19–20.

18. *Ibid.*, pp. 20–21.

19. Michael Castleman. "Sunscam." *Mother Jones* 23 (May/June, 1998): 27.

20. *Ibid.*, pp. 27–28.

21. Kathleen Fackelmann. "Melanoma madness." *Science News* 153 (June 6, 1998): 360.

22. *Ibid.*, pp. 360, 363.

23. W. T. Loesch III. "Responsible sun protection in the media whirlwind." *Drug & Cosmetic Industry* 163 (August, 1998): 10.

24. "The link between sunscreen and melanoma." *Shape* 23 (May, 2004): 127.

25. Alex Kuczynski. "For tans, it's sprays vs. rays." *New York Times*, June 13, 2004, p. 9.

26. *Ibid.*

27. Ken Landow. "Do sunscreens prevent skin cancer?" *Postgraduate Medicine* 116 (July, 2004): 22.

28. Gina Kolata. "A dermatologist who's not afraid to sit on the beach." *New York Times*, July 20, 2004, p. F5.

29. *Ibid.*

Chapter 10

1. "Sunburn, poison ivy, and seasickness." *Fortune* 36 (August, 1947): 113.

2. J. C. Furnas. "The truth about suntan." *Saturday Evening Post* 221 (July 31, 1948): 65–66.

3. "A place in the sun." *New York Times*, July 15, 1949, p. 18.

4. Ruth Adler. "Fun to fry." *New York Times Magazine*, July 9, 1950, p. 32.

5. Bernadine Bailey. "Sun tan pro and con." *Today's Health* 28 (July, 1950): 45, 55.

6. "Personal business." *Business Week*, July 27, 1957, p. 141.

7. Leo Orris. "The sun: friend or enemy?" *Mademoiselle* 53 (May, 1961): 143.

8. Allan Grant. "Sun pleasures and perils." *Life* 51 (August 4, 1961): 87, 91.

9. "Mlle plots the perfect tan." *Mademoiselle* 59 (July, 1964): 40.

10. *Ibid.*

11. *Ibid.*, pp. 40–41.

12. Russell Baker. "Observer: the strangest shores." *New York Times*, June 27, 1965, sec 4, p. 10.

13. "Brown as a..." *Newsweek* 68 (August 1, 1966): 58–59.

14. "Sun ban." *Time* 89 (May 12, 1967): 65.

15. "Sun talk." *Mademoiselle* 73 (May, 1971): 210.

16. Eugenia Sheppard. "Love affair with the sun." *Harper's Bazaar* 104 (June, 1971): 94–95.

17. *Ibid.*, p. 95.

18. Lee Edson. "Warning: prolonged exposure to the sun can be harmful to your health." *New York Times*, August 8, 1971, sec 10, p. 1.

19. L. Stambovsky. "Suntanning under siege." *Drug & Cosmetic Industry* 111 (July, 1972): 40–41.

20. *Ibid.*, pp. 119–121.

21. James C. G. Conniff. "Bask, don't burn." *New York Times Magazine*, July 7, 1974, pp. 13, 15.

22. "Sensitivity to sunburn." *Science* 67 (June 15, 1928): sup 12, 14.

23. *Ibid.*

24. "Sunburn meter is shown." *New York Times*, June 24, 1949, p. 25.

25. Stacy V. Jones. "Sun-bathing now mechanized." *New York Times*, January 30, 1954, p. 21.

26. "Sunglasses with alarm." *New York Times*, August 7, 1971, p. 33.

27. "Sunburn doses measured." *New York Times*, September 6, 1975, p. 31.

28. Robert Brody. "Avoiding a sunburn with pills and patches." *New York Times*, July 24, 1988, sec 3, p. 17.

29. Edmund L. Andrews. "In the sun too long? Device sounds an alarm." *New York Times*, April 27, 1991, p. 38.

30. "For sun lovers: a yellow badge of caution." *Newsweek* 119 (June 8, 1992): 44.

31. Toddi Gutner. "Protection racket." *Forbes* 150 (August 17, 1992): 90.

32. Bernice Kanner. "The selling of suntans." *New York* 16 (August 8, 1983): 19.

Chapter 11

1. Claudia Wallis. "Bring back the parasol." *Time* 121 (May 30, 1983): 46.

2. "Love of a suntan." *New York Times*, June 12, 1984, p. C7.

3. Stephen Rae. "No fear of frying." *New York Times*, May 27, 1985, p. 19.

4. Deborah Blumenthal. "Some doubts about new cosmetics for tanning." *New York Times*, January 16, 1988, p. 33.

5. "Tanning debate: heavy vs. healthy." *New York Times*, May 11, 1988, p. C10.

6. Mary McIver. "The sun's killing rays." *Maclean's* 101 (June 13, 1988): 38–39.

7. "For sun lovers, tan is worth the risk." *New York Times*, July 24, 1988, p. 31.

8. *Ibid.*

9. Robert Brody. "A tanless society by the year 2000?" *New York Times*, July 24, 1988, sec 3, p. 17.

10. "Fear of frying." *New Republic* 199 (September 5, 1988): 4.

11. Arthur G. Miller, William A. Ashton, John W. McHoskey and Joel Gimbel. "What price attractiveness? Stereotype and risk factors in suntanning behavior." *Journal of Applied Social Psychology* 20 (September, 1990): 1275–1280.

12. *Ibid.*, p. 1282.

13. *Ibid.*, pp. 1294–1298.

14. Alexandra Greeley. "No safe tan." *FDA Consumer* 25 (May, 1991): 21.

15. Marita Broadstock, Ron Borland and Robyn Gason. "Effects of suntan on judgments of healthiness and attractiveness by adolescents." *Journal of Applied Social Psychology* 22 (January 16, 1992): 157–158.

16. *Ibid.*, pp. 161–171.

17. Nathaniel C. Nash. "Ozone depletion threatening sun worshippers." *New York Times*, March 27, 1992, p. A7.

18. Simon Chapman, Robin Marks and Madeleine King. "Trends in tans and skin protection in Australian fashion magazines, 1982 through 1991." *American Journal of Public Health* 82 (December, 1992): 1677–1679.

19. "Good-bye summer tan." *Glamour* 91 (May, 1993): 234–240.

20. *Ibid.*, pp. 236, 238.

21. Judith Waldrop. "Under the sun." *American Demographics* 15 (July, 1993): 4.

22. Peter Marks. "Don't bother me: I'm catching some rays." *New York Times*, July 2, 1995, sec 4, p. 6.

23. "The tan man." *New Yorker* 71 (September 18, 1995): 42.

24. Patrick Perry. "Safe under the sun." *Saturday Evening Post* 268 (September/October, 1996): 43.

25. Emily Prager. "The taming of the tan." *Harper's Bazaar* 129 (May, 1996): 127, 186.

26. Susan Brink. "Sun struck." *U.S. News & World Report* 120 (June 24, 1996): 62.

27. Howard K. Koh. "Sunbathing habits and sunscreen use among white adults: results of a national survey." *American Journal of Public Health* 87 (July, 1997): 1214–1215.

28. *Ibid.*, pp. 1215–1216.

29. "Beauty and health." *Glamour* 95 (July, 1997): 58.

30. Shannon Dortch. "There goes the sun." *American Demographics* 19 (August, 1997): 4, 6–7.

31. Lawrence Van Gelder. "Chronicle." *New York Times*, August 19, 1997, p. B6.

32. Deborah Netburn. "Young, carefree and hooked on sunlamps." *New York Times*, May 26, 2002, sec 9, p. 7.

33. *Ibid.*

34. "Deceptive tans and health risks." *New York Times*, June 8, 2002, p. 14.

35. Karen Thomas. "Gold is not just for the statues." *USA Today*, March 9, 2004, p. D2.

Chapter 12

1. Don Baker. "Employees get a sun tan in Westinghouse offices." *American Business*, 21 (July, 1951): 22–23.

2. "F.D.A. proposes standards for control of sunlamps." *New York Times*, December 30, 1977, p. A22.

3. Diane Weathers. "90-second sun-

tans." *Newsweek* 94 (December 24, 1979): 68.

4. *Ibid.*

5. "Sun salons." *Time* 115 (February 11, 1980): 59.

6. *Ibid.*

7. "Sunshine: hazardous to your health." *Consumers' Research Magazine* 63 (April, 1980): 33–34.

8. "How to survive a season in the sun." *Consumer Reports* 45 (June, 1980): 352.

9. "Suntan parlors to post warnings." *New York Times*, August 21, 1980, p. B6.

10. "Risks of tanning booths." *New York Times*, January 27, 1981, p. C2.

11. "Tanning parlors fade from franchise scene." *New York Times*, May 26, 1981, p. D1.

12. *Ibid.*, pp. D1, D4.

13. *Ibid.*, p. D4.

14. Richard Zoglin. "Going for the bronze." *Time* 1215 (February 25, 1985): 82.

15. *Ibid.*

16. William E. Schmidt. "Even in the South, they tan indoors." *New York Times*, June 1, 1985, p. 48.

17. "Tanning salons may face licensing." *New York Times*, March 29, 1987, p. 42.

18. *Ibid.*

19. *Ibid.*

20. David Brand. "Perils of the tanning parlor." *Time* 131 (May 23, 1988): 76.

21. "Some tanning salons found to violate rules." *New York Times*, March 28, 1991, p. B8.

22. Jennifer A. Oliphant, Jean L. Forster, and Colleen M. McBride. "The use of commercial tanning facilities by suburban Minnesota adolescents." *American Journal of Public Health* 84 (March, 1994): 476–477.

23. *Ibid.*, pp. 477–478.

24. *Ibid.*, p. 478.

25. Peter Marks. "Don't bother me: I'm catching some rays." *New York Times*, July 2, 1995, sec 4, p. 6.

26. Richard C. Palmer. "Indoor tanning facility density in eighty U.S. cities." *Journal of Community Health* 27 (June, 2002): 191–196.

28. *Ibid.*, p. 198.

29. Lauren Lyster. "The bronze age." *Los Angeles Magazine* 48 (March, 2003): 38.

30. Jaime deBlanc-Knowles. "Dangerous tans." *E: The Environmental Magazine* 15 (September/October, 2003): 11–12.

31. Ian Mylchreest. "Retailer sets out to shake up valley tanning salons." *Las Vegas Business Press* 21 (February 2, 2004): 19.

32. Richard Webster. "Indoor tanning remains popular despite doctors dire warnings." *New Orleans City Business*, April 5, 2004, p. 34.

33. Jane Schwanke. "Study shows alarming upward trend in teen use of indoor tanning facilities." *Dermatology Times* 25 (June, 2004): 55.

34. Alex Kuczynski. "For tans, it's sprays vs. rays." *New York Times*, June 13, 2004, p. 9.

35. *Ibid.*

36. Eric Nagourney. "Good day, sunshine: why they tan." *New York Times*, July 13, 2004, p. F1.

37. Jennifer Saranow. "States crack down on indoor tanning." *Wall Street Journal* (eastern ed.), January 26, 2005, p. D1.

38. "Bottled sunburn." *Los Angeles Times*, September 21, 1912, sec 2, p. 10.

39. "Not even skin deep is beauty." *Los Angeles Times*, September 2, 1923, sec 3, p. 15.

40. J. C. Furnas. "The truth about suntan." *Saturday Evening Post* 221 (July 31, 1948): 66.

41. "A suntan in a capsule." *Life* 40 (May 7, 1956): 89–90.

42. Ray J. Shrick. "Next: suntan pills." *Science Digest* 40 (July, 1956): 41–42.

43. Harry Kursh. "The new sun tan pill." *American Mercury* 83 (July, 1956): 139.

44. Wesley S. Griswold. "Take a powder: get a suntan." *Popular Science* 169 (July, 1956): 103.

45. "Suntan pills scored." *New York Times*, December 14, 1956, p. 19.

46. "Sunproofing for all?" *Newsweek* 52 (December 22, 1958): 52.

47. "Man-tanning products make golden getaway." *Printers' Ink* 270 (March 4, 1960): 11.

48. *Ibid.*, pp. 11–12.

49. "Man-Tan zooms to $1,800,000 tv budget." *Sponsor* 14 (March 15, 1960): 40–41.

50. "Dark, dark, darker." *Newsweek* 55 (May 23, 1960): 84.

51. *Ibid.*, pp. 84, 87.

52. "Sunshine comes in bottles (and tubes)." *Advertising Age* 31 (May 30, 1960): 2, 96.

53. "NBBB issues copy guide suggestions for tanning ads." *Advertising Age* 31 (July 4, 1960): 68.

54. "Sun tan in a bottle: the real story." *Good Housekeeping* 151 (October, 1960): 197–198.

55. *Ibid.*, p. 198.

56. *Ibid.*

57. "Those artificial tans." *Newsweek* 56 (October 31, 1960): 80.

58. William R. Vath. "Suntan in a bottle: how safe? How effective?" *Today's Health* 39 (June, 1961): 26–27.

59. *Ibid.*, pp. 65–66.

60. Fred Dickenson. "Suntan, straight from the bottle." *Reader's Digest* 79 (August, 1961): 69–71.

61. Lorraine Baltera. "Suntan products leaning to protection themes." *Advertising Age* 46 (May 12, 1975): 12.

62. Louise Fenner. "The tanning pill, a questionable dye job." *FDA Consumer* 16 (February, 1982): 23.

63. *Ibid.*, pp. 23, 25.

64. Lisa Belkin. "Warning about pills for getting early tan." *New York Times*, March 23, 1985, p. 48.

65. Terry Trucco. "Getting a sunless tan is easier than ever." *New York Times*, May 16, 1992, p. 30.

66. Jean Seligman. "No day at the beach." *Newsweek* 119 (June 8, 1992): 44.

67. "Sunless side up." *New Orleans* 38 (March, 2004): 80.

68. Alex Kuczynski. "For tans, it's sprays vs. rays." *New York Times*, June 13, 1004, p. 9.

69. "How to get a good tan without the sun." *Consumer Reports* 69 (October, 2004): 7.

Bibliography

Abele, John J. "Suntan lotions enjoying day in sun." *New York Times*, July 13, 1957, pp. 21, 24.

Adams, Mildred. "Modern worshippers of that old god, the sun." *New York Times Magazine*, July 7, 1929, sec 5, pp. 12–13.

Adler, Ruth. "Fun to fry." *New York Times Magazine*, July 9, 1950, pp. 32–33.

Adler, T. "Sunscreen can't give blanket protection." *Science News* 145 (January 22, 1994): 54–55.

"The advantage of tan." *Literary Digest* 78 (September 22, 1923): 27–28.

"Advises bathers against sunburn." *Los Angeles Times*, July 31, 1917, sec 1, p. 4.

"All shades of tan are now seen on New York's streets." *New York Times*, August 19, 1928, sec 7, p. 9.

Alsop, Gulielma F. "Health via sunlight." *The Woman Citizen* 11 (July, 1926): 37.

"A.M.A. describes tanning hazards." *New York Times*, July 25, 1989, p. C7.

Andrews, Edmund L. "In the sun too long? Device sounds alarm." *New York Times*, April 27, 1991, p. 38.

Angier, Natalie. "Theory hints sunscreens raise melanoma risks." *New York Times*, August 9, 1990, p. B10.

"Are you a heliophobe?" *Literary Digest* 106 (August 2, 1930): 26.

"Asks solariums in Chicago." *New York Times*, July 20, 1930, sec 2, p. 3.

"Athletics rising greatly in Soviet." *New York Times*, August 31, 1930, sec 3, p. 4.

"Auto toll laid to sun bathing." *Los Angeles Times*, August 5, 1937, p. 4.

"Babies and sunshine." *Literary Digest* 79 (December 1, 1923): 27.

Bailey, Bernadine. "Sun tan pro and con." *Today's Health* 28 (July, 1950): 44–45+.

Baker, Don. "Employees get a sun tan in Westinghouse offices." *American Business* 21 (July, 1951): 22–23.

Baker, Russell. "Observer: the strangest shores." *New York Times*, June 27, 1965, sec 4, p. 10.

"Balms away! Sun worshippers face heavy ad barrage from lotion makers this summer." *Advertising Age* 34 (June 10, 1963): 18–19.

Baltera, Lorraine. "Suntan products leaning to protection themes." *Advertising Age* 46 (May 12, 1975): 10, 12.

"Bare heads and sunshine." *New York Times*, July 14, 1905, p. 6.

"Beauty and health." *Glamour* 95 (July, 1997): 58+.

"Beauty and sunburn." *New York Times*, August 15, 1931, p. 12.

Bechet, Paul E. "Common sense under the sun." *Hygeia* 20 (July, 1942): 507+.

Belkin, Lisa. "A fierce fight over the sun." *New York Times*, May 31, 1986, pp. 35, 37.

_____. "Warning about pills for getting an early tan." *New York Times*, March 23, 1985, p. 48.

Bennett, William. "Sun: the new wisdom." *Vogue* 179 (June, 1989): 204–206.

"Beware the unruly sun." *Newsweek* 133 (June 21, 1999): 81–82.

"Big sky, big burn." *Time* 24 (December 14, 1959): 72.

Bigelow, Frederick S. "Colds and where to catch them." *Saturday Evening Post* 208 (November 30, 1935): 34.

Bjerklie, David. "Does sunscreen save your skin?" *Time* 141 (May 24, 1993): 69.

Blum, Harold F. "Skin cancer and sunlight." *Science* 145 (September 18, 1964): 1339–1340.

Blumenthal, Deborah. "Some doubts about new cosmetics for tanning." *New York Times*, January 16, 1988, p. 33.

"Bottled sunburn." *Los Angeles Times*, September 21, 1912, sec 2, p. 10.

"The bottom line." *Economist* 320 (September 14, 1991): 33.

Brady, William. "The sun cure." *The Independent* 79 (September 21, 1914): 414.

Brand, David. "Perils of the tanning parlor." *Time* 131 (May 23, 1988): 76.

Brink, Susan. "So much for sunblock." *U.S. News & World Report* 126 (June 14, 1999): 65.

_____. "Sun struck." *U.S. News & World Report* 120 (June 24, 1996): 62–67.

Broadstock, Marita, Ron Borland and Robyn Gason. "Effects of suntan on judgments of healthiness and attractiveness of adolescents." *Journal of Applied Social Psychology* 22 (January 16, 1992): 157–177.

Brody, Jane E. "Protecting skin from sun's rays." *New York Times*, May 22, 1985, pp. C1, C10.

Brody, Robert. "A tanless society by the year 2000?" *New York Times*, July 24, 1988, sec 3, p. 17.

_____. "Avoiding a sunburn with pills and patches." *New York Times*, July 24, 1988, sec 3, p. 17.

_____. "Playing the numbers for a lighter tan." *New York Times*, July 24, 1988, sec 3, p. 17.

"Brown as a..." *Newsweek* 68 (August 1, 1966): 58–59.

Bunker, John W. M. "Light and life." *American Journal of Public Health* 16 (July, 1926): 676–686.

Castleman, Michael. "Beach bummer." *Mother Jones* 18 (May/June, 1993): 32–37.

_____. "Sunscam." *Mother Jones* 23 (May/June, 1998): 27–28.

Chapman, Simon, Robin Marks and Madeleine King. "Trends in tans and skin protection in Australian fashion magazines, 1982 through 1991." *American Journal of Public Health* 82 (December, 1992): 1677–1680.

"Changes eased in sunburns." *New York Times*, August 22, 2002, p. A18.

Chase, Stuart. "Confessions of a sun-worshipper." *The Nation* 128 (June 26, 1929): 762–765.

"Chicago sun-bathers must wear something." *New York Times*, March 22, 1932, p. 4.

"Children at Cornell bask in violet rays." *New York Times*, March 27, 1932, p. 25.

Clark, Matt. "Suntans and skin cancer." *Newsweek* 99 (June 14, 1982): 85.

Conley, Veronica Lucey. "While you tan." *Today's Health* 30 (July, 1952): 34–35.

Conniff, James C. G. "Bask, don't burn." *New York Times Magazine*, July 7, 1974, pp. 12–13+.

"Cornell to fight colds." *New York Times*, May 3, 1930, p. 30.

"Credits 60,000 cures to artificial sun." *New York Times*, October 2, 1924, p. 24.

Dale, Crag. "Beware of sunburn." *Popular Mechanics* 49 (May, 1928): 754–757.

"Dark, dark, darker." *Newsweek* 55 (May 23, 1960): 84, 87.

Davis, Donald A. "Boggy ground." *Drug & Cosmetic Industry* 154 (March, 1994): 22.

_____. "Defining the sunscreen market." *Drug & Cosmetic Industry* 153 (December, 1993): 28+.

_____. "Sunscreen." *Drug & Cosmetic Industry* 153 (August, 1993): 24–26.

deBlanc-Knowles, Jaime. "Dangerous tans." *E: The Environmental Magazine* 15 (September/October, 2003): 11–12.

"Deceptive tans and health risks." *New York Times*, June 8, 2002, p. 14.

Dickenson, Fred. "Suntan straight from the bottle." *Reader's Digest* 79 (August, 1961): 69–71.

"Doctor sun." *Literary Digest* 58 (August 31, 1918): 26.

"Doctors urge care in using ray lamps." *New York Times*, January 9, 1929, p. 33.

Dortch, Shannon. "There goes the sun." *American Demographics* 19 (August, 1997): 4+.

"Eating sunshine to cure tuberculosis." *Current Opinion* 76 (June, 1924): 831–832.

"Economic loss from sunburn is put at $1,400,000 a year." *New York Times*, June 8, 1931, p. 1.

Edson, Lee. "Warning: prolonged exposure to the sun can be harmful to your health." *New York Times*, August 8, 1971, sec 10, pp. 1, 14.

"Environment helps accelerate consumer demand for sunscreens." *Drug & Cosmetic Industry* 149 (August, 1991): 30+.

Ephraim, Jerome W. "The truth about sunburn." *American Mercury* 35 (July, 1935): 364–367.

"Exposure to sun helps prevent cancer deaths." *Science News Letter* 37 (March 30, 1940): 198–199.

Fackelmann, Kathleen. "Melanoma madness." *Science News* 153 (June 6, 1998): 360–361+.

Falkner, Leonard. "The burning question." *American Magazine* 110 (August, 1930): 50–51+.

"F.D.A. proposes standards for control of sunlamps." *New York Times*, December 30, 1977, p. A22.

"Fear of frying." *New Republic* 199 (September 5, 1988): 4.

Fenner, Louise. "The tanning pill, a questionable inside dye job." *FDA Consumer* 16 (February, 1982): 23–25.

Fields, Helen. "Burned by SPF." *U.S. News & World Report* 135 (July 21, 2003): 51.

Fitzgerald, F. Scott. *The Beautiful and Damned.* Middlesex, England: Penguin, 1966.

Fitzgerald, Robert E. "Perrysburg — a mecca for heliotherapy." *American Journal of Public Health* 16 (September, 1926): 893–895.

"For people who have fair skins, suntans may raise gallstone risks." *New York Times*, February 5, 1992, p. C12.

"For sun lovers: a yellow badge of caution." *Newsweek* 119 (June 8, 1992): 44.

"For sun lovers, tan is worth the risk." *New York Times*, July 24, 1988, p. 31.

Forkan, James P. "Sun shines on marketers of tanning, sunburn products." *Advertising Age* 41 (June 22, 1970): 3, 72.

Free, E. E. "Tan fad to furnish new facts to science." *New York Times*, August 11, 1929, sec 9, pp. 3, 10.

Freudlich, Naomi. "The sun vs. your skin: a survival guide." *Business Week*, July 1, 1991, pp. 90–91.

Fugh-Berman, Adriane. "Sunscreen or smoke screen." *Ms* 5 (July/August, 1994): 19–21.

Funk, J. Clarence. "Sun worshippers in Pennsylvania." *American Journal of Public Health* 15 (September, 1925): 764–766.

Furnas, J. C. "The truth about suntan." *Saturday Evening Post* 221 (July 31, 1948): 28–29+.

"Glass houses for health." *New York Times*, July 1, 1927, p. 20.

"The good and evil of getting tanned." *Literary Digest* 106 (August 23, 1930): 30.

"Good-bye summer tan." *Glamour* 91 (May, 1993): 234–241.

Grant, Allan. "Sun pleasures and perils." *Life* 51 (August 4, 1961): 78–85+.

Greeley, Alexandra. "No safe tan." *FDA Consumer* 25 (May, 1991): 16–21.

Griswold, Wesley S. "Take a powder: get a suntan." *Popular Science* 169 (July, 1956): 103–105.

Gutner, Toddi. "Protection racket." *Forbes* 150 (August 17, 1992): 90.

Hamilton, Joan C. "Sun protection? There's a rule." *Business Week*, June 11, 1990, pp. 22–23.

Harrington, John W. "Sun-bathers on increase." *New York Times*, July 5, 1936, sec 10, p. 5.

Harris, D. T. "The biological action of light." *Scientific Monthly* 21 (November, 1935): 503–505.

Harris, Marvin. "The rites of summer." *Natural History* 82 (August, 1973): 20–22.

Harris, R. I. "Heliotherapy in surgical tuberculosis." *American Journal of Public Health* 16 (July, 1926): 687–694.

Harrow, Benjamin. "Meet doctor sunshine." *Hygeia* 5 (November, 1927): 579–582.

Hazen, H. H., and Florence B. Biase. "Sunlight and the skin." *American Journal of Nursing* 33 (August, 1933): 747–749.

"Heavy coat of tan is called harmful." *New York Times*, September 28, 1929, p. 20.

"Heliotherapy arrives." *New Statesman* 21 (April 28, 1923): 75–76.

"Housing heads urge end of smoke evil." *New York Times*, January 31, 1929, p. 15.

"How to get a good tan without the sun." *Consumer Reports* 69 (October, 2004): 7.

"How to survive a season in the sun." *Consumer Reports* 45 (June, 1980): 350–356.

"How to take a sun bath." (ad) *Los Angeles Times*, July 25, 1926, p. K27.

Hubbard, Henry D. "New vistas opened by invisible rays." *New York Times*, October 18, 1931, sec 9, p. 4.

Hutchinson, Woods. "Light refreshments." *Saturday Evening Post* 197 (May 2, 1925): 16–17+.

Johnson, Allen S. "Hot weather hazards." *Hygeia* 15 (June, 1937): 508–510.

Jones, Stacy V. "Sun-bathing now mechanized." *New York Times*, January 30, 1954, p. 21.

Kaempffert, Waldemar. "Invisible light is put to work for man." *New York Times Magazine*, May 6, 1927, sec 4, pp. 4–5+.

Kanner, Bernice. "The selling of suntans." *New York* 16 (August 8, 1983): 19–20.

Kolata, Gina. "A dermatologist who's not afraid to sit on the beach." *New York Times*, July 20, 2004, p. F5.

Kuczynski, Alex. "For tans, it's sprays vs. rays." *New York Times*, June 13, 2004, p. 9.

Kursh, Harry. "The new sun tan pill." *American Mercury* 83 (July, 1956): 139–140

Landow, Ken. "Do sunscreens prevent skin cancer?" *Postgraduate Medicine* 116 (July, 2004): 22.

Laurens, Henry. "Sunlight and health." *Scientific Monthly* 42 (April, 1936): 312–324.

Lawrence, D. H. "Sun." in *The Complete Short Stories,* vol II. New York: Penguin, 1976, pp. 528–545.

"The link between sunscreen and melanoma." *Shape* 23 (May, 2004): 127.

"Linking cancer and sun bathing." *New York Times*, July 30, 1933, sec 4, p. 5.

Liptak, Adam. "Mother is jailed after children are sunburned." *New York Times*, August 21, 2002, p. A10.

Loesch, W. T. III. "Responsible sun protection in the media whirlwind." *Drug & Cosmetic Industry* 163 (August, 1998): 10+.

"Love of a suntan." *New York Times*, June 12, 1984, p. C7.

Lyster, Lauren. "The bronze age." *Los Angeles Magazine* 48 (March, 2003): 38.

"Made her beautiful." *Los Angeles Times*, January 13, 1901, p. 5.

"Man-Tan zooms to $1,800,000 tv budget." *Sponsor* 14 (March 5, 1960): 40–41.

"Man-tanning products make golden getaway." *Printers' Ink* 270 (March 4, 1960): 11–12.

Markel, Howard. "So what's a responsible sun worshipper to do?" *New York Times*, August 25, 2002, sec 4, pp. 1, 3.

Marks, Peter. "Don't bother me: I'm catching some rays." *New York Times*, July 2, 1995, sec 4, p. 6.

Mayer, Edgar. "Sun-bathing and sun-lamps." *The American Journal of Nursing* 33 (August, 1933): 739–746.

McIver, Mary. "The sun's killing rays." *Maclean's* 101 (June 13, 1988): 36–42+.

"Medical progress." *New York Times*, January 9, 1929, p. 30.

"Miami's icon of kitsch faces toppling over the bottom line." *New York Times*, August 25, 1991, p. 28.

Miller, Arthur G., William A. Ashton, John W. McHoskey, and Joel Gimbel. "What price attractiveness? Stereotype and risk factors in suntanning behavior." *Journal of Applied Social Psychology* 20 (September, 1990): 1272–1300.

"Mlle plots the perfect tan." *Mademoiselle* 59 (July, 1964): 40–41.

"Modern sun worship: II — its history." *New Statesman* 18 (October 8, 1921): 10–12.

"Modern sun worship III — its high priest and his temple." *New Statesman* 18 (October 15, 1921): 42–43.

"More light." *New Statesman* 18 (November 12, 1921): 162–166.

"More solar surgery." *Literary Digest* 48 (June 13, 1914): 1432–1433.

"More sunlight." *Literary Digest* 66 (September 11, 1920): 128, 130.

Mylchreest, Ian. "Retailer sets out to shake up valley tanning salons." *Las Vegas Business Press* 21 (February 2, 2004): 19.

Nagourney, Eric. "Good day, sunshine: why they tan." *New York Times*, July 13, 2004, p. F1.

Nash, Nathaniel C. "Ozone depletion threatening Latin sun worshippers." *New York Times*, March 27, 1992, p. A7.

"NBBB issues copy guide suggestions for tanning ads." *Advertising Age* 31 (July 4, 1960): 68.

Netburn, Deborah. "Young, carefree and hooked on sunlamps." *New York Times*, May 26, 2002, sec 9, pp. 1, 7.

"The new sun worship." *The Survey* 49 (October 15, 1922): 109–110.

"Newport to war on smoking by women." *New York Times*, May 3, 1908, p. 11.

"Not even skin deep is beauty." *Los Angeles Times*, September 2, 1923, sec 3, p. 15.

O'Gara, Gerald J. "Health rays." *Sunset Magazine* 65 (July, 1930): 11–14.

Ogle, Jane. "Facing up to sunning." *New York Times* Magazine, June 14, 1981, pp. 108, 120.

"Old doctor sun." *Literary Digest* 87 (October 17, 1925): 28.

Oliphant, Jennifer A., Jean L. Forster, and Colleen M. McBride. "The use of commercial tanning facilities by suburban Minnesota adolescents." *American Journal of Public Health* 84 (March, 1994): 476–478.

Orris, Leo. "The sun: friend or enemy?" *Mademoiselle* 53 (May, 1961): 142–143+.

"Our energy due to the sun." *New York Times*, May 15, 1911, p. 3.

"Paba for sunburn." *Newsweek* 21 (May 17, 1943): 70.

Palmer, Richard C., et al. "Indoor tanning facility density in eighty U.S. cities." *Journal of Community Health* 27 (June, 2002): 191–202.

"Paris doctor warns against sun bathing." *New York Times*, June 25, 1933, p. 1.

Parker, Martha. "Danger in the sun." *New York Times* Magazine, July 9, 1944, p. 32.

Parsons, Floyd. "Sun worship." *Saturday Evening Post* 202 (November 16, 1929): 28–29+.

Parsons, Floyd W. "What price sunshine?" *Saturday Evening Post* 198 (July 25, 1925): 6–7+.

"Perils of the summer sun." *Literary Digest* 86 (August 15, 1925): 20–21.

Perry, Patrick. "Safe under the sun." *Saturday Evening Post* 268 (September/October, 1996): 42–47+.

"Personal business." *Business Week*, July 27, 1957, p. 141.

Peters, Lulu Hunt. "Diet and health." *Los Angeles Times*, July 6, 1922, sec 2, p. 8.

"A place in the sun." *New York Times*, July 15, 1949, p. 18.

Praeger, Emily. "The taming of the tan." *Harper's Bazaar* 129 (May, 1996): 126–127+.

"Pretty on $1 a week." *Los Angeles Times*, January 27, 1907, sec 7, p. 2.

"Preventing sunburn and promoting tan." *Consumers' Research Bulletin* 23 (June, 1949): 13–15.

"Puts ban on sun bathing." *New York Times*, July 19, 1930, p. 28.

"Questions the need to abolish disease." *New York Times*, May 21, 1926, p. 14.

Rae, Stephen. "No fear of frying." *New York Times*, May 27, 1985, p. 19.

"Return of the red skin." *The Commonweal* 16 (June 15, 1932): 173.

Reuben, David. "Suntan can kill you." *Reader's Digest* 136 (June, 1990): 119–123.

Revell, Madelein G. "A place in the sun." *Public Health Nurse* 19 (November, 1927): 538–541.

"Revolving sun baths." *Scientific American* 125 (September 3, 1921): 170.

"Risks of tanning booths." *New York Times*, January 27, 1981, p. C2.

Rudolph, Barbara. "Don't let the sunshine in." *Forbes* 129 (June 21, 1982): 80–81.

Saleeby, C. W. "The advance of heliotherapy." *Nature* 109 (May 20, 1922): 663.

_____. "Sunlight and disease." *Nature* 111 (April 28, 1923): 574–576.

Saranow, Jennifer. "States crack down on indoor tanning." *Wall Street Journal* (eastern ed.), January 26, 2005, p. D1.

Saunders, Dero A. "New under the sun." *Forbes* 144 (August 7, 1989): 134.

"Says cancers yield to electrosurgery." *New York Times*, September 7, 1932, p. 7.

"Says we will sleep under violet rays." *New York Times*, February 11, 1931, p. 28.

Schmidt, William E. "Even in the South, they tan indoors." *New York Times*, June 1, 1985, p. 48.

Schwanke, Jane. "Study shows alarming upward trend in teen use of indoor tanning facilities." *Dermatology Times* 25 (June, 2004): 55.

Seligman, Jean. "Catching dangerous rays." *Newsweek* 105 (June 24, 1985): 69.
_____. "No day at the beach." *Newsweek* 119 (June 8, 1992): 44.
"Sensitivity to sunburn." *Science* 67 (June 15, 1928): sup 12, 14.
Sheard, Charles. "Cheeks of tan." *Hygeia* 5 (May, 1927): 221–223.
Sheppard, Eugenia. "Love affair with the sun." *Harper's Bazaar* 104 (June, 1971): 94–95.
Shrick, Ray J. "Next: suntan pills." *Science Digest* 40 (July, 1956): 41–43.
Sloan, Pat. "Coppertone ads tout beauty on the beach." *Advertising Age* 60 (March 6, 1989): 67.
_____. "Getting a tan, family-style." *Advertising Age* 64 (January 25, 1993): 12.
_____. "Here comes the sun care." *Advertising Age* 49 (May 29, 1978): 3, 32.
_____. "Suncare marketers raise their screens." *Advertising Age* 58 (May 25, 1987): 1, 66.
_____. "Suncare '82 outlook partly cloudy." *Advertising Age* 53 (February 15, 1982): 45.
_____. "Sunscreens shine in cosmetics." *Advertising Age* 56 (May 6, 1985): 70.
_____. "Tan is back, and new brands skimp on protection." *Advertising Age* 68 (June 2, 1997): 22.
_____. "UV index backs sunscreen surge." *Advertising Age* 66 (January 30, 1995): 11.
Slosson, Edwin E. "The progress of science." *Scientific Monthly* 21 (November, 1925): 551–554.
"Smoker's cancer laid to sunburn." *New York Times*, April 8, 1941, p. 18.
"Some tanning salons found to violate rules." *New York Times*, March 28, 1991, p. B8.
"A spectrum of sun protection." *Consumer Reports* 63 (May, 1998): 20–23.
"SPF: the sun-profit factor." *Newsweek* 111 (June 27, 1988): 44.
Stambovsky, L. "The suntan business." *Drug & Cosmetic Industry* 102 (May, 1968): 42–44+.
Stambovsky, L. "Suntanning under siege." *Drug & Cosmetic Industry* 111 (July, 1972): 40–41+.
"The sun: a doubt." *The New Statesman and Nation* 4 (September 10, 1932): 281–282.
"The sun also burns." *Time* 81 (June 21, 1963): 43.
"The sun as a surgeon." *Literary Digest* 48 (February 28, 1914): 427.
"Sun ban." *Time* 89 (May 12, 1967): 65.
"Sun bathers warned to beware of liquor." *New York Times*, July 1, 1935, p. 21.
"Sun baths for chilly babies." *Los Angeles Times*, November 4, 1915, sec 2, p. 3.
"Sun baths in London planned by Lansbury." *New York Times*, September 19, 1929, p. 34.
"The sun cure." *Scientific Monthly* 16 (May, 1923): 555–557.
"Sun devotionals." *New York Times*, July 6, 1929, p. 12.
"Sun lamps to tan cheeks of members of Congress." *New York Times*, February 13, 1929, p. 1.
"Sun ray baths save baby." *New York Times*, October 18, 1925, p. 6.
"Sun salons." *Time* 115 (February 11, 1980): 59.
"Sun talk." *Mademoiselle* 73 (May, 1971): 210–211.
"Sun worship." *Today's Health* 48 (June, 1970): 36–39.
"Sun-bathers seek Manhattan roofs." *New York Times*, July 10, 1932, sec 10 & 11, p. 1.
"Sunburn beneficial only when gradually acquired." *New York Times*, July 29, 1928, sec 8, p. 2.
"Sunburn delays draft." *New York Times*, June 22, 1943, p. 21.
"Sunburn doses measured." *New York Times*, September 6, 1975, p. 31.
"Sunburn index gauges risk." *Prevention* 38 (August, 1986): 7–8.
"Sunburn jelly." *Newsweek* 27 (January 21, 1946,): 89.
"Sunburn leads to death." *New York Times*, July 17, 1925, p. 7.
"Sunburn meter is shown." *New York Times*, June 24, 1949, p. 25.
"Sunburn, poison ivy and seasickness." *Fortune* 36 (August, 1947): 110–115+.
"Sunburn preventives." *Consumer Reports* 15 (July, 1950): 291–294.
"Sunglasses with alarms." *New York Times*, August 7, 1971, p. 33.
"Sunless side up." *New Orleans* 38 (March, 2004): 80.
"Sunlight." *Hygeia* 8 (August, 1930): 704.
"Sunlight and cancer." *New York Times*, October 30, 1933, p. 16.

"Sunlight declared the enemy of man." *New York Times Magazine,* April 21, 1907, sec 5, p. 2.

"Sunlight therapy's value certain in tuberculosis." *New York Times,* March 2, 1924, sec 9, p. 18.

"Sunny sea beaches good for children." *New York Times,* September 14, 1924, sec 8, p. 11.

"Sunproofing for all?" *Newsweek* 52 (December 22, 1958): 52.

"Sunshine comes in bottles (and tubes)." *Advertising Age* 31 (May 30, 1960): 2, 96.

"Sunshine: hazardous to your health." *Consumers' Research Magazine* 63 (April, 1980): 32–36.

"Sunscreen lowers risk of melanoma." *New York Times,* October 14, 1993, p. B9.

"Sunscreens." *Consumer Reports* 56 (June, 1991): 400–406.

"Sunscreens." *Consumer Reports* 66 (June, 2001): 27–29.

"Suntan." *Life* 11 (July 21, 1941): 55–58.

"A suntan in a capsule." *Life* 40 (May 7, 1956): 89–90.

"A sun-tan mode." *New York Times,* June 16, 1929, sec 8, p. 8.

"Suntan parlors to post warnings." *New York Times,* August 21, 1980, p. B6.

"Suntan pills scored." *New York Times,* December 14, 1956, p. 19.

"Sun-tan preparations." *Consumer Reports* 26 (July, 1961): 394–397.

"Suntan preparations." *Consumer Reports* 36 (July, 1971): 408–411.

"Suntan preparations." *Consumers' Research Magazine* 58 (August, 1975): 20–23.

"Suntan — safe or dangerous?" *Consumer Bulletin* 41 (May, 1958): 26–29.

"Sun's actinic rays are magnet for tourists." *New York Times,* January 18, 1925, sec 8, p. 18.

"Sun's rays the great healer." *The Canadian Magazine* 73 (April, 1930): 43.

Sweet, Cheryl A. "Healthy tan — a fast-fading myth." *FDA Consumer* 23 (June, 1989): 11–13.

Sweet, Holland. "Back to the bronze age?" *Harper's Bazaar* 126 (May, 1993): 130–131+.

Symes, Mrs. Henry. "Chats with correspondents on health and beauty topics." *Los Angeles Times,* September 20, 1903, p. E10.

_____. "How to be healthy and beautiful." *Los Angeles Times,* August 3, 1902, p. C7.

"Take your sunshine in small doses." *Literary Digest* 98 (August 4, 1928): 22.

"The tan man." *New Yorker* 71 (September 18, 1995): 42.

Tannen, Mary. "Seeing the light." *New York Times Magazine,* May 11, 1997, pp. 54–55.

"Tanning debate: heavy vs. healthy." *New York Times,* May 11, 1988, p. C10.

"Tanning parlors fade from franchise scene." *New York Times,* May 26, 1981, pp. D1, D4.

"Tanning salons may face licensing." *New York Times,* March 29, 1987, p. 42.

Taylor, Angela. "All about the sun: a new turn on tans." *New York Times,* June 1, 1977, p. C9.

Thompson, Larry. "Trying to look sunsational." *FDA Consumer* 34 (July/August, 2000): 15–21.

Thomas, Karen. "Gold is not just for the statues." *USA Today,* March 9, 2004, p. D2.

"Those artificial tans." *Newsweek* 56 (October 31, 1960): 80.

Tisdale, Frederick F. "Sunlight and health." *American Journal of Public Health* 16 (July, 1926): 694–699.

"To tan without burning." *Consumers' Research Bulletin* 33 (June, 1954): 31–33.

Tobey, James A. "Curing disease by sunlight." *Current History Magazine* 22 (June, 1925): 455–456.

"Topics of the Times." *New York Times,* June 27, 1921, p. 12.

Trucco, Terry. "Getting a sunless tan is easier than ever." *New York Times,* May 16, 1992, p. 30.

"Ultra-violet rays used in an office." *New York Times,* December 28, 1931, p. 14.

"Upholds ultra-violet ray." *New York Times,* January 29, 1930, p. 2.

"Urges sunlight hour for sunlight." *New York Times,* October 6, 1929, sec 3, p. 6.

"Use sunlight on rickets." *New York Times,* June 15, 1927, p. 48.

Van Gelder, Lawrence. "Chronicle." *New York Times,* August 19, 1997, p. B6.

Vath, William R. "Suntan in a bottle: how safe? how effective?" *Today's Health* 39 (June, 1961): 26–27+.

Waldrop, Judith. "Under the sun." *American Demographics* 15 (July, 1993): 4.

Wallis, Claudia. "Bring back the parasol." *Time* 121 (May 30, 1983): 46.

Walsh, James J. "Sun tan: the latest fad." *The Commonweal* 10 (August 7, 1929): 358–359.

Wandycz, Katarzyna. "Safe sun." *Forbes* 152 (July 19, 1993): 212–213.

"Want a shot of sunshine?" *Time* 138 (December 2, 1991): 85.

"Warns against sunburn." *New York Times*, July 19, 1924, p. 4.

"Warns as to sun bathing." *New York Times*, February 18, 1929, p. 10.

"Ways to get a stylish tan." *New York Times*, June 23, 1929, sec 5, p. 19.

Weathers, Diane. "90-second suntans." *Newsweek* 94 (December 24, 1979): 68.

Webster, Richard. "Indoor tanning remains popular despite doctors dire warnings." *New Orleans City Business*, April 5, 2004, pp. 33–35.

Weir, June. "Care under the sun." *New York Times Magazine*, February 17, 1985, p. 84.

_____. "Summer sense." *New York Times* Magazine, May 9, 1982, p. 77.

Whitaker, Alma. "Sun tans win in movieland." *Los Angeles Times*, July 27, 1930, pp. B9, B17.

Wilkinson, Donna. "Why do men get sunburned?" *New York Times*, June 21, 2004, p. F5.

"Woman near death from beach sunburn." *New York Times*, June 25, 1921, p. 2.

"Woman tells a suntan-oil company how to soothe her." *New York Times*, July 28, 1979, p. 41.

"Wynne warns of sunburn peril." *New York Times*, July 31, 1930, p. 10.

Zoglin, Richard. "Going for the bronze." *Time* 125 (February 25, 1985): 82.

Index